Skills for Living

Group Counseling Activities for Young Adolescents

Volume 2

Rosemarie Smead

Research Press
2612 North Mattis Avenue
Champaign, Illinois 61822
www.researchpress.com

Composition by Jeff Helgesen
Printed by McNaughton & Gunn, Inc.

ISBN 0–87822–420–3
Library of Congress Catalog Number 89–61588

CONTENTS

Handouts

ACKNOWLEDGMENTS _____

This book is lovingly dedicated to Dr. Connie Deuschle, counselor educator from Indiana University at South Bend, colleague, and co-leader. Over the past 6 years working with me through the Indiana Department of Education, Connie has devoted boundless energy to organizing and coordinating our in-depth trainings for school counselors, psychologists, and social workers throughout the state. Together we have shared the joys and healing skills of group work with hundreds of group leaders. My appreciation and affection for her support and friendship are everlasting.

The *Skills for Living* series is the result of a 10-year journey with fellow travelers from Research Press: Ann Wendel, Russ Pence, Karen Steiner, and everyone else. I am deeply indebted to them for their encouragement of my work. This volume is especially precious because we all flexed to make these groups even more user-friendly to an ever-increasing number of counselors, counselors-in-training, and students.

PART 1

INTRODUCTION

In the decade before the twenty-first century, challenges abounding, we have experienced overwhelming societal problems with our children and youth. Violence in the schools is alarming, as is a litany of problematic behaviors that affect our youth, families, schools, and society. Since the publication in 1990 of *Skills for Living: Group Counseling Activities for Young Adolescents,* as well as publication in 1994 of *Skills for Living: Group Counseling Activities for Elementary Students,* counseling research has broadened its focus to include process, providing us further hope and incentive to pursue this medium for making a positive impact on youth.

The decade of the 1990s has seen a multipronged approach to intervention in maladaptive behaviors of youth. First, the "at-risk" population has been more clearly identified, and organized programs on their behalf have been funded at the federal, state, and local levels. The student assistance profession has organized in response to the at-risk movement, offering a breadth of services to youth identified as engaging in unproductive behavior and having the potential for developing more entrenched negative behavior patterns. Sequential, closely monitored training programs have been conducted to provide activities to teach social skills, problem-solving skills, relationship skills, and self-management strategies. Such programs have been impressive in identifying and mediating problematic behaviors.

Group counseling adds a content-plus-process approach to the picture. Youth with established issues are selected on the basis of their appropriateness for treatment and are offered a special opportunity to learn new ideas, perspectives, and attitudes. They are exposed to new behavioral skills to replace existing maladaptive behaviors and can practice these behaviors in a safe, supportive environment. Essential to the therapeutic process is the expression and redirection of affect. Group counseling encourages the expression of affect related to life's painful experiences and supports the interactive relationships among members that can result in healing and growth.

This book provides youth of middle school and junior high school age with the opportunity to experience positive growth and change in the group setting. A number of topic areas are covered:

Girlfriends: Understanding and Managing Friendships

Jugglers: Middle School Transition Issues

Dating and Relating: Male/Female Relationship Issues

"Teaching Tolerance": Understanding and Valuing Individual and Cultural Differences

Give a Little, Take a Little: Relationships at Home

The Brain Laundromat: Cognitive Coping Skills

Agree to Disagree: Learning to Manage Anger

Guys' Club: Issues from a Male Perspective

The topic-oriented group experiences in this book are based on common problematic issues and behaviors. In addition to these, you might want to develop some of your own topics that would better fit your population or be more relevant at a specific time. You might also want to have one or two "freebie" sessions for which the youth earn the opportunity to decide what they would like to discuss. Indeed, a whole group experience may be based on your population's needs. It is important to keep in mind, however, that professional good practice and the research base for group work with youth suggest that some structure be followed in terms of session pattern so the experience doesn't degenerate into gripe and complaint sessions, with no therapeutic focus or outcome.

WHY GROUP COUNSELING?

The Association for Specialists in Group Work developed a descriptive model of specializations of group work in 1991 (ASGW, 1991). This model helps us to understand and visualize where group counseling with youth falls in terms of group goals, leadership issues, training requirements, applicable techniques, and types of members. Specializations include the following major categories: task/work groups, guidance/psychological education groups, group counseling, and group psychotherapy. In order for this book to achieve its intended purpose and to maximize the growth experience for the youth involved, it is important to distinguish among the types of group work, especially between group guidance/psychological education and group counseling.

This book and the two others in the *Skills for Living* series are intended for group counseling rather than psychological education, usually referred to as *group guidance* in a school setting. Guidance is an educational experience intended for large groups, such as the classroom. The American School Counselor Association (1998–1999) recommends a program of structured guidance for all ages/grades on a regular basis, to provide youth with information and instruction on issues such as decision making, understanding feelings, STD's, problem solving, drugs/alcohol, and career choices. Guidance is content oriented and designed to be preventive. Preventive can mean preventing problems altogether or preventing problems from becoming more serious. Guidance can be conducted by a professional with specific training and experience in that area—for example, a school nurse might offer guidance activities in a classroom on the topic of drugs and alcohol.

Group counseling is distinctly different. Group counseling is a healing and learning process, conducted by a counselor or another mental health professional with specific training in this modality. It is intended for youth with established problems who are willing and psychologically able to face and make progress working on their issues. The purpose of the group counseling activities presented here is to engage, on a short-term basis (8 to 12 weeks), with topic- or problem-driven issues, dealing directly with the affective, behavioral, and cognitive needs of group members. Although the group agendas in this book have specific content, leaders must realize that process is as important as content and be willing to let content go at any time in the life of the group that a process issue arises. Group content refers to the *what* of the group, the topic or subject of conversation. Group process involves the inter-actions among group members—the *how* of what is happening. When embarking on a group experience based on the topics in this book, leaders must inch continually toward the interpersonal processes and relationships of group members rather than remain strictly married to the content of the agendas! It is in dealing with the process/relationship issues in the immediacy of the moment that the true learning, growth, and healing of group counseling take place.

Classrooms are of necessity content driven. Counseling sessions must allow process to occur. Group counseling allows group members to experience new ideas and attitudes about behavior, to practice new behaviors, and to examine their feelings about an issue and how they are learning from relationships. The approach is primarily remedial, although as noted it can keep established difficulties from developing into more serious problems and is in that sense preventive.

ORGANIZING THE GROUP EXPERIENCE

Conducting a time-limited topic- or issue-driven group counseling experience is a process. It begins before the first session and continues after the last session. The following pages describe a series of steps, not necessarily in sequence, covering nearly all of the group leadership responsibilities connected with the group. Some of these tasks overlap, and some can be omitted according to the setting and circumstances.

In general, as leader you will cover 12 steps when conducting a group experience:

Step 1—Conduct needs assessment.

Step 2—Develop written proposal.

Step 3—Advertise the group.

Step 4—Obtain informed consent from parent/guardian.

Step 5—Conduct pregroup interviews.

Step 6—Select group members.

Step 7—Conduct pregroup session.

Step 8—Administer pretest.

Step 9—Conduct sessions.

Step 10—Administer posttest.

Step 11—Conduct postgroup follow-up.

Step 12—Write up group evaluation.

Step 1: Conduct Needs Assessment

In order to provide appropriate services for your young clients, it is essential to tap in to the population you are serving and invite them to share their perceptions of what services are needed. In a school setting, the youth and their parents, teachers, and administrators are your constituency. In an agency, clients, their families, the community, and other service providers can make recommendations and referrals.

A needs assessment is a formal opportunity for you to link with other key players in the provision of services for youth. Demonstrating respect for and interest in these individuals' opinions goes a long way to encourage positive relationships between counselor and other professionals. Parents, teachers, and administrators will be more likely to permit youth to leave the classroom for group if they understand the purpose and goals to be accomplished. In addition, after the group has been conducted, the needs assessment (along with posttest results) can be used to demonstrate accountability to the administration.

In general, a needs assessment is valuable about every 2 years in a school setting, unless a particular event causes a shift in the population's needs. Both formal and informal needs assessments can be used to gather information. An informal needs assessment might involve verbally asking administrators, teachers, parents, and youth what they think are the three most important needs/issues of the school population. This technique will gather a wide variety of responses, and the information can be recorded along with information obtained from more formal methods. The examples of faculty and student needs assessments in Appendix A of this book are of this type.

Step 2: Develop Written Proposal

When you have selected the topic or issue your group will address, the next step is to organize your ideas and describe, on paper, how the process will develop. If you are just beginning to do group work or this is the first time you have conducted a group on this topic, it is essential that you spend time in preparation so that you can conduct the sessions in an organized manner. Often other professionals, the youths themselves, and their parents do not understand what group counseling means. You might have to deal with some resistance, questioning, and even pressure to do things in a way that is not helpful or considered good practice in the profession, so a thoroughly written proposal lends strong support. Astute administrators will recognize your knowledge, organizational skills, and training in this specialty and will be more likely to be supportive after reading your proposal.

The written proposal should include the following information.* In addition to dealing with these general points, the proposal can include specific outlines for each group meeting. These outlines should spell out the exact goals, materials, and processes involved. (The group agendas in this book provide a framework for organizing group content.)

Description and Rationale

What is the purpose of the group?

Whose needs does it meet?

What kind of group will it be (skill building, personal growth, decision making, problem solving, other)?

What topics are going to be explored in the group?

Objectives

What objectives do you have in mind for the group?

Can your objectives be accomplished reasonably by participants the age and with the abilities of your members?

Are your objectives clear? Measurable? Reasonable in terms of number of sessions proposed?

Logistics

Who will lead the group? What are the leader's qualifications?

Will there be only one leader, or will you have a co-leader? Is either of the leaders a student rather than a fully licensed/qualified professional?

What responsibilities does the leader have toward the student co-leader?

---

*These guidelines are based generally on recommendations provided by G. Corey and M. S. Corey in *Groups: Process and Practice* (5th ed.), 1997, Pacific Grove, CA: Brooks/Cole.

Who will assure that the group will be conducted in an ethical and professional manner?

How will the group members be selected?

When will the group meet? If during regular class time, do all parties (teachers, students, parents) agree?

How many members will be selected, and what are the criteria for inclusion? Is there a plan to provide services for those who are not selected?

Where will the group meet, and for how long?

Will the group be closed or open to new members as the group progresses? How will requests to drop out be handled?

Procedures

What kind of techniques will you be using? (Possibilities include relaxation, role-playing, behavioral modeling, self-improvement exercises, props to help focus on an idea, and so on.)

How and when will you explain the risks of being involved in a group?

How will you protect members from being hurt physically or psychologically?

Will you take special precautions because participants are legal minors?

How will you explain confidentiality and its limits?

How will you handle parents or others who might want you to divulge a child's confidences?

How will you obtain informed assent from the group member and informed consent from parents/guardians?

Will you require both parents to sign an informed consent if there is a noncustodial parent?

Are you seeking permission to use any experimental techniques, conduct any research, or use any recording devices?

Evaluation

How do you plan to determine whether a member has changed due to exposure to the group experience?

How are you going to determine whether your goals and objectives have been met?

What follow-up procedures do you anticipate?

How will you protect the confidentiality of members as you write up an evaluation of the group? Who will receive evaluation data?

How will evaluation data be stored? Who will have access?

How do you plan to evaluate leader and co-leader (if appropriate) performance?

Step 3: Advertise the Group

Having enough members seems to be a major concern of beginning counselors or counselors in training. Actually, it is very common to find that you have many more applicants than you can include in the group, and the issue of turning down potential members occurs. Nonetheless, there are many ways to advertise the group, as well as several populations that need to be kept informed about it. A good place to start recruiting group members is with the individuals who have the most contact with your client population: administrators, mental health professionals, teachers, and students. Parents, school psychologists, school social workers, student assistance professionals, and school nurses might also refer students.

Administrators

In many schools, the assistant principal sees students who are having academic or behavioral difficulties and will be in a position to refer or recommend candidates. Special education committees who review and recommend services also can be included. After approval or organization of your group, you will want to let all of the school administrators know what group(s) will be occurring during the year.

Teachers

You can inform teachers through personal contact, news/notes from the counseling office, bulletin board notices, faculty meeting announcements, or mini-meetings before or after school for those interested. An introductory announcement can be put in all teachers' mailboxes. The sample letter to school faculty included in Appendix A could serve this purpose. If you have an electronic or computerized bulletin board, the information can be listed there.

Counselors

Your agency or school colleagues in the counseling office will be familiar with students who are having problems coping in different areas and will be a good source for referrals. Ask them to mention the group to the youth and parents with whom they work. You or other counselors could make a brief announcement about the group in homeroom classes, inviting students to talk with you about membership. You can also post signs or use direct contact to let students know about the group.

Step 4: Obtain Informed Consent from Parent/Guardian

In many schools, parents or legal guardians must provide a written informed consent in order for minor children to participate in group counseling. Raised awareness to children's rights, as well as a "consumer's movement" in counseling, has influenced provision of services in all venues. The purpose of providing informed consent originally was empowering the client, but the current shift distinctly focuses on protecting the counselor from litigation. Brown (1994) has used the term *empowered consent*, meaning complete and meaningful disclosure in an interactive way that supports the client's freedom of choice. Obtaining consent involves the provision of specific information about the group so the client (and, in the case of the minor child, the parent/guardian) can make an intelligent decision about whether or not to participate. Cormier and Cormier (1991, 1998) believe the counselor is acting in good faith and protecting the client's rights and welfare by providing the following information about strategies:*

1. A description of all relevant and potentially useful treatment approaches for this particular client with this particular problem

2. A rationale or purpose for each procedure

3. Description of the counselor's role

4. Description of the client's role

5. Description of possible risks or discomforts

6. Description of expected benefits

7. Estimated time and cost of each procedure

_____

*Items 1 through 7 are from W. H. Cormier and L. S. Cormier (1998, p. 288). Items 8 through 11 are from Cormier and Cormier (1991, p. 306).

8. Offer made to answer client's questions about strategy

9. Client advised of the right to discontinue strategy at any time

10. Explanations given in clear and nontechnical language

11. Summary and/or clarifications used to explore and understand client reactions

The importance of obtaining informed consent from the parent/guardian, as well as informed assent from the student, cannot be overstated. One good way to provide the necessary information is to use a letter and form similar to the samples provided in Appendix A. Check your school policy on the requirement for consent from both custodial and noncustodial parents, and be sure to look into this matter before making any final selection of members. It might not be advisable to select a child whose noncustodial parent refuses to give permission. The noncustodial parent's objection may influence the custodial parent and become a source of confusion for the child, resulting in the child's inability to participate fully or possible dropout. Loss of a member affects the cohesion of the entire group, setting back the group process.

Step 5: Conduct Pregroup Interviews

The ethical guidelines of our counseling specialty require us to screen potential group members so that we may obtain informed consent (or, in the case of minors, assent). It is appropriate to give prospective members certain initial information as a group—for example, information about the group's purpose, goals, expectations, and normative behaviors (such as the right to "pass" on sharing thoughts, feelings, and behaviors). However, youth may not be ready or willing to disclose other information in front of their peers. Thus, it is essential that part of the pregroup interview be done individually, giving potential group members the privacy to disclose information in response to questions such as "Are you going to any other counselors or psychologists for counseling in a group or by yourself?" "What self-change goals are you willing to work toward?" and "On a scale of 1 to 10, how much do you want to be in the group?" Young adolescents are highly influenced by their peers and tend not to give the same answer in front of their peers as they would privately with the counselor. This can skew the counselor's decision to include or exclude a particular member from the group. Another major reason for part of the interview to be private is that group counseling has the potential to be harmful under certain conditions. It is our responsibility to look for potential problems and screen out children who are not appropriate candidates—for example, children who have suicidal or homicidal ideation or who are involved in family sexual abuse.

Screening helps you ask the right questions to determine whether the group setting is appropriate for a particular youth. The TAP-In Student Selection Checklist, included as Appendix B, is designed to help you objectify and standardize the interview process. The acronym TAP stands for *Tell, Ask,* and *Pick*. It will help remind you of the information you need to give the child, the questions you need to ask the child, and the guidelines you need to follow to help you make the selection—thus helping you "tap-in" to the student's world.

In the interview, it is a good idea first to talk to the student for a while about expectations for the group and what his or her interests are in participating. Then, before going through the checklist, you could say something like "Being a member of the group is very special. There are a number of things I need to tell you and ask you, so I have them written down so I won't forget, OK?" It is especially important to use language the student can understand to describe what will be involved in the group.

For reasons of safety and security for both youth and counselor, it is recommended that leaders duplicate the TAP-In Student Selection Checklist and use one in interviewing each potential group member. Even if the member is not at risk for interaction with the court system or more serious problems, a copy of the selection process document frequently is useful in justifying nonselection, as well as for reference if this youth seeks admission to a future group. This last issue occurs more frequently than one can imagine!

Step 6: Select Group Members

One of the most critical factors in the preparation for group counseling is preselection of group members. George Gazda, one of the founders of the ASGW and father of exhaustive research on developmental group counseling for youth, said at a workshop presented at the American Counseling Association in the early 1980s that selection of members for youth group

work is 50 percent of what it takes to get your group to "fly"—that is, make it to the working stage. Unfortunately, this point is often neglected or discounted by beginning group counselors. Pressure from others to select students who are inappropriate candidates or who do not assist in balancing roles may be overwhelming if leaders are not firmly grounded in the ethics and knowledge of appropriate selection procedures.

Each time you lead a group, there is the potential for tremendous personal growth in each member. There also exists the risk of personal harm for each member. Because of its many intertwining relationships, a group has a life of its own. This is a description of the *group process*, the powerful dynamic that generates healing in a group. Whatever happens to one member affects all members. Thus, it is the responsibility of the leader to select participants who will be most likely to have a positive experience and to screen out those who are at risk for harm to themselves or others. Group counseling presents a distinctly unusual contradiction. On the one hand, it is a diluted form of help: If there are eight members, each youth is getting only one-eighth of the pie, in terms of the amount of therapeutic work. In other words, one-eighth of the leader's energies are focused on each of the group members. If one member is so emotionally needy that he or she needs half of the pie, or the whole pie, then perhaps that member needs individual counseling instead of a group experience, or perhaps a minigroup of four youths, in order to receive what he or she needs and not impede other group members from receiving their share of the group's energy. On the other hand, the group experience involves intense interaction among members, and therefore the possibility exists that helping will be potentiated instead of diluted. The group members who are not speaking and interacting at any particular time may also be getting valuable information and insights from observing the interactions of the members who are more active. Such intensity may be detrimental to some members, and thus vulnerable youth should not be included in the group.

Frequently, counselors have difficulty explaining to teachers, parents, or administrators why group counseling is not appropriate for a student who seems to have great need for counseling services. One way to explain this is to use the following analogy: Suppose you decide you would like to have cosmetic surgery. You choose a reputable surgeon, make an appointment, and discuss what you would like to have done. Does the surgeon say, "See our scheduling coordinator and set the date?" NO! The surgeon will conduct some type of an assessment, perhaps ask you to complete a questionnaire about how this surgery might affect your self-image, and send you to the lab for other tests. It is the surgeon who decides, based on all of the information, whether you are an appropriate candidate for surgery. If you are a suitable candidate for this surgery, then you may find yourself getting ready to go under the knife. If results indicate that for some reason you would not be a good candidate, you will be informed that it would not be in your best interest to proceed. It is the same way with group counseling. Just as the physician is the expert and makes the decision regarding surgery, the group counseling leader is the expert and is bound by ethical and professional guidelines to select group members who are appropriate for this very intense type of therapeutic experience. Yes, recommendations and referrals are welcome, but the group counselor should never bow to others' pressure to accept a youth who isn't suited. This type of pressure could come from well-meaning adults, as well as from the youth him- or herself. Some youth simply are not appropriate candidates for group counseling, according to best practice guidelines in the profession. When youth have multiple acting-out problems, they may appear very needy. They definitely need help, but the screening process may reveal reasons a group is not best. As noted earlier, such youth may need more intense individual work or, if they are involved in a personal crisis, may not work well in the group at this time.

Homogeneity and Heterogeneity

The factors of homogeneity and heterogeneity are paramount in selecting group members who will be likely to work together for everyone's benefit. *Homogeneity* refers to selection on the basis of likenesses (for example, youth who have all experienced a death in the family or youth who are not able to express anger in appropriate ways). In short-term groups, there needs to be a major uniting factor for members to relate to one another quickly. This factor promotes a perception of universality (we are alike in our problem), as well as a sense of cohesion, or "we-ness." These factors are considered major reasons group work is helpful and healing, so it is integral to foster them through the selection process.

Despite the value of homogeneity, *heterogeneity* is often the crucial ingredient in the success of the group counseling effort. Why? Because heterogeneity provides the differences that are needed for each child to have a role model from which to learn. After all, learning from models is what group counseling is all about. What seems confusing about this issue is the term *role model*. One ordinarily thinks of a role model as someone who is perfect or nearly so, at least in some dimensions. Why take up space in a group with a "perfect" (well-adjusted) youth when so many need help? The response is that we are not talking about the "together" youth, who seems to have no issues. There are two types of models, the mastery model and the coping model (Cormier & Cormier, 1998). A *mastery model* is the perfect performance model, while a *coping model* is a person who is making progress working on an issue or behavior but who still demonstrates needs and errors. A coping model is what we are looking for in a group—youths who have the same (homogeneous) major issue but who are different in terms of experiences and personality. Some of these differences are as follows:

Different coping skills to deal with situations

Different stage of dealing with the problem

Different attitude about the problem situation

Different values regarding the situation

Different disclosure levels (high, average, low)

Different emotional response levels (high, average, low)

Different cultural heritage

Different socioeconomic levels

Different levels of resiliency

Example 1
Homogeneous for topic: Divorce

Heterogeneous for skills, adjustment, and other qualities

Choose eight members from some of these or other categories:

1–2 members whose parents have remarried and who have half-siblings

1–2 members who have one parent remarried

7

1–2 members with adjustment problems whose parents have both remarried

1–2 members whose parents are dating

1–2 members where only one parent is present (the other may be living elsewhere, in prison, or deceased)

1–2 members where the custodial parent has a live-in partner

Example 2

Homogeneous for topic: Difficulty dealing with anger

Heterogeneous for skills, adjustment, and other qualities

Choose eight members from some of these or other categories:

2–3 members who ACT OUT their anger

- Contact with juvenile justice system
- Early sexual activity
- Aggressive, antisocial behavior

2–3 members who ACT IN their anger

- Somatization of anger (physical illnesses caused by psychological stress, such as asthma attacks or stomachaches)
- Emotional problems, such as depression or suicidal ideation

1–2 members who CHANNEL their anger

- Excellence in sports, academics, hobby, or other area but still having difficulty expressing anger appropriately

Role-balancing is essential for a short-term group. By selecting on heterogeneous factors, group members with similar problematic behaviors and situations can observe and learn from others who have a variety of different coping skills and perspectives. This provides a powerful therapeutic experience. Every member selected must bring to the group some positive aspect to model. A lack of heterogeneity is why short-term groups that are overloaded with youth having a particular problem usually are unsuccessful. If you have a group in which all the youth have failed the last two grading periods, how are you going to model enjoying studying, being successful taking exams, and wanting to learn? There will be no one in the group who has overcome academic problems, and therefore these experiences

won't be modeled. What if the group is overloaded with youth who have problems acting out anger? Again, these youth will have no models for other, more appropriate ways to behave.

General Selection Guidelines

Specific guidelines are given in the introduction to each group agenda to help you select youth who might be appropriate candidates for a group on that topic. Although research is inconsistent on the exact selection of members, the following general guidelines of good practice will help you decide. Use your best judgment in selecting members and develop your own feelings on what will work in your setting and for your topic. If you select members outside these guidelines, be aware that you may have to deal with the types of problems that the guidelines protect against.

Select

1. A range of participants so each student will have at least one positive behavioral model

2. Youth who are no more than 2 years apart chronologically

3. Youth with approximately the same social, emotional, intellectual, and physical maturity

4. Youth who respond well to social influence (one high-status boy and girl)

5. Youth who are able to work in other group situations (class projects, teams)

6. Youth of different racial, cultural, ethnic, and socioeconomic backgrounds, if possible

7. Youth of both sexes, unless the topic would cause one sex to be very uncomfortable (for example, a male student in a group of pregnant females)

Do Not Select

1. Best friends, worst enemies, or siblings. There are other dynamics going on in these relationships that prohibit appropriate self-disclosure.

2. Youth who are suicidal or homicidal, or who have seriously considered attempting either of these actions recently, without psychological treatment

3. Youth who are involved in ongoing sexual activity (homosexual or

heterosexual) if such behavior is exceptional within the peer group

4. Youth who habitually lie and steal for attention

5. Youth experiencing an ongoing or recent crisis (unless the group is specifically geared to deal with this conflict)

6. Youth whom you know or strongly suspect are being abused or are under investigation for abuse

7. Youth who are extremely aggressive physically and/or verbally

8. Youth whose parents are divided about having the youth participate

9. Youth who are too "different" from the rest of the group (for example, one student from an ethnic minority, one student who has a developmental disability)

Even though they might not be appropriate candidates for a counseling group, students who fall into the "do not select" category are certainly still in need of services. You could work with these students individually or in a family group, or you could refer them to another counselor or a mental health agency.

A final issue in selection concerns letting students know they have not been chosen. One way to prevent having to deal with a large number of students not selected is to interview the youth whom you know or have assessment information on first—in other words, those who have the highest potential for being selected. Interview only enough to get eight members, with perhaps two alternates. It is not required that you interview everyone who wants an interview! Even though it helps to mention clearly and frequently during the advertising and interviewing processes that not everyone who wants to be in the group can be included, some students may interpret not being selected as a significant adult rejection. If more groups on the topic are planned later on, and the student is a genuine candidate, you could relate this information. Otherwise, individual counseling or referral may be the solution.

Step 7: Conduct Pregroup Session

Before the group is ready to proceed with sessions devoted to the content or topic of the group, a number of "business" items must be addressed:

1. Going over the purpose and goals of the group

2. Thoroughly explaining confidentiality and its limits

3. Conducting an activity to develop ground rules

4. Doing a get-acquainted activity

5. Establishing thinking-feeling-behaving definitions

You can begin to address the first three items—purpose and goals, confidentiality, and ground rules—in the pregroup interview, but you will need to go over these issues again with the whole group, as well as conduct a getting-acquainted activity and a thinking-feeling-behaving activity. (I'll have more to say about these activities under discussion of the first session.) School-based group sessions are frequently limited by the prevailing class time period (40 or 50 minutes). Completing the preliminary business will take longer than that, so other arrangements must be made.

Probably the best approach is to have a *pregroup session,* in which the group you have tentatively selected from the pregroup interview phase convenes for the sole purpose of conducting some of this preliminary business: going over purpose and goals, confidentiality, and perhaps ground rules. Having this session will greatly facilitate getting your group to the working stage. In addition, if you are having some doubts about potential members, the pregroup session gives you an opportunity to screen them out before the group officially starts. If the group starts and a member must be asked to leave, it may damage developing cohesion and get the group off on the wrong foot.

The following technique is helpful in making final selection decisions at the pregroup session: Pass out index cards during the pregroup meeting. Ask potential group members to respond to three questions:

1. Is your best friend, worst enemy, or relative here in the pregroup session? Please name.

2. Is there anyone here who would make it so uncomfortable for you that you could not or would not feel comfortable talking about your thoughts and feelings?

3. This session gave you more information about what the group will be like, such as the goals of the group, some of the

ground rules, who the other members will probably be, and what confidentiality means. Please share on a scale of 1 to 10 (1 meaning not at all and 10 meaning very much) how much you want to participate in this group experience.

The information you can get from using this technique is extremely valuable. It is certainly worth the time and effort more times than not, especially when you find yourself at the third or fourth session with several group members not participating or dropping out due to issues directly related to these questions.

If you cannot schedule a pregroup session, another approach is to schedule the first session of your group during a double period. (Times before or after school can be used, but this does not work in all settings.) Yet another way of handling preliminary business is to extend your group experience from eight to perhaps ten sessions. You can use the first 40- to 50-minute session to deal thoroughly with some of these issues. You can then use the beginning of the second session to finish the group business.

Step 8: Administer Pretest

Accountability is an important issue in group work. A pretest and posttest can give you valuable information about whether the group counseling experience has been effective in changing the skills, attitudes, and/or behaviors of individual group members and the group as a whole.

If a main purpose of your group counseling activity is to conduct research, you will probably want to use a standardized instrument. On the other hand, if you would be satisfied with more general information about the attitudes of participants, a counselor-constructed Likert-type scale like those provided in Appendix C for each of the groups would be sufficient. It is important to point out that the scales included in this book are not sophisticated, norm-referenced instruments, nor are they meant to give proof of anything. However, these informal measures can allow you to estimate what might have happened as a result of the group experience and take a look at attitudes that have changed. Another benefit of the informal approach is that it allows you to construct items to fit the goals and objectives of each session.

In addition to providing information about the impact of sessions on participants, the pretest can be used to help you select members

for the group. For example, if you administer a pretest designed to assess self-esteem, you might want to eliminate some youths whose self-esteem is very high in favor of balancing roles in the group. It is important to point out, however, that self-report measures of this type are subject to inaccuracies. You might therefore want to augment the information from the measure with teacher and/or parent reports of whatever factor you are assessing.

If the pretest is used as a screening tool, it could be administered during the pregroup interview to all students who are thinking about participating. If other selection criteria are used, the pretest could be given any time after selection and before the first session. Never use the first session for pretesting and/or the last session for posttesting.

Step 9: Conduct Sessions

The next step is to conduct the sessions. Some of the procedures described have more than enough stimulus material for one session and can be used for two sessions, especially if your time is limited to 40 minutes. Sessions under 40 minutes are not recommended, as the dynamics of the group experience cannot unfold if the sessions are too crowded with content. You can easily extend the eight sessions to ten, twelve, or more by eliminating part of the content and allowing for more discussion and processing. Fewer than eight sessions does not allow the group process to evolve, nor does it allow for the issues and topics to be covered in enough depth to result in attitudinal changes.

A flexible approach to extending the group is to have members select topics or activities every so often. For example, if members participate and work well in three sessions, the fourth session could be a free topic, then the eighth session could be a free topic, and so forth until the main content of the agenda is finished. The "Jugglers" agenda lends itself well to free topics, but you could use the approach for any of the groups. Keep in mind that free topics should use the same ground rules and format as the structured ones. You will need to ask group members for some goals at the beginning of the session and keep the focus on the chosen topic so members do not get the idea that the "freebie" topic is an opportunity to gripe about peers and teachers.

Step 10: Administer Posttest

After the group has ended, use the same instrument you used as a pretest for your posttest. It is important not to wait more than a week or two to give the posttest; if you do, you increase the chance that you are really measuring maturation and/or learning from other sources, and your results thus may be contaminated. You could have the group members stop by your office for a few minutes to take the posttest and give you any other feedback you need to make changes in the group format or content. You might also develop some type of evaluation form on leader skills, if you are willing to accept the feedback. Such a form should allow for responses to questions like "What did you like about the way the leader lead the group?" and "What do you think needs to be changed?"

Step 11: Conduct Postgroup Follow-up

At the last session of the group, it is appropriate to tell the members that they will have another opportunity to get together and discuss their thoughts and feelings about the group, and to share support, ideas, or encouragement for goals they are still working on. This follow-up session (or two if you wish) is usually held about 4 weeks after the last session. Group members can share their accomplishments and perceptions of what happened to them during the group and get new ideas about how to keep working on their issues. Follow-up meetings also offer an opportunity for mutual support in reaching behavior-change goals, setting new ones, and overcoming obstacles. Encouragement and a renewal of commitment to work on behavior change are reinforcing and helpful. One idea for the postgroup follow-up session is to invite group members to have lunch with you. They can bring their lunch trays or brown-bag it to your office or another place where you will have privacy.

Step 12: Write Up Group Evaluation

The postgroup evaluation is essential for accountability and can be used for the following purposes:

To inform administrators, teachers, and/or parents of the direction of change that may have occurred in the group as a result of participation

To compare pretest with posttest responses for each member to help that member achieve current and future goals

To provide information helpful in assisting group members with any problems that may have developed due to focusing on areas covered in the group

To assist the group leader in improving the group in the future

To obtain an idea of the group leader's effectiveness

Write a brief report describing your experience and giving generalized data results from the pretest/posttest comparison. A two-page narrative and posting of means would be sufficient for most settings. Remember that the data from these tests belong to the students taking the tests and must be kept confidential. Except in extreme circumstances, individual scores may not be shared unless the youth gives permission. Be sure to omit all identifying information on reports of general data.

GUIDELINES FOR GROUP SUCCESS

Group counseling is a science and an art. The leader is the artist, adding the gift of personhood to the experience. The richness of the relationships provides potential for a magical growth experience in group process, but there must be knowledge of the science and skillful application of theory, techniques, and organizational logistics. This section deals with some of the mechanics, based on good practice and research in the profession.

Logistics

Logistical issues in conducting your group involve group size, scheduling of sessions, and aspects of the group setting.

Group Size

The recommended number of group members for preadolescents or adolescents is six to eight. This number allows all of the members to be heard on a regular basis, sharing thoughts, feelings, and behaviors, and practicing new skills. Fewer than eight members limits the sharing and input, which is the grist for the mill in group counseling. Too few members may cause the group to become too intense, with more pressure on each member to participate. If there are more than eight members (you have a hoard!), the shy or unassertive youth will have less opportunity to become involved, and you may spend a great deal of time drawing out the low disclosers and cutting off the monopolizers or more frequent participants. A rule of thumb: The younger the members, and/or the more severe the problem(s), the smaller the number in the group. If you are working with youth with severe problems, with no opportunity to select a better heterogeneous mix, four members may be what is needed to make it work. Even numbers facilitate use of dyads during get-acquainted, role-play, and other activities.

Scheduling of Sessions

Each of the group counseling experiences outlined in this book has a minimum of eight sessions. In terms of group counseling, eight is a very small number of sessions to have expectations for permanent behavior change—the best that can be hoped for is some attitudinal change. Some youth will make changes based on eight sessions, but you cannot expect permanent behavior change in established maladaptive actions. Although school personnel and parents often expect counseling to work miracles, this is usually not the case. Before youth can make deliberate behavior changes, they must raise their awareness of what they are thinking, feeling, and doing in a situation that produces unhelpful behaviors. It is two sides of a coin: First comes awareness, then comes behavior change. Changes that take place in group counseling often do not produce visible results for some time.

Devoting more than 8 to 12 weeks to group counseling in a school setting is usually unrealistic, and the eight or so sessions outlined per topic in this book are scheduled for 40 to 50 minutes each. These sessions can be expanded according to the group's needs or otherwise adapted to suit your particular circumstances.

It is recommended that you meet with the group once weekly. When planning the schedule, be sure to consider school vacation times: If you miss one week, it may be difficult to regenerate the level of trust, cohesion, and commitment that members have developed so far. Two weeks is a long time for young adolescents.

Another issue relating to scheduling concerns the need to avoid causing students to be frequently absent from classes. One way of avoiding this conflict is to schedule the group sessions during a study hall, free period, club period, activity period, or before or after school. Another option is to use a different class period for each weekly session. For example, the first group session would be scheduled for first period in the morning; the next week it would be during second period. In this way students who are having academic difficulties do not miss the same class several times.

Setting

Confidentiality is a major issue in group counseling, and ensuring that youth have a place where they feel comfortable disclosing without someone overhearing helps them develop a feeling of security. Choose a room that closes completely and be sure to hang a "Do Not Disturb" sign on the door reminding people not to enter once the group has started. If you are beginning to do group counseling, you may need to discuss this issue with your colleagues and school secretaries, letting them know your group is not to be disturbed unless there is an emergency. It is up to you to set a professional, serious tone and let others know up front how important the issue of privacy is to group counseling.

You will need enough chairs, cushions, pillows, or bean-bag chairs for each member, including yourself. Do not sit around a table, as it is a distraction and barrier. If you have a small room with a table in the center, move the table to one side so it can still be used for drawing and other activities. Be sure each youth in the group can see you and the other members clearly. You will need an easel pad to write on occasionally and, of course, a box of tissues! Taking the group outside in nice weather is an appealing possibility; however, this would not be a good idea if distractions such as a nearby physical education class or another activity would interfere with the group's work.

Session Organization

Each group session outlined in this book is divided into three parts: Opening Time, Working Time, and Processing Time. Opening Time should be about one-quarter of the time allotted to the group. For example, if you are having a 40-minute session, you will have about 10 minutes for the Opening Time business. Working Time claims one-half of the session time, or 20 minutes of a 40-minute session. Processing Time occupies the other one-quarter of the time, or the last 10 minutes of a 40-minute session. Each of these sections of the group session includes tasks to be accomplished. No matter what the topic, problem, issue, or age of participants, it is extremely important for you to manage the time so the youth do not miss the special opportunities that each of these sections presents. After a session or two, when the members learn that you are going to say, "We need to end our Working Time now so that we can process," they can be included and even given the "clock watcher" responsibility to help. Making a definite statement for transitions between sections of the session helps members realize they cannot gab about nonessentials and must learn to use the time they have to help themselves and one another make personal changes. Specific language also provides structure for youth who have AD/HD or who for other reasons exhibit low tolerance for frustration, poor organizational skills, or the inability to plan ahead.

The First Session

The initial session's content will vary according to how much preliminary business you have been able to accomplish before the group's first formal meeting. As noted previously, you must accomplish certain tasks before you can move on to the content of the group experience. I'll repeat these tasks here, with the addition of processing, and assign them some approximate time spans:

1. Going over the purpose and goals of the group (5 minutes)

2. Thoroughly explaining confidentiality and its limits, and encouraging comments and questions from members regarding their understanding, acceptance, and compliance with this requirement (15 minutes)

3. Conducting an activity to develop ground rules (15 minutes)

4. Doing a get-acquainted activity (20 minutes)

5. Establishing thinking-feeling-behaving definitions (25 minutes)

6. Processing what was learned (5 to 10 minutes)

This adds up to a total of 85 to 90 minutes, roughly twice as long as the average 40- to 50-minute session typical in most school settings. How can you do all of this at the first session? You can't! This is why I recommended that you hold a pregroup session (as described in Step 7), arrange for double time the first session, or add a session and complete these tasks over the first two sessions, starting the topic with the third session. If these preliminary business tasks are omitted, they will have to be "caught up" during another session's time, adding to the confusion. It is frustrating for leader and members alike to try to cram too much into one session. Doing so will probably leave everyone feeling the experience has been annoying rather than pleasant. So, even though you must work extra hard at the beginning, your effort will pay off in subsequent sessions.

The first-session Opening Time in each of the groups describes procedures for the first four tasks: purpose and goals, confidentiality, ground rules, and getting acquainted. Instead of a topical activity, Working Time is primarily devoted to a thinking-feeling-behaving activity. Processing Time is similar to that for subsequent sessions.

Purpose and Goals

First, you will need to welcome members and briefly describe the purpose and goals of the group. To convey the overall purpose, you might say something like "The purpose for us getting together and sharing difficulties about dating and getting along in relationships is so everyone can learn better ways of making relationships work—to make our relationships less emotionally painful and more loving and joyful." Some goals for a group on this topic might be identifying personal values in a relationship, learning how to be more assertive in getting one's needs met, learning to empathize with others' feelings and needs, and so on.

Confidentiality and Its Limits

At the heart of the group process is confidentiality. Without it, group members will be unwilling to self-disclose, and the group will go nowhere. You can define confidentiality in very clear, age-appropriate language as the "no-blab" rule, telling group members, "What is said in group, stays in group." Give many examples of what other kids or adults might say that would pressure members to break confidentiality. For instance:

I heard you talk about other kids in that group. What did Sherrin say about me?

Did anyone tell about the stuff we smoked on Friday?

You know Tenisha and I broke up. What is she saying about me in that group?

Only crazy people need to go to group. What is Juan doing in there?

It is also important for you to explain the limits of confidentiality—in other words, the fact that as the group leader, you are required to share information about what goes on in group under certain circumstances, covered by the ideas of harm, abuse, and courts:

Harm means anything that would indicate that the member has harmed, is harming, or will do harm to self or others. This includes overt behaviors—for example, a member who makes comments about suicide or "getting even" with someone. It also includes covert behaviors, as in the case of a member who believes she is pregnant but who has not confirmed this fact or received any medical care.

Abuse refers to knowledge of child abuse. All states have laws that a counselor divulge information to the proper authorities if a member reports being abused or knowing that another youth is being abused. Some states have laws requiring the counselor to report adult and elder abuse. Group leaders should be familiar with the reporting requirements in their own states.

Courts means that if a judge subpoenas records, the counselor may have to reveal information that would otherwise be held confidential. In addition, the counselor may need to report knowledge of felony criminal activity to the proper authorities.

One way to remind group members of the limits of confidentiality is to share the Limits of Confidentiality sign included in Appendix A as a handout (or as a poster you display each session). It is also helpful to give several examples of what "harm" means:

You say you have been thinking about running away.

You say you know about two guys who are going to get in a serious fight where someone would get hurt.

You say you are thinking about suicide or homicide.

You say you thought you were pregnant, or had some disease, or were exhausted

all the time and couldn't sleep (you could be harming yourself if the problems aren't taken care of by a professional).

You say you know of an older youth or adult who is harming someone under 18 years old in any way—physically, sexually, or emotionally.

Ground Rules

The third piece of business of first-session Opening Time is assisting group members in developing a set of ground rules that helps them become more comfortable with the new experience of disclosing personal ideas, feelings, behaviors, and opinions to one another. Ground rules are a specific type of group norm, or expected behavior, of group members. (Other norms are discussed later in this introduction.) Ground rules are explicit, written, agreed-upon rules developed for the purpose of group safety. At the first session, you can describe a few basic ground rules, in addition to confidentiality, for all groups in that setting:

Come to group on time.

Everyone has the right to "pass" (not share unless that's comfortable).

Respect others' opinions.

You can then invite the members to develop some ground rules of their own, for the purpose of making the group a safe and inviting place to share private thoughts and feelings. These might include the following:

Everyone gets equal time to talk.

No fighting or put-downs.

Take turns.

Try to help members frame their rules in a positive rather than negative form (for example, "Respect others' opinions" versus "No put-downs"). If group members develop some of their own ground rules and feel "ownership" of them, they will be more likely to use them to govern their own behavior. If you develop and impose all of the rules, then group members will likely see them as just another set of adult controls and tune them out. Ground rules need to be worked out, no matter how long it takes. Sometimes more assertive group members control this activity, and it is up to you to listen carefully and use your skills to encourage everyone to participate so the rules truly represent the group. Otherwise, this issue will come up again, sometimes as a hidden agenda.

One way to reinforce ownership is to ask group members to write the ground rules out on a poster that will be displayed during each group session. They can do this as a project—perhaps the first one in the life of the group. They can choose one member to be the "scribe" and write the rules on the poster, or each one can take a turn writing a rule. Once the rules are written, each member can sign his or her name to the poster to signify acceptance and agreement. Beginning the group with a shared responsibility is a powerful technique that helps build cohesion.

Getting Acquainted

The getting-acquainted activity helps group members begin to develop a sense of "we-ness" or cohesion and gives them the opportunity to see how the group will work. The groups in this book include a number of different types of activities for this purpose. Many of the activities involve dyads. Especially if you have members who are somewhat reluctant to speak up, the dyad is an excellent choice for a getting-acquainted activity. Ordinarily it is much easier to speak to one person than to face the whole group and make even low-level self-disclosures. After sharing something like name, favorite pizza topping, and one thing each member hopes to learn from the group experience, the dyads then disclose this information to the rest of the group. If you will be asking the dyads to share with the larger group, be sure to let them know this beforehand. Some dyad work you won't ask everyone to share, just those who want to: Group members may feel more free to brainstorm and self-disclose with a partner if they know the information will not necessarily be shared with everyone else.

Thinking-Feeling-Behaving

Other group business that must be covered before you begin talking deeply about content is to be certain that group members know how thinking, feeling, and behaving are different. You will be referring to these three modalities constantly, and you don't want to find yourself at the third or fourth session with members still not able to tell the difference between a feeling and a behavior!

Each group's first session includes an idea for teaching group members to discriminate among the three and name words that apply to each one. For instance:

Thinking: Imagining, deciding, examining, learning, organizing, remembering, wondering

Feeling: Annoyed, confused, elated, furious, humiliated, jealous, motivated, resentful, weary

Behaving: Arguing, digesting, flirting, gossiping, imitating, laughing, smiling

A number of groups use the metaphor of interlocking gears to help group members understand the concept of interrelationship. Other metaphors include the roots, trunk, and leaves of a tree, or a head, heart, and hand. Once group members have mastered these distinctions, you can ask them to use their new terminology to share their goals related to the group's topic. You can ask, for example, "What do you want to be thinking, feeling, and doing differently about (your anger, your loss, your boyfriend/girlfriend problem, and so on) at the end of the group?"

Subsequent Sessions

During sessions after the first, the Opening Time has two business items. The first is to ask, using open-ended questions, what concerns group members have about confidentiality, then about the ground rules. Do not ask *if* group members have any concerns. Instead, say, "What concerns or questions about confidentiality do you have?" Open-ended questions assume they do have comments, questions, or concerns. This gives them permission to say what they want, rather than just saying no. The second item is to refer to the topic of the session before, then ask another open-ended question that will allow anyone who has taken the risk to try some between-session self-improvement practice a chance to share how it went. Say, for example, "Who would like to share what it was like to try using I-messages?" Let them share and reward them profusely for even thinking about attempting practice or changes.

Working is the term used in group counseling for the psychological business that is conducted. In the session, the Working Time provides a stimulus activity designed to bring about the goals of the session. In selecting an activity, be sure to keep in mind that it cannot take longer than half of the total session time. If it goes longer, you "hit the wall"—in other words, the bell rings, the kids leave, and there is no time for processing!

Finally, and most important, is Processing Time. Processing Time is devoted to maximizing the learning experiences of the session. The idea of processing applies to session-related learning for members and leaders, before- and after-session dynamics, group termination, and follow-up of the group experience. Here we are talking about the processing that takes place during each session. There are actually two processing activities in most sessions. The first involves the formal, open-ended questions the leader asks, or has the members ask, specifically related to the ongoing Working Time learning activity. For example, if you are conducting the thinking-feeling-behaving activity in the first session, you might want to know if indeed everyone understands the concept and might ask, "What questions do you have about the differences between thinking and feeling? What feelings might be more difficult to express than others?"

The second type of processing is a formal time set aside after the Working Time to maximize individual and group insight into what transpired that session. This type of processing occurs on four levels:

Intrapersonal (What were you thinking or feeling while we talked about _____ ?)

Interpersonal (What did you notice about the other group members today? or What was it like to be a group member today?)

New learning (What new ideas, feelings, or behaviors do you have now as a result of coming to group?)

Application (How can you use what you learned today to help you this week?)

These levels reflect areas of insight from an individual's perspective, but responses are heard by and therefore stimulate insights in other members. Some of the sessions give more than one question for each level. By selecting at least one question from each of the four levels, you can provide each member with the opportunity to grow and can encourage connections, empathy, and relationship skills in all members.

The importance of leaving sufficient time for end-of-session processing cannot be overstressed. If the time is eroded, the youth may leave the session without a clear idea of what they have experienced and no time to make commitments for behavioral practice. (I promise to be on you like a duck on a June bug if you fail to save time for processing!)

Group Norms

One of the most important leadership tasks is to establish norms for behavior and interaction in the group. Norms are implicit, expected ways of behaving that are reinforced by the leader and other group members. Most norms are unwritten codes of behavior that you as the leader encourage from the beginning session. When a member deviates from the expected behaviors, there is usually some kind of pressure to conform, such as teasing, questioning, criticism, or expression of irritation. As a behavioral model for the group, you take responsibility for demonstrating and reinforcing these norms. Group members will pick up the norms quickly if you are consistent in setting and reinforcing them. Some major norms for you as the leader are as follows:

To bring up and protect confidentiality of members each session, giving members an opportunity to discuss any related material and dealing with breaches of confidentiality immediately

To bring up and discuss between-session behavioral homework, reinforcing members for any and all attempts to make changes

To respect and help group members respect one another's feelings and ideas, using empathy statements frequently

To protect members against physical and emotional threats, coercion, and undue peer pressure

To work to ensure equal participation of members

To convey that attendance is a serious commitment

To help members address one another directly, not talk unilaterally to the leader

To praise and help members praise one another for efforts, not just for results

Some norms are deliberately set by the group leader for the purpose of having a positive effect on the group goals, such as respecting members' right to pass and encouraging members to appreciate one another's efforts at change. Sometimes negative norms get started and work against achieving behavioral change. For example, if a member comes to group late with no excuse and no one questions this, it could become a negative norm to come late.

Another negative norm that needs to be stopped happens when someone shares a nonmajority opinion for which he or she is criticized or teased. If this is accepted, others will refrain from giving such opinions.

LEADERSHIP ISSUES

The personhood of the counselor, leadership style, and the issue of co-leadership are among the most important issues involved in a group experience.

Personhood of the Counselor

The approach to group counseling described in this book requires that the leader share aspects of his or her own personhood (personal behavior, attitudes, ideas, and feelings) with members. For this reason, it is neither possible nor desirable to behave in one way in the counseling session and another way outside of it. All of us have areas where we are not using our potential to the fullest, and all of us engage in behaviors that are less than admirable. If a counselor purports to be a model for young adolescents, then that counselor needs to be striving to be as authentic a person as possible. As Gerald Corey (1995) states in his text *Theory and Practice of Group Counseling*, "The most effective group direction is found in the kind of life the group members see the leader demonstrating and not in the words they hear the leader saying" (p. 53). Many other experts in the field have expressed similar opinions regarding the personhood of the counselor (Carkhuff, 1971; Rogers, 1980; Yalom, 1975). The counselor's knowledge of procedures, activities, and evaluation methodology are certainly important, but the journey to developing one's potential remains the counselor's most important long-term task.

Leadership Style

Leadership style can be thought of as a continuum of control over a group. At one end of the continuum is *leading*, or complete control over the content and expectations of an experience. This type of leadership is often found in a classroom, or perhaps a classroom guidance activity, in which the subject is presented in lecture style and each youth interacts independently with the teacher and the books or materials presented. Questions are also unilateral, between teacher and student, and little if any interaction takes place among the class members. The leader is prepared to assess the degree to which the youth have assimilated the material presented through exams. Group counseling, however, does not follow this model. We are attempting a totally different approach, building an atmosphere of trust, warmth, support, encouragement, and self-disclosure, all necessary for group process to take place. This approach, closer to the other end of the control continuum, is termed *facilitation*. Facilitation involves shared responsibility for what happens in the session; the leader provides stimulus material, but the focus is on interpersonal actions, not on learning specific content. Group classroom guidance and skills training are content oriented, whereas group counseling is process oriented, with content as a stimulus. In group counseling, the purpose is to provide a safe environment for youth to explore their feelings, values, attitudes, and ideas about themselves and their behaviors, with behavior and attitudinal changes as a result. The group members are encouraged to participate fully by making connections with one another and being supportive and encouraging of one another's situations and attempts to change behavior. In other words, the focus is not totally on content but on the process of becoming a better human being.

This concept may be new for someone accustomed to the content-oriented approach of the educational setting. But letting go of some control needs to happen for group counseling to succeed. Although content and skills are presented in the groups in this book, they are meant only as stimuli—they are not cast in concrete. Leaders must be willing to give up the agenda for the needs of the moment. Many times in group work with youth, a member will arrive with a raw issue related to the topic and obviously be hurting over the incident or situation. If the procedures are rigidly followed, the youth with the issue will not be psychologically present in the group, and the other members will likely wonder what is going on. Perhaps the youth will behave in an uncharacteristically aggressive way or be very withdrawn. If it is appropriate in the specific situation, it is your responsibility as leader to forego the plan and help the member deal with the issue in the context of the group.

Difficulty giving up control is most often a leader problem, as youth will readily accept opportunities to share group leadership responsibilities. To encourage group members to take on responsibility, you could ask, for example, "Who would like to do the Opening Time questions today?" Write out the major questions about confidentiality, the ground rules, and behavioral homework from the previous session, and let one of the members conduct this part of the session. The same can be done with Processing Time. The opening session of the "Dating and Relating" group shows a humorous way to involve members in group leadership; the technique can be extended to any of the other group agendas.

In this way, the youth learn responsibility for their own personal growth and acquire life skills they will have from then on. It's their nickel! The group belongs to the youth, not the leader—turn it over to them at every opportunity to solve their own problems, and encourage, encourage, encourage.

Co-leadership

Another aspect of leadership concerns whether one or two leaders will be involved. Selection of a co-leader is an extremely important decision and should not be made randomly or according to convenience. Every aspect of the group is impacted by both leaders, and insufficient attention to this process can have a negative effect from the beginning. There are many advantages to having a co-leader: Members gain from two perspectives, especially if it is a female/male leadership team, by receiving extra support and encouragement. Beginning co-leaders, such as student counselors or counselors just learning group work, can receive support and modeling from the more experienced partner. Co-leaders can learn new skills and techniques from each other, as well as fill in if one or the other is absent.

The issue of co-leadership is a complex one. Suffice it to say here that the essential requirements for co-leaders to work out well are, not surprisingly, the same qualities and values needed for members to have a healing experience—trust and respect. Co-leaders must also have a desire to learn from each other and nurture a climate of safety so that each can disclose growth areas, limitations, and concerns without fear of reprisal. All major decisions need to be made together. The following questions may help:

How are we going to share preparation for the group responsibilities?

When will we meet to plan for each session and debrief after each session?

Who will open and close each session, and who will manage timekeeping?

How will conflicts between leaders and members be handled?

What theories and techniques will be followed/used?

How will we end, conduct follow-up, and evaluate the group?

Consider the co-leadership model only if there is a great deal of trust, respect, honesty, and willingness to put the time in to make this work. The group members deserve no less than a fully functioning therapeutic team. If you select a student co-leader, it is essential to know what the university supervisor's expectations are for that student before agreeing to co-lead with the student. A dominant leader who does not share the leadership responsibilities and tasks cannot provide the appropriate growth opportunities for the student.

THE "MAGICAL GLUE" OF GROUPS

If the topic or subject being discussed is one side of the content coin, the other is *group process*. This is not to be confused with the previously mentioned skill of processing, although the two are related. Group process has to do with the *how* of groups—that is, with what is happening in the relationships between and among group members and leader in the here and now, not in the there and then. It is the essential ingredient that makes group work therapeutic. Without fostering process, the group is a psychoeducational group or perhaps a task group, but not group counseling. Balancing between the content of the group (topic) and the process (what is happening in relationships) is the major and likely the most difficult task you will have as group leader.

Why is learning to deal with the here-and-now process issues so difficult for beginning group counselors? Because we grow up in a content-driven educational system, geared to get the information across to students so they can be tested and ranked and move on to more content. As a group counselor, you have either been a teacher or a student, so you are geared toward delivering content. Only with sufficient studies and supervision in group counseling does a leader become process-oriented rather than content-oriented. This concept is very difficult for professionals unfamiliar with group work and for parents to understand, as they are not exposed to these ideas. This is most likely why they remain in the content domain, expecting the counseling to "fix" a youth through a direct education process—and, of course, this does not happen.

How do you balance content and process in a session? Deal with issues in this order:

1. What is presently happening in the group

2. Current events outside the group

3. Past events outside the group

Start with the content suggested to focus the group, but whenever something is happening in the group, change the focus to that event. Some examples of statements to refocus the group on process are as follows:

> What is happening right now? (It could be a private conversation going on between two group members; someone is mad, bored, hurt, crying; someone is absent.)
>
> What is it like to watch other group members whispering in the group?
>
> What are you feeling right now?
>
> How much trust are you feeling in the group right now?
>
> It feels like some disrespect is going on—what do you think?
>
> What would you like someone to say to you?
>
> Whom do you link or connect with?
>
> Jana, would you share what is going on with you?
>
> How do you feel about Jeremy's saying he is mad at you? Tell Jeremy.
>
> I'm wondering where the tension is coming from—what do you think?

It's magic—but it's magic the leader stimulates to happen! These are the process issues/statements that make group work, that make the experience healing and growthful. Some group leaders stick with the content because of lack of knowledge of what to say to make process happen and sometimes because it is scary to deal with these issues. But it is absolutely worthwhile to take the risk to learn to switch between process and content as needed

so you and your group members can experience the highs of healing.

ETHICAL ISSUES

Thorough discussion of the complex matter of group work ethics is beyond the scope of this introduction, yet the counselor who provides services for young adolescents has a responsibility to adhere to ethical practice even greater than that of a counselor working with adults. Youth are in a position of vulnerability and risk. They come to the counseling experience trusting the counselor to be completely knowledgeable, professional, and ethical in every aspect of delivery of group counseling services. The counselor has the responsibility to practice group work ethically not only for the sake of the young clients, but also for their parents, the school administration, and the profession. It is a matter of trying to serve many masters at once while keeping in mind the complex issues associated with confidentiality, participant rights, and psychological and physical risk.

The best practice guidelines developed by the Association for Specialists in Group Work (1998) are reprinted as Appendix D in this book. Before undertaking a group, review these guidelines carefully and investigate the recommendations of any other professional organization to which you may belong. It will also be helpful to review discussions of ethical responsibility found in various other group counseling resources (for example, Corey & Corey, 1997; Gazda, 1989).

TECHNIQUES FOR GROUP SUCCESS

The group leader can employ hundreds of skills and techniques to improve the individual effectiveness, process, and overall outcome of the group experience. Over the course of conducting the topical groups in the *Skills for Living* series—as well as groups for adults in prison, private practice, and mental health settings—I have found that certain techniques consistently add significantly to the experience for leader and members. These techniques range from widely used general counseling techniques, such as using open-ended questions and dyads, to specific props that enhance understanding of therapeutic concepts. The following section highlights these useful and growth-engendering methods. A complete discussion of these and other techniques is included in my book *Skills and Techniques for Group Work with Children and Adolescents* (Smead, 1995).

Self-Improvement Exercises

Although the primary goal of group counseling is not skills training, in which the development and transfer of training to everyday situations is the goal, the group sessions do provide the opportunity for members to practice new skills. Self-improvement exercises (also known as behavioral homework) are between-session activities selected by the youth to practice improved ways of thinking, new skills, or more adaptive behaviors. This practice allows youth to try out new behaviors without pressure from peers or group leaders who may be observing, at their own pace, and as frequently as desired. There are three major guidelines: First, youth select their own exercises. Second, the counselor ensures that the youth have a clear idea of what to do. Finally, reinforcement for effort occurs at the beginning of the next session.

There is an essential difference between self-improvement exercises (behavioral homework) and traditional academic homework. Academic homework is assigned by a classroom teacher who expects every child to comply. Self-improvement exercises are selected by the youth and undertaken only if the youth is ready, with the leader's guidance and careful encouragement. Practicing new behaviors outside of group is a risk for a child and may have strong, swift negative repercussions. For example, if a shy, passive child uses I-messages with an abusive parent, the result could be more abuse. If the counselor has *assigned* rather than *encouraged* the use of I-messages, an obvious risk is present. At the end of each session, during the Processing Time, the final processing question is a version of "What are you willing to do between sessions to use what we learned today to help move closer to your goals?" The counselor invites group members to think about and perhaps make a commitment to practice.

Be sure your group members do not think this practice is a requirement. Say that practice is optional in several ways—for example, "Only choose something to practice if you think you are ready to do it, and if the time comes and you are scared or too worried, don't try it yet." Also, encourage group members for even thinking about trying out something new between sessions. Stop escalating commitments immediate-

ly. For example, if one youth says, "I'll try using the I-message with _____ ," and a second youth says, "I'll try using I-messages ten times," immediately stop and say, "If you just think about using it, or try it one time, that is a wonderful thing, and we will all be very proud of you. You don't have to do it more times." The younger your population, the more likely this is to occur.

During the Opening Time of the next session, you must bring this topic up, rewarding and reinforcing even tiny steps forward. Failure to do so will severely damage your treatment compliance: If you don't remember, in the next session group members are not likely to commit to behavioral practice!

Open-Ended Questions

Closed-ended questions usually begin with *do, is,* and *are.* They are used to elicit specific information, such as "Did you take your medication?" "Are you going to practice today?" and "Is your homework finished?" Continued use of this type of questioning frequently puts the receiver on the defensive, and the responses to closed-ended questions are usually one or two words. This type of question is not helpful in group counseling. Leave these questions at the door unless you absolutely need some specific information.

In the group experience, you are trying to encourage higher level cognitive thinking. Open-ended questions are more helpful in stimulating such responses. This type of questioning provides the opportunity for the youth to consider their thoughts, feelings, and behaviors. If you want to prompt introspection and ability to think about thinking (metacognition) and think about feelings (meta-emotion), use open-ended questions nearly all of the time. Skillful use of such questions consistently respects members' ability to think for themselves, to dig deeper into their emotional and intellectual resources, and to come up with responses that are healing to self and others. You will notice throughout this book that the Opening Time and Processing Time questions follow this format. For example:

What was it like when (you got in trouble)?

What were you (thinking, feeling, doing) when this happened?

What have you done so far (about your anger) that has worked?

What could you do differently in that situation?

What would you be willing to do to improve this situation?

What do you think you could do between sessions to get a tiny bit closer to your goal?

The question to avoid completely begins with the *why* word. The usual answer to the question "Why?" is "Because": Because she said it was OK, because he hit me first, and so forth. Asking why won't get you an answer and does not promote introspection or healing. It just puts youth on the defensive. There are very few times when the "Why?" question is appropriate in group counseling!

The Share-Around

Nearly every group counselor uses the technique of a *go-around*, an invitation to members to respond to a specific stimulus question or word. This technique is used in the classroom and other areas, usually beginning with the teacher's or leader's looking at a particular group member, with the direct or indirect expectation for that person to start, and the next member's feeling obligated to continue. I prefer to use a different technique in groups, which I call a *share-around*. In each group there are going to be high, average, and low self-disclosers. Given this natural group dynamic, you can allow high self-disclosers to choose going first. The share-around allows average and low self-disclosers the opportunity to watch and listen to models before taking a risk to speak up, teaching group members that you respect their individual needs and differences in terms of self-disclosure and encouraging them to do the same. In this way, the share-around models the philosophy that group work is really teaching love skills based on interpersonal respect. The invitation goes like this: "Let's hear from everyone on this. Everyone will have a chance to talk. Whoever would like to go first may go first, and then whoever wants to go next can talk. We won't go in a circle." You might have to stop them from going in order a time or two until this norm is established.

Using Props

The groups described in this book are not talk psychotherapy: The natural medium of chil-

dren and youth is play, not discussion. Even middle and high school youth love play. The activities in this book therefore are geared toward a particular issue with an element of play involved. Many of the activities use props to get the point across. For example, one session uses pacifiers to help group members identify childish behaviors that worked at one time but now need to be discarded for more adult behaviors. Another uses "alien" dolls to discuss feeling alienated and to identify different values. Plastic chameleons focus the group's attention on how we change our values to be accepted by a certain person/group. I have found the use of frogs to be particularly helpful in playfully expanding the metaphor of surviving difficult life situations. The idea is that if frogs can go through a complete metamorphosis from egg to tadpole, growing legs and lungs, then coming out on land or lily pad, then you can grow and change into the person you want to be, too. The hundreds of multicolored poison dart frogs represent our many human races and cultures; if they can survive their hardships, you can survive your parents' divorce.

Youth love these props and talk about them for a long time after the group is finished—and they remember the concepts better than if they were only described. If you are going to do group work with youth, a good investment would be fun and interesting props to get your points across in a memorable way.

Using Dyads

Young adolescents are particularly concerned about meeting other youth and disclosing personal information. By using the dyad technique early on in the life of the group, you can enhance their comfort level in sharing this new experience. In most cases it is easier to talk to one person than it is to a whole group. In the first session, the get-acquainted activity can be done by having the group members pair up, share certain information, then regroup and share the information with the rest of the group. You can use dyads again a time or two during the first few sessions to reduce tension about talking to several other youth in a "close-up" manner, as well as at any other time the group seems stuck. (Partners can draw something or work on a task together, then report back to the group.) After using the dyad structure a few times, try other configurations, or work together as a whole group. If you overuse the dyad, members will tire of the format.

Hope Statements

Youth who commit suicide have no hope. They are unable to see any possible way of dealing with their situation, as they have no behavioral referent for its improving. Many youth come to group with little sense of hope about growing up to lead productive lives, doing something they really like. You cannot hope there will be hope—you have to kindle, encourage, and support the idea of hope. One way you can do this is by using a *hope statement* at the end of every group, thus having the members hear over and over that one significant adult who cares about them has hope they will succeed and can improve. Some examples of hope statements are as follows:

> I have a great deal of hope that we are going to have a growthful experience together during this group.

> It's so exciting to know you are making progress and inching forward toward your goals.

> I can see and hear you getting better and better each session, and want you to know I have so much hope and confidence in each of you.

This is a beautiful, positive, and loving gift to give the group as each session ends.

Invitation

Youth have heard thousands of times over their academic careers statements like "You're going to do _____ " or "I want you to (be quiet, get to work, whatever)." Group counseling is different in so many ways, providing a supportive, encouraging environment. As the leader, you respect each group member individually. You are a safe, nonjudgmental, noncontrolling, no-power-plays type of person. You don't act, talk, or behave like other persons in the youths' life because you have a different mission. One special way for you to demonstrate this is to use the phrase "I'd like to invite you to (take part in an activity, share in a share-around, think about a new way of doing something, make a commitment to behavioral improvement exercises, and the like)." This technique is extremely powerful if used continually throughout the group to demonstrate your respect and belief in the youth—and they are in desperate need of someone's believing in them!

Linking and Connecting

When youth come to the first session, they are individuals who may or may not know one another. You can use the *linking and connecting* skill to help healing "we-ness" grow and flourish. One of the most powerful and simple of all group work techniques, it can be taught quickly to children down to about third grade. Linking is a deliberate way of teaching group members to make thinking, feeling, and behavioral connections to one another. By using the linking format a few times, you can teach them the skill. Group members from about fourth grade on will usually start using the skill on their own because it helps them feel in control of what is happening, and, as they say, "cool."

For youth, use a three-part statement. For example:

- DaLena, when you said your dad forgot to pick you up last Saturday,
- I felt sorry for you
- because my dad forgets to pick me up sometimes.

- Chele, when you said your boyfriend dumped you,
- I know what you felt then
- because I got dumped, too.

After a group member makes a linking statement to someone, encourage the person linked with to say one short sentence back, such as "Thanks, DaLena. I needed someone to understand that" or "I appreciate your sharing that with me, Chele." Use of the linking technique will encourage your group members to become a group more quickly, rather than remaining individuals who don't have any connections or sense of cohesion.

HOW TO STOP NEEDING THIS BOOK

Leading a group counseling experience is a little like conducting a symphony orchestra. Like leading, conducting is determined by the culture that you are in, the sophistication of the participants, the temperament and skills of the conductor/leader, and many other variables. When learning to conduct, a person needs to consider who he or she is and how best to express that sense of individuality, as well as the various technical aspects of the art. The person needs to apply a great deal of sensitivity to understand and provide the input each member of the orchestra needs. Some orchestra members will be watching the conductor carefully for every nuance of instruction. Others might need very little in the way of input to play their instruments and the particular piece in a masterful fashion. So it is with the group.

As you develop your group counseling leadership skills, it is essential that you tune in to the needs of the youth in your group. By nur-turing both skills and caring, you will begin to develop a balance in your professional life that will allow group work to meet the needs of many more of your clients.

So, how do you stop needing this book? According to the story, when one famous concert violinist was asked by a passerby how to get to Carnegie Hall, the violinist said, "Practice, practice, practice!" It seems that there are so many skills, tasks, and issues related to the work of group counseling that one wonders if providing services for a number of youth at once saves any time at all. What you need, then, is practice, and practice comes only after you have the courage to get started.

REFERENCES AND SUGGESTED RESOURCES FOR PROFESSIONALS

American School Counselor Association. *Role Statement: The school counselor membership resource guide.* Alexandria, VA: Author.

Association for Specialists in Group Work. (1991). *Ethical guidelines for group counselors.* Alexandria, VA: Author.

Association for Specialists in Group Work. (1998). *Best practice guidelines.* Alexandria: VA: Author.

Begun, R. (Ed.). (1996). *Ready-to-use social skills lessons and activities for grades 7–12.* Old Tappan, NJ: Center for Applied Research in Education.

Benard, B. (1993). Fostering resiliency in kids. *Educational Leadership, 51*(3), 44–48.

Berkovitz, I. H., & Sugar, M. (1975). Adolescent psychotherapy, group psychotherapy, family psychotherapy. In M. Sugar (Ed.), *The adolescent in group and family therapy.* New York: Brunner/Mazel.

Berube, F., & Berube, L. (1997). Creating small groups using school and community resources to meet student needs. *School Counselor, 44,* 294–301.

Bowman, R. P. (1987). Small group guidance and counseling in schools: A national survey of school counselors. *School Counselor, 34,* 256–262.

Brown, L. S. (1994). *Subversive dialogues: Theory in feminist therapy.* New York: Basic.

Carkhuff, R. (1971). *Helping and human relations* (Vols. 1 & 2). New York: Holt, Rinehart & Winston.

Carrell, S. (1993). *Group exercises for adolescents: A manual for therapists.* Newbury Park, CA: Sage.

Carroll, M., Bates, M., & Johnson, C. (1997). *Group leadership* (3rd ed.). Denver: Love.

Carroll, M., & Wiggins, J. (1990). *Elements of group counseling: Back to the basics.* Denver: Love.

Cartledge, G. (1996). *Cultural diversity and social skills instruction: Understanding ethnic and gender differences.* Champaign, IL: Research Press.

Cartledge, G., & Johnson, S. (1997). Cultural sensitivity. In A. P. Goldstein & J. C. Conoley (Eds.), *School violence intervention: A practical handbook.* New York: Guilford.

Cohen, E. G. (1994). *Designing group work: Strategies for the heterogeneous classroom* (2nd ed.). New York: Teachers College Press.

Corey, G. (1995). *Theory and practice of group counseling.* Pacific Grove, CA: Brooks/Cole.

Corey, G., & Corey, M. S. (1997). *Groups: Process and practice* (5th ed.). Pacific Grove, CA: Brooks/Cole.

Corey, G., Corey, M. S., & Callanan, P. (1998). *Issues and ethics in the helping professions* (5th ed.). Pacific Grove, CA: Brooks/Cole.

Cormier, W. H., & Cormier, L. S. (1991). *Interviewing strategies for helpers* (3rd ed.). Pacific Grove, CA: Brooks/Cole.

Cormier, W. H., & Cormier, L. S. (1998). *Interviewing strategies for helpers* (4th ed.). Pacific Grove, CA: Brooks/Cole.

Dansby, V. S. (1996). Group work within the school system: Survey of implementation and leadership role issues. *Journal for Specialists in Group Work, 21,* 232–242.

DeVito, J. A. (1981). *Human communication: The basic course.* New York: HarperCollins.

Donigian, J., & Malnati, R. (1997). *Systemic group therapy.* Pacific Grove, CA: Brooks/Cole.

Egge, D. L., Marks, L. G., & McEvers, D. M. (1987). Puppets and adolescents: A group guidance approach. *Elementary School Guidance and Counseling, 21,* 183–192.

Ferrara, M. L. (1992). *Group counseling with juvenile delinquents: The limit and lead approach.* Newbury Park, CA: Sage.

Foster-Harrison, E. S. (1989). *Energizers and icebreakers: For all ages and stages.* Minneapolis: Educational Media Corporation.

Foster-Harrison, E. S. (1994). *More energizers and icebreakers: For all ages and stages.* Minneapolis: Educational Media Corporation.

Gazda, G. M. (1989). *Group counseling: A developmental approach* (4th ed.). Needham Heights, MA: Allyn and Bacon.

Gibbs, J. C., Potter, G., & Goldstein, A. P. (1995). *The EQUIP program: Teaching youth to think and act responsibly through a peer-helping approach.* Champaign, IL: Research Press.

Gladding, S. T. (1998). *Counseling as an art: Uses of the creative arts in counseling* (2nd ed.). Alexandria, VA: American Counseling Association.

Gladding, S. T. (1999). *Group work: A counseling specialty.* Columbus, OH: Prentice Hall.

Goldstein, A. P., & McGinnis, E. (1997). *Skillstreaming the adolescent: New strategies and perspectives for teaching prosocial skills* (rev. ed.). Champaign, IL: Research Press.

Gudykunst, W. B. (Ed.). (1983). *Inter-cultural communication theory: Current perspectives.* Newbury Park, CA: Sage.

Gysbers, N. C., & Henderson, P. (1988). *Developing and managing your school guidance program.* Alexandria, VA: American Association for Counseling and Development.

Hewitt, G. (1998). *Today you are my favorite poet: Writing poems with teenagers.* Portsmouth, NH: Heinemann.

Holcomb, E. L. (1996). *Asking the right questions: Tools and techniques for teamwork.* Thousand Oaks, CA: Corwin.

Kaminer, Y. (1994). *Adolescent substance abuse: A comprehensive guide to theory and practice.* New York: Plenum Medical/Plenum.

Khalsa, S. S. (1996). *Group exercises for enhancing social skills and self-esteem.* Sarasota, FL: Professional Resource Press.

Malekoff, A. (1997). *Group work with adolescents.* New York: Guilford.

McWhirter, J. J., & McWhirter, E. H. (1989). Adolescents-at-risk: Poor soil yields damaged fruit. In D. Capuzzi & D. R. Gross (Eds.), *Working with at-risk youth: Issues and interventions.* Alexandria, VA: American Association for Counseling and Development.

Morganett, R. S. (1990). *Skills for living: Group counseling activities for young adolescents.* Champaign, IL: Research Press.

Morganett, R. S. (1994). *Skills for living: Group counseling activities for elementary students.* Champaign, IL: Research Press.

Oaklander, V. (1978). *Windows to our children: A gestalt approach to children and adolescents.* Moab, UT: Real People Press.

O'Rourke, K., & Worzbyt, J. C. (1996). *Support groups for children.* Bristol, PA: Accelerated Development.

Paperbacks for Educators. (1998–1999). *Bibliotherapy for children catalog.* Washington, MO: Author.

Paperbacks for Educators. (1998–1999). *School counselor catalog K–8 and 9–12.* Washington, MO: Author.

Paperbacks for Educators. (1998–1999). *Special children, special teens catalog.* Washington, MO: Author.

Parham, T. (1991, April). *Effective counseling interventions for promoting wellness among African American males.* Paper presented at the American Association for Counseling and Development national convention, Reno, Nevada.

Payne, R. K. (1995). *Poverty: A framework for understanding and working with students and adults from poverty.* Baytown, TX: RFT Publishing.

Rambo, T. (1997). The use of creative arts in adolescent group therapy. In S. T. Gladding (Ed.), *New developments in group counseling.* Greensboro, NC: Educational Resources Information Center.

Richardson, R., & Evans, E. T. (1996). *Connecting with others: Lessons for teaching social and emotional competence* (Grades 6–8). Champaign, IL: Research Press.

Riddle, J., Bergin, J. J., & Douzenis, C. (1997). Effects of group counseling on the self-concept of children of alcoholics. *Elementary School Guidance and Counseling, 31,* 192–203.

Rogers, C. (1980). *A way of being.* Boston: Houghton Mifflin.

Savin-Williams, R. C. (1995). Lesbian, gay male, and bisexual adolescents. In A. R. D'Augelli & C. J. Patterson (Eds.), *Lesbian, gay, and bisexual identities over the lifespan.* New York: Oxford University Press.

Scearce, C. (1992). *100 ways to build teams.* Arlington Heights, IL: IRI/Skylight Training and Publishing.

Schilling, D. (1996). *50 activities for teaching emotional intelligence* (Level II, Middle School, Grades 6–8). San Pedro, CA: Innerchoice.

Schmidt, J. J. (1993). *Counseling in schools: Essential services and comprehensive programs.* Needham Heights, MA: Allyn & Bacon.

Seifert, K. L., & Hoffnung, R. J. (1993). *Child and adolescent development* (2nd ed.). Boston: Houghton Mifflin.

Smead, R. (1995). *Skills and techniques for group work with children and adolescents* [Book and Video Series]. Champaign, IL: Research Press.

Thompson, C. L., & Rudolph, L. B. (1996). *Counseling children* (4th ed.). Pacific Grove, CA: Brooks/Cole.

Vernon, A. (1998). *The Passport program: A journey through emotional, social, cognitive, and self-development* (Grades 6–8). Champaign, IL: Research Press.

Wolfe, D. A., Wekerle, C., Gough, R., Reitzel-Jaffe, D., Grasley, C., Pittman, A., Lefebvre, L., & Stumpf, J. (1996). *The youth relationships manual: A group approach with adolescents for the prevention of woman abuse and the promotion of healthy relation-ships.* Thousand Oaks, CA: Sage.

Yalom, I. D. (1975). *The theory and practice of group psychotherapy.* New York: Basic.

PART 2

GROUP AGENDAS

Girlfriends: Understanding and Managing Friendships ———

The need for affiliation is at its height in preadolescent and adolescent girls. Girls who hardly speak to their parents often spend hours on the phone or hanging out with other girls, seeking desperately to validate and support their burgeoning selves. Young adolescence is a time of deep questioning—"Who am I?"— and a major influence on this process is relationships with other girls and eventually with guys (Gilligan, 1982). Although parents fight to protect and nurture their daughters, young girls are busily defining their own individuality from a select few other girls whom they consider their friends/role models, as well as from magazines, music videos, and movies—and so the cultural indoctrination goes on (Pipher, 1994).

Peers are everything. Parents are in the way. Even girls who previously had warm and healthy relationships with their parents are frequently turned off by the parental frustration that results from their constant testing and experimenting with limits, new values, and friendships with schoolmates of questionable reputation. Girls set the standard for one another, and those who don't measure up to the current "in" behaviors (dress, language, dating habits, values) frequently are scapegoated (Orenstein, 1994). Girls who are different are bullied, teased, harassed, shunned, and pressured in hundreds of ways, with the message always the same—conform, or it's social suicide for you.

The peer culture of today is more intense than that of earlier decades because of the presence of alcohol, "designer drugs," crack cocaine, gangs, and so on. Girls have pressures their parents never experienced and are more in need of assistance to deal with these issues, which adults often don't understand or don't accept. The reality is, girls do have stressors they are physiologically and emotionally not prepared to cope with, and a supportive, interactive group experience can be a point of light in the darkness.

This group is a different kind of friendship group. It is designed for girls who are having difficulty coping with the pressures generated by the need to affiliate with peers or to feel competent and accepted, and who use or abuse friendships in unhealthy ways. It is an opportunity for girls to gain insight into why they hate, hurt, and humiliate one another, rather than help, develop hope in, and support one another.

The sessions in this topic area are as follows:

Session 1—Getting Started

Session 2—Sorting Things Out

Session 3—Aliens

Session 4—The Guys

Session 5—The Green Gossip Monster

Session 6—My True Colors

Session 7—Flirting or Harassment?

Session 8—That's a Wrap

GROUP GOALS

1. To facilitate development of a trusting, supportive environment in which members feel secure to risk and share, in particular about issues that cause difficulties relating to girls and women

2. To promote the group norms of becoming a supportive, encouraging person

3. To ensure that members can discriminate thinking, feeling, and behaving

4. To assist members in assessing their own trouble spots in relating to other females

5. To encourage recognition and awareness of major issues related to girl-boy relationships

6. To raise members' awareness of pressures to affiliate that take a toll on one's identity and detract from self-development

7. To discuss the concept of gossip and its personal and social consequences

8. To encourage and support positive choices in dating behavior

9. To provide an opportunity to learn concepts relating to sexual harassment and its effects on self and others

10. To review the group experience and set goals for future personal work

SELECTION AND OTHER GUIDELINES

Choose high, medium, and low self-disclosers, and be sure to role-balance. You will want to select a heterogeneous group of girls, each of whom brings a skill, ability, talent, attitude, set of values, or energy from which other group members can learn. A good mix would include one or two girls who are of high social status who have other friendship needs, such as learning to be more accepting and tolerant. Also include girls who are shy, somewhat different, those who pressure and those who are pressured, and perhaps girls who do well in academics but not in friendships. It is essential that neither best friends nor worst enemies be selected, as this mix will inhibit disclosure and trust, ultimately shutting down the experience.

REFERENCES AND SUGGESTED RESOURCES FOR PROFESSIONALS

Abner, A., & Villarosa, L. (1995). *Finding our way: The teen girl's survival guide.* Scranton, PA: HarperPerennial.

Brown, L. S. (1994). *Subversive dialogues: Theory in feminist therapy.* New York: Basic.

Gadeberg, J. (1997). *Brave new girls: Creative ideas to help girls be confident, healthy, and happy.* Minneapolis: Fairview.

Gilligan, C. (1982). *In a different voice: Psychological theory and women's development.* Cambridge, MA: Harvard University Press.

Johnson, A. (1997). *Girls speak out: Finding your true self.* New York: Scholastic.

Koff, E., & Rierdan, J. (1995). Preparing girls for menstruation: Recommendations from adolescent girls. *Adolescence, 30,* 795–811.

Lewis, B. (1997). *What do you stand for? A kid's guide to building character* (Grades 5–10). Minneapolis: Free Spirit.

Orenstein, P. (1994). *Schoolgirls: Young women, self-esteem, and the confidence gap.* New York: Doubleday.

Pipher, M. (1994). *Reviving Ophelia: Saving the selves of adolescent girls.* New York: Ballantine.

Sonnenblick, M. D. (1997). The GALSS club: Promoting belonging among at-risk adolescent girls. *School Counselor, 44,* 243–245.

Getting Started

GOALS

Affective

To begin to become comfortable with self-disclosing and the group experience

Behavioral

To thoroughly discuss confidentiality and its limits

To establish ground rules with other members to encourage ownership

To participate in a getting-acquainted activity

Cognitive

To understand the purpose and general goals of the group

To learn what confidentiality is and understand its importance

To clarify the concepts of thinking, feeling, and behaving

To begin to select personal goals

MATERIALS

Limits of Confidentiality sign (see Appendix A, page 270)

Thinking-Feeling-Behaving Gears (see Appendix A, page 271)

Easel pad or posterboard and marker

Large sheet of newsprint

Colored markers

Healthy snacks (such as fruit, crackers, juice, raisins)

GROUP SESSION

Opening Time

> For sessions after this first one, Opening Time will take up about one-fourth of the typical 40- to 50-minute session time, or about 10 minutes. For this session, however, you will need to plan on more time to discuss confidentiality, develop ground rules, and conduct a getting-acquainted activity. See the book's introduction for some ideas on how to schedule this extra time.

1. Welcome girls to group and go over the group's name, purpose, and goals. Stress that this group is going to help them deal with some of the difficulties they may be having from growing up female in our society and with how being a girl can be painful due to pressures from others as well as choices we make that are not in our own best interest.

2. Thoroughly discuss confidentiality (the "no-blab" rule): What is said and done in the group stays in the group. Be sure to give some examples of things adults or peers outside the group might say to pressure group members to share what happens in group. For example:

    What do you guys talk about in group anyway?

    Shara shouldn't be in the group—what's she doing there?

Do you tell who smokes and drinks beer in that group?

After members are clear on what confidentiality is, share the Limits of Confidentiality sign (either as a handout or poster) and discuss: Let group members know you are bound by the confidentiality rule but that as the leader you are required to tell about what goes on in the group if you think someone will do harm to self or others, if someone says anything about child abuse or criminal activity going on, or if a judge orders you to turn over information.

3. Explain that in addition to confidentiality, the group needs a few other basic rules so members can feel safe. Present the ground rules you have decided on for your group. For example:

    Take turns.

    Everyone has the right to "pass" (not share unless that's comfortable).

    Respect others' opinions (no put-downs).

    Come on time.

Don't move on until the group agrees on the ground rules. Write or have the group write the rules on an easel pad or piece of posterboard and have each member sign the document to show agreement. You can then post these rules every session.

---

4. To help group members get acquainted, have them form dyads and share their names, what secret name they would like to have, and what they like most and least about being a girl. Set a time limit for the activity so they can share equally and tell them they will also be sharing this information with the rest of the group.

5. Reassemble in the group circle and let the pairs introduce each other and share the information.

Working Time

Working Time will be half of a typical session, or about 20 to 25 minutes.

---

1. Introduce the idea that thinking, feeling, and behaving are three major parts of who we are. Show the group the Thinking-Feeling-Behaving Gears and explain, in your own words:

    In group, we will be talking about what we are thinking, feeling, or doing to add to our problems in coping with life, and how we can change thinking, feeling, and doing to live more effective and happy lives. Thinking, feeling, and behaving are just like these three interlocking gears—whatever one is doing affects the others. In this group it is important that each of you understand what is being said when we ask, "What are you thinking?" "What are you feeling?" and "What are you doing?"

2. Write the three categories on the easel pad or posterboard and invite the group to give examples of each type. For instance:

    Thinking: Imagining, deciding, examining, learning, organizing, remembering, wondering

    Feeling: Annoyed, confused, doubtful, joyful, humiliated, jealous, motivated, resentful, weary

    Behaving: Arguing, digesting, eating, flirting, gossiping, imitating, laughing, smiling

3. As a fun way to clarify these ideas, invite the group to make a drawing to show the three types of words in some connected way, similar to the Gears drawing (but not gears). For example, for a tree, the ground and roots could represent thinking words; the trunk,

behaving words; and the branches, feeling words. For a butterfly, the head could be the place for thinking words, the body for behaving words, and the wings for feeling words. Let the girls decide how they are going to represent the three concepts and, as a group, draw them with the colored markers on the newsprint. They can sit on the floor or do this at a table. The only rule is that everyone must agree on the concept and participate in some way in the drawing. Encourage and praise as they decide together what to draw. Be sure to give them a time limit for the drawing so they will have the opportunity to present their work.

4. When the girls have finished their drawing, have them place it in the middle of the floor in the center of the group and share what their picture represents and how they came to decide on the format. After sharing, they may sit on the floor or chairs in a circle. Ask the following questions:

> What are some of the things that you *think* about being a girl?
>
> What are some of the *feelings* you have about being a girl?
>
> What are some things you *do* or *don't do* because you are a girl?

5. Ask, "What would be a realistic goal for you in this group?" Girls might express some realistic goals by finishing this sentence: "By the end of this group I want to . . ."

> Stop saying negative things about my body.
>
> Learn to stand up for myself and my ideas.
>
> Speak up when I get blamed for things others do.
>
> Take more time getting ready for school so I look better.
>
> Not worry about how I look so much.
>
> Take classes I want to take, not what others want me to take.

Processing Time

Processing Time takes one-quarter of a typical session, or about 10 minutes.

---

1. Ask at least one question from each of the four processing levels:

INTRAPERSONAL

Today was our first session. What have you been thinking or feeling during the time we have been together?

INTERPERSONAL

What did you notice about being a member of the group today? What did you notice about the other group members?

NEW LEARNING

What ideas or feelings have you experienced today that are new for you?

APPLICATION

What can you take from the group today that you can use to help you between now and the next session?

2. Give the group a hope statement like the following example:

I feel confident that each of you will be successful in identifying and making progress on changes that improve things for you—your friends, family, and schoolwork.

3. Remind them of the day and time of the next session, then share the snacks.

Sorting Things Out

GOALS

Affective

To relax and lessen stress involved in disclosing personal information

Behavioral

To learn and practice the use of the linking and connecting skill

Cognitive

To introduce the concept of friends as a support system and sounding board for answering the question "Who am I?"

To become aware of choices of friends who are accepting as well as self-defining

MATERIALS

Easel pad or posterboard and marker

Healthy snacks

GROUP SESSION

Opening Time (¼ session time)

1. Welcome the girls back to group. Ask what ideas, concerns, or questions the group might have concerning confidentiality. Ask if anyone had to deal with outside-of-group queries about what was happening in group, and reinforce anyone who did for dealing with the situation appropriately. Ask the group how they think the current ground rules are working for them. Are any changes needed?

2. Review in a few sentences the topic and activity from the first session (thinking-feeling-behaving and personal goals for the group). Address any specific interpersonal issues (disagreements, lack of trust, and so forth) from the first session that might need revisiting.

Working Time (½ session time)

1. Invite the group to participate in a share-around for the purpose of hearing what each one believes is important about having both a "best friend" and lots of girls as friends. Work the share-around until everyone responds or passes. Use the following scaling question:

   On a scale of 1 to 10, how important is it to you to have a best girlfriend? One means not important at all and 10 means that you absolutely must have an identified best girlfriend at all times.

2. Without processing that information, go on to a second scaling question:

   On a scale of 1 to 10, how important is it to you to have several girlfriends to hang out with? One means it is not important to you at all and 10 means it is absolutely essential for you to feel you have several friends who like and accept you.

3. Begin building cohesion by teaching the girls the linking and connecting skill. In your own words, share:

I noticed while you were sharing how important a best friend and a group of friends are to you that you were watching each other and some were nodding and smiling at others. This shows that you were thinking or feeling the same thing as the one you were acknowledging. Let's begin to communicate directly with one another, instead of to me or through me because this is your group—you are the most important. Tell whomever you linked with that you made a connection with her, using this formula. It will be stiff and funny at first, but after you do it a time or two, it will feel great to know that someone else is thinking and feeling the same as you.

4. Write the following formula on the easel pad or posterboard:

   _____ *(name)*, when you said . . .

   I thought (or felt) . . .

   because . . .

   Be sure that group members say the person's name, that they linked with the person about whatever, and what they thought or felt about that situation. Be sure the person linked with has time to say something back. (It's a good idea to post a chart with this linking statement somewhere in the group room and refer to it as needed during each session.)

5. Ask: "Would you be willing to share with the group some of the reasons you value having a best friend and perhaps several other close girlfriends in your life? Tell everyone." Encourage group members to share their ideas.

6. Invite responses to the following questions:

   How can you tell if a friend is for you, meaning a person who will not do harm to you in any way, or against you, someone you cannot trust not to hurt you in some way?

   How does it feel to be influenced for a long time by someone you feel deep down inside is not good for you? What can you do if you feel stuck in that situation?

   By staying in a friendship that influences you to do things you aren't comfortable with and causes you to get in trouble or lose good things you have, what are you really saying about yourself? (I care more about others than I do about myself; it is more important to be liked by the "right" people than to be my own person; I need to work on my own self-esteem and let go of people who drag me down.)

7. Ask and invite sharing:

   Can you think of someone who has been a positive influence on you—your parents or another older member of your family—for many years?

   How do you feel about trusting the rest of the girls in our group to keep on coming to group and sharing, in confidence, your ideas about friendships?

Processing Time (¼ session time)

1. In your own words, explain, then ask at least one question from each of the four processing levels:

   Today was our second time together, and we talked about some serious ideas and some fun ideas about identifying how girlfriends are a special and wonderful part of our lives, who also can cause us a lot of emotional pain and irritation.

   INTRAPERSONAL

   What have you been thinking and feeling inside yourself about girl friendships during our time together today?

INTERPERSONAL

What was it like to be a member of the group today? What did you notice about the other group members?

NEW LEARNING

What did you learn today about yourself and your ideas and feelings, or about how other girls think about friendships?

APPLICATION

If during the time before our next session you watched and listened as other girls interact, what do you think you might learn? Would anyone be willing to try this before the next session and let us know what you learned?

2. Thank group members for their participation and give them a hope statement about how friendships are very powerful and can influence us to behave in ways that are either positive and growthful for us or negative and hurtful for us. Say, "We are now ready to explore what personal challenges each one of you wants to work toward resolving."

3. Remind members of the day and time for the next session, then share the snacks.

Aliens

GOALS

Affective

To have fun with the concept of "aliens" coming to the school

To get in touch with feelings associated with attracting, having, and losing girlfriends

Behavioral

To explore the stresses and pressures close friendships bring

Cognitive

To become aware of the importance of choosing friends carefully because they have strong positive and negative influences on us for a long time

MATERIALS

Three representations of an alien creature, such as dolls, pictures, videotape jackets, posters, puppets, and so on. Good "aliens" are available from Oriental Trading Company (1–800–228–2269). If you can find candy or treats in the form of aliens, great!

Healthy snacks

GROUP SESSION

Opening Time (¼ session time)

1. Welcome girls back to group. Ask if there are any concerns or questions about confidentiality. How are the ground rules working for everyone at this time?

2. Briefly connect with the previous session, on choosing friends who are good for you, and ask if anyone noticed anything about their own choice of friends in the past week. What was it about another girl that made that person valuable as a friend or potential friend? What negative influences might they have noticed?

Working Time (½ session time)

1. Paraphrase the following:

   Sometimes you find a group of girls that you really want to be like and be with. You really want to be part of their group, but for some reason they don't want you. Maybe they are subtle about it, and maybe they are rude and just tell you to get lost. How do you feel?

2. After some discussion, say, "Who else in the group might be thinking and feeling like you? Tell them you linked with them." Review the linking and connecting formula described during the last session and encourage group members to use it. Then move on.

3. Show the group the alien dolls/representations and ask what group members think these objects are. Pass the aliens around for everyone to see and hold. Let the group have a few minutes to talk about who or what an alien is, what *alien* means, and the whole concept of alien as being someone or something we think might come from outer space—a creature that "doesn't belong here."

4. Point out that *alien* can also mean a feeling we have when we are the "outsider" and thought of as different. Ask: "Have you ever felt like an alien when you wanted to be part of a group and the group didn't want you? What was that like?" Encourage differences of opinion and

ways of looking at this issue of belongingness and discuss how important it is to feel part of a group, or at least to have one or two girlfriends you can count on to go places with and be there for you.

5. Tell this story:

> *Now suppose some really cool alien girls named Zanta, Phanta, and Yxinta, from Planet X, come to your school. They're very smart, beautiful in a weird sort of alien way, have really cool alien clothes made out of shiny metallic stuff that has its own built-in computer signals, and know the best places to hang out to have fun and meet cool guys. All of the girls in your class want to be best friends with Zanta, Phanta, and Yxinta. There is only one little problem, and that is the alien girls have certain requirements for anyone who wants to be in their exclusive friends' club. One of the requirements is that everyone in the group of friends will make fun of other kids who are different in any way, such as kids from another country or culture or kids who look different, like some students with special needs. This is very strange indeed, because the aliens are the most different of anyone in the school! The aliens insist that their friends use put-downs and negative, hurtful gossip about other kids and teachers, even if it isn't true. They also require anyone who is in their friendship club to smoke "doedoe weed," rolled up in rhododendron leaves. Doedoe weed makes your mouth and clothes smell like disgusting rotting eggs, as well as doing away with some of your IQ points.*

6. Remind the group that they really want to be friends with these aliens, then ask the following questions:

> What would you be willing to do to be best friends with the aliens? What would you not be willing to do?

> What positive influences on you do you think the aliens would have—what could you learn from them that would help you in your life?

> What negative effects do you think hanging out with the aliens might have?

> Why do you feel like an alien when you are rejected by real girls you highly value? Why does it bother you? Why not just forget it and find someone else who would be glad to be your friend?

> When you do feel like an alien, how do you handle it? What kinds of feelings do you have and how do you deal with those feelings, even when they might be overwhelming?

> What kind of stresses do you have that are caused by trying to make and keep desirable friends? Do you think an alien from outer space might have those same stresses on earth? (Just joking!)

> What kinds of feelings do you experience when you have a good friend and then all of a sudden you lose your friend, either because the friend moves away or because your friend ends the friendship with you?

> Are close friendships with other girls worth the emotional pain that you have to go through to make, keep, and maintain?

Processing Time (¼ session time)

1. Begin by saying, "Today we talked about some imaginary friends you could have. Even though this isn't real for us right now, it gave us an interesting way of thinking about real friends." Then ask at least one question from each of the four levels of processing:

INTRAPERSONAL

While we were talking about what some people might want us to be like to have them as friends, what were you thinking and feeling?

INTERPERSONAL

How are you feeling about our group right now—how does it feel to be a member of our group today?

NEW LEARNING

What new ideas or insights did you have about girlfriends today?

APPLICATION

What changes might you need to make to have friends who are more helpful and who don't cause you to have negative experiences? Who would be willing to think about this outside the group and notice what is going on in their friendships? (Explain that this information will help the group plan skills they could learn in group and figure out what skills might be available from other sources.)

2. Thank group members for coming and give them a hope statement. Remind them of the next session's day and time, then enjoy the snacks.

The Guys

GOALS

Affective

To increase feelings of self-esteem and efficacy through participating and helping others

Behavioral

To learn about new social and coping skills to deal with dating pressures

Cognitive

To become aware of a variety of opinions about dating and learn to be comfortable with personal decisions about dating at this time

To realize that other girls have the same kinds of pressures and problems

To become aware of personal resources to take control of some situations

MATERIALS

Ski rope (Three-foot lengths, one for each group member. Put a knot at each end of each length to keep it from unraveling. Fifty-foot lengths are generally available at discount stores for about 3 dollars.)

Paper and pencils

Healthy snacks

GROUP SESSION

Opening Time (¼ session time)

1. Welcome girls back to group. Ask what concerns or questions they might have about confidentiality. After three sessions, what thoughts do they have about the ground rules—do any need to be amended or added? Briefly connect with the previous session's topic ("aliens" and pressures to belong).

2. Ask if anyone noticed things about their friendships with other girls that might need to be changed. Ask, "If these things can't be changed and are a source of problems for you, do you think the friendship will have to be ended?" (No long-winded storytelling.)

Working Time (½ session time)

1. Pass out the lengths of rope, one to each group member. In your own words, explain:

   There is a lot of pressure on you now to date, to have a steady boyfriend, to have sex before you want to or are ready to, and to do other things about dating. When we feel stressed out about anything, whether it is about dating or a school project, a fun activity like cheerleading, or whatever, our bodies tell us we are stressed by giving us certain physiological signals. For example, when some people get stressed, they begin to perspire, or their stomach feels like it has butterflies in it, or their face and/or neck gets all red. Usually our bodies know we have reached our limits before we actually become aware of it ourselves. Can you think of a time when you had a dating pressure and felt like you were all in knots about it?

2. Let group members respond about how they could tell and what the situation was, then summarize:

So, if we listen and pay attention to our bodies, we can really be in tune with what is going on. Our bodies don't lie to us—they react when there is too much stress. We can't fool our bodies! But sometimes we can fool the mind by denying that something is wrong when deep down inside we know it is wrong for us. In some situations if we admit that a person or a situation is likely to be trouble for us, we may have to give it up, like going to a cool party where you know there are going to be drugs and beer available. Or say you hear from three or four girls that a particular boy is bad news and that the girls who have been hanging out with him end up with big problems, but you keep telling yourself,"No, he couldn't be that bad—besides, he wouldn't get me in trouble." Deep down inside you are scared because what the other girls say does happen and you are just denying it. Sometimes we convince ourselves and others that nothing is wrong, but our bodies tell us something is wrong. Which is accurate? What we want to believe or what our bodies and our intuition are telling us?

3. Ask the group if they have ever heard the saying "I feel like I have knots in my stomach" to mean having a lot of worries and stress. Explain that the group will be using the ropes to represent how they feel inside about some dating situations that are causing them a lot of stress, like they have knots inside. Have each member take her rope and tie a few knots in it. Say, "These will represent problems you have with guys. Or if you just have one huge problem, make one big knot by tying several small knots right on top of each other." Explain that next the girls will choose knots and share some of their big relationship worries/problems—the ones that give them knots in the stomach. Sharing will help them make plans to relax these knots.

4. When group members have finished making their knots, continue:

    Now sometimes we think that a guy or guys or other people are responsible for our feeling awful, but we are going to learn that to control the situation we need to take responsibility ourselves because we can't change other people, we can only change ourselves! Let's have a share-around about what your knot represents—pick one and share with us so we can begin to help one another.

5. Let as many share a painful dating/relationship situation as want to. Do not try to solve problems—just let the sharing itself take place.

6. Ask, "What do you need to do to make a change in this situation? What can you do to take responsibility for correcting things in the situation/relationship?" Let them all suggest something they can do. If someone doesn't know what to do, say, "If you don't know what to do, and you have tried everything you know, we'll write this problem down and try to come up with some new skills to help you improve the situation or relationship or end it." Go on to the next person who wants to share, and come back to those who need help. Encourage the group to give the ones who still need help some suggestions and supportive ideas. Reinforce them for giving support.

Processing Time (¼ session time)

1. Ask at least one question from each of the four processing levels:

    INTRAPERSONAL

    What were some of the things you were thinking and feeling when you heard other girls in the group share about their dating problems and pressures?

    INTERPERSONAL

    What about being a group member was helpful to you today?

NEW LEARNING

What new ideas did you learn from group today?

What do you think about learning that you have to take responsibility for making changes, not wait or expect others to change?

APPLICATION

How are you going to use what you learned today to help you deal with pressures about dating that have been causing you knots in your stomach?

What would you be willing to do before the next session to inch toward your goals?

2. Tell the group that, after four sessions with them, you are feeling very proud of their accomplishments and progress in being mature and taking control of their lives. Tell each girl something positive about her progress.

3. Thank group members for coming and give them a hope statement. Remind them of the day and time for the next session, then share the snacks.

The Green Gossip Monster

GOALS

Affective
To increase sense of community with the group by working and practicing together

Behavioral
To practice the use of coping statements to deal with gossip about self and others

To learn the use of "I-messages" as a coping and assertion skill

Cognitive
To be able to identify what is and what isn't gossip

To realize how gossip affects both the sender and the receiver

To identify concerns about how words wound one's reputation

MATERIALS

Green Gossip Monster Situations (Handout 1)

One or more containers of green slime, apple jelly, or Jello

A spoon or ladle to deliver the green goo

Some napkins or paper towels and a bowl or bucket of water—or a nearby sink!

Green candy (if possible)

Healthy snacks

GROUP SESSION

Opening Time (¼ session time)

1. Welcome girls to group and ask what concerns about confidentiality group members might have. Inquire about the ground rules: How are they working at this point?

2. Briefly connect with the previous session's topic of dating decisions. Ask and encourage members to share experiences:

    Who would like to share ideas or steps they took toward dealing with dating issues or feeling OK about where they are about their dating status at this time?

    What dating pressures (knots) were you able to notice between sessions, either for yourself or for friends?

Working Time (½ session time)

1. Ask the girls to form dyads, then give each pair a copy of the Green Gossip Monster Situations (Handout 1). Show them the green gooey stuff and tell them it represents how sticky, spreading, and hard to clean up gossip is . . . and that they are to keep the goo in their hands for a while, until the end of the activity: "Keep thinking of how yucky it is and how it manages to slink around your hands and get into every crack—like gossip you can't get back!" Then give each girl a big spoonful of green goo.

2. Assign one of the Green Gossip Monster Situations to each dyad. Request that they come up with a way to resolve the gossip situation and *keep the green goo off the paper!*

3. Let the dyads read and discuss their situations for about 5 minutes. Tell them to try to identify who is being hurt and how the gossip affects the sender (person who starts the rumor or gossip) and the receiver (person who is the target of the hurtful statements or person who hears about the hurtful statements and knows the target person). They must keep holding the goo and the paper in some way!

4. After they have discussed the situations, have them come back to the group circle. One member of the dyad reads the situation to the rest of the group. Ask them both to share what exactly the gossip is, who the target of the gossip is, and what thoughts and feelings they have about how damaging this situation is to the people involved. Go through all four situations, still holding the goo!

5. Ask the following questions. Don't drop the goo!

    How do untruthful, mean-spirited words wound you when you are the target of gossip? (Encourage the group to share feelings of helplessness, rage, desire to retaliate, and so forth.)

    How does gossip affect others when you are involved?

    If you are angry at those who gossip about you and want to get *revenge*, what could you expect from the situation? (More of the same, no resolve, more wounding words, perhaps physical fights where someone is violent and both parties are in danger of being expelled from school or involved with the law.)

6. Say:

    Even though you might not be able to change other people who have already done damage to you, you do have the right to tell them how you feel and how it affects you. One way you can do this is to use I-MESSAGES. Here are some examples:

    When you say things about me that are untrue, I feel hurt and angry because you do not have the right to damage me, and I want you to stop it immediately.

    I feel furious when you spread lies about me because I have the right to respect, and I want you to treat me the same way you want to be treated.

    I feel outraged when you spread hurtful gossip because it is untrue and hurts your reputation as someone who can be believed, and I want you to respect yourself as well as me in the future.

7. Continue:

    When you are in a situation where people are spreading untrue or hurtful things about other people, such as a teacher or other students, you can express yourself by making COPING STATEMENTS. Here are some examples:

    I'm going to respect other people the same way I want to be respected, and I'd appreciate it if you would do the same.

    Gossip is hurtful, and I choose not to be that way.

    Gossip hurts everyone involved. I'm outta here!

    Sorry guys, I'm taking the high road on this one.

8. Explain:

    Yes, you might have to take some ribbing from your friends, but YOU CAN TAKE IT! The gossipers know they are wrong, so just walk away. It's not the worst thing that could happen, and you are showing your individuality and courage—others will respect you in the long run.

9. Have the girls look at their hands with the green goo on them. Ask:

> What was it like to have this awful green stuff, like sticky gossip, all over your hands?

> Was it possible not to get it all over your paper, maybe even your clothes?

> How is the goo like gossip? (Can't take it back once it's out!)

> What did you learn from having to deal with this stuff?

10. Let them clean up and get the green goo off. Perhaps have some green candy to reward them and replace the green goo.

Processing Time (¼ session time)

1. Ask and discuss at least one question from each of the four levels of processing:

   INTRAPERSONAL

   When you were reading the situations about gossip about yourself or other people, what were you thinking and feeling?

   INTERPERSONAL

   What did you notice about the rest of the girls in our group when we were trying to figure out how to deal with these situations?

   NEW LEARNING

   What new ideas about gossip do you have now that you didn't have before you came to group today?

   APPLICATION

   What would you be willing to do between this session and the next about the issue of gossip among your friends?

   How could you make a change in how you do things or how you act in situations where gossip happens?

2. Thank them for coming, give them a hope statement, and remind them of the time and day for the next session. Enjoy the snacks!

Green Gossip Monster Situations

GREEN GOSSIP SITUATION 1

You and your best friend, both eighth graders, and some other girls are eating lunch in the cafeteria. Two of the seventh-grade girls say that they heard Alyssa and Allison, who aren't there, are lesbians and do weird and sinful things. They say that all the seventh-grade girls know it now, so you and the eighth-grade girls might as well know it, too. You and your girlfriend know this isn't true and are mad as wet hens when you hear these mean-spirited seventh-grade girls are spreading this around. What would you say? (*Gossip about others*)

GREEN GOSSIP SITUATION 2

You finally get a date with Josh, a cool guy you really like. He is nice and fun, and you get along great on the date. You had to beg your mom to let you go out, and she trusted you to go out the first time without a group of other friends. Renee, a girl who used to like Josh, is jealous he went with you—she even lives on your street. When you get home your mom confronts you with the information that some neighbor kids said they saw you and Josh with cans of beer in his car when you went on the date. Your mom is furious. You know this isn't true, but the trusting relationship with your mom has been damaged. It was probably Renee who made up this vicious lie. You try your best to convince your mom that this is the case. What would you say? (*Gossip about you*)

GREEN GOSSIP SITUATION 3

This guy named Rob has been giving you a ride to school for a month, since he got his license. He is really mean and talks dirty when he is driving. He also drives too fast, taking chances passing people he should stay behind. But going to school with him has saved you a lot of time, and you can practice cheerleading with your friends because you get there early when Rob drives. Now you hear that Rob has been bragging to his friends that you have been having sex with him on the way to school. The rest of your friends are really disgusted with you when they hear this. You try to tell them Rob is making this up, but he has them pretty well convinced. Your reputation is the pits. What would you say? (*Gossip about you*)

GREEN GOSSIP SITUATION 4

You are at the mall shopping for earrings with your two best friends. They start saying that they heard Mr. Michaels, the French teacher, used to be in prison, and that he smokes dope at the football games. You are shocked that they would say something damaging that might not be true about Mr. Michaels. They said that some sixth graders just made it up, and now the whole school is starting to believe it, and because they are afraid of Mr. Michaels, they laughed at him, too. What do you think? (*Gossip about others*)

My True Colors

GOALS

Affective

To experience a risky disclosure of very personal foibles and frailties

Behavioral

To identify some stable aspects of "who I am"

To explore what aspects of friendship are truly important

To share with others errors in thinking and behavior

Cognitive

To learn that we can "sell ourselves out" as girls and women in order to be accepted

To plant the seeds of the idea that we must love ourselves first before we can be loved by others

MATERIALS

Eight or more plastic chameleons. (These are plastic fish bait; they come in packages in the fishing equipment section at discount stores, usually alongside plastic worms!)

Healthy snacks

GROUP SESSION

Opening Time (¼ session time)

1. Welcome girls back to group and ask what concerns they might have about confidentiality. How do they think the ground rules are working out?

2. Briefly connect with the previous session's topic (gossip). Ask who would be willing to share what they realized about gossip or what they did in situations to deal with gossip, either about themselves or about others.

Working Time (½ session time)

1. In your own words, explain:

    At this time of your life there are so many things happening around you and to you that sometimes it's like there is nothing stable, nothing you can count on. What your parents value and what your friends value seem to be so different, from music to careers to ideas about dating, curfews, and everything that makes a difference in your life. You have lived with yourself and know yourself the best of anyone! You might be trying out some new ideas and values now, but there are some things about yourself that you like and choose and want to stay the same. What are some of the values you want to hang on to, not throw away because others are pressuring you?

    Let them name some of their values. For example:

    Sticking up for a friend

    Working hard to get something you want

    Being a good sport

    Being helpful to people who need or ask for your help

Standing up for your rights

Making good choices that are helpful, not hurtful, to yourself

Avoiding using drugs or alcohol

Not taking chances or doing risky behaviors that could be harmful to yourself and others

2. Summarize:

Girls and boys have different ways of dealing with things. As you know, girls very much like to have other girls to share their feelings, ideas, dreams, problems, and just "girl talk." Guys don't always tell their thoughts and feelings to other guys as much as girls share with other girls. It is extremely important to girls to have other girls to help process all the stuff that is going on in life! It is important to guys to be "in control"; they often deal privately with their problems and hurts, not discussing them with other guys.

Sometimes it becomes so important to have a particular friend, or to have a boyfriend, that girls "sell out": That means they deny their real thoughts and feelings and change their behavior in order to be liked or accepted by others. THIS IS NOT GOOD! If you have to give up being your own true self to have friends, then who are you, anyway? If you can't stand up to others and speak up for yourself, your self-esteem is the pits. You don't like yourself enough to be an individual, your own true, beautiful self. Do you know anyone like this?

3. Allow some time for responses, then show the group the chameleons. Say:

What are these? Well, we are going to call them chameleons, even though they are really plastic fish bait! What is it that is unique about chameleons? (They change colors in different situations to protect themselves from predators.) What color person would you say you are, if you have to choose one color? For example, I am a (purple, yellow, whatever) person. What color are you?

4. Let each girl choose a chameleon and say what color person she is. Continue:

Now suppose you were in this situation: Some really neat girls ask you to be part of their group . . . to hang out with them. You have been wanting to get into this crowd all year! You are so excited that they want you to be with them, because they are so cool! So you say, "Sure, I'd love to!" Then you find out that all of them smoke pot when they get together on the weekends. It has always been your value to keep healthy and eat right because you are in gymnastics. Your coach is very supportive but strict about good health habits. What do you do? Do you stand up for your value of not using drugs, or do you change your color, give up your "true colors," to be part of the group?

5. Let the group discuss this, then ask the girls to share situations in which they faced making a change from their true colors, like a chameleon, to be accepted by a group, a boyfriend, or someone in another situation. Let as many share as want to.

6. Ask the following questions:

What happens to you if you give up on yourself to be liked by others? On a scale of 1 to 10— 1 means very easy and 10 means extremely hard—how hard is it to stand up for your values, for your true colors?

How do you feel about yourself if you give in?

How would your friends who really know and love you feel if you change yourself just to buy friendship?

How can you keep good friends and be true to yourself also?

Processing Time (¼ session time)

1. Ask at least one question from each of the four processing levels:

    INTRAPERSONAL

    What kind of feelings did you experience today when we were talking about giving up or selling out our true colors, our real values and feelings, in order to have friendships?

    INTERPERSONAL

    What happened in group today that resulted in your feeling more or less part of the group?

    NEW LEARNING

    What new ideas or thoughts do you have about being true to yourself, liking yourself?

    APPLICATION

    What would you be willing to do between now and the next session to stand up for being yourself?

2. Thank group members for their very personal sharing and give them a hope statement. Remind them of the time and day for the next session and let them know that there is only one working session left—the last session will be a review and celebration. Share the treats.

Flirting or Harassment?

GOALS

Affective

To identify feelings and values about sexual harassment

Behavioral

To learn the definitions of sexual harassment

To learn and practice choosing ways to deal with situations in a group that is being harassing

Cognitive

To identify the difference between flirting and harassment

To determine what to do if you believe you are being harassed

To become aware of how flirting "works" and how it affects self and others

MATERIALS

Flirting or Harassment Situations (Handout 2)

Healthy snacks

GROUP SESSION

Opening Time (¼ session time)

1. Welcome the girls back to group and remind them that this is the next-to-last session, so today will be the last time a new topic will be discussed. The very last session will be a review, planning for future goals, and a celebration of what's been learned. Ask what concerns about confidentiality the group has at this time. How are the ground rules—are any changes necessary?

2. Ask who would like to share what they experienced since the last session related to the topic of being pressured or feeling pressured to give up, change, or hide part of your identity or values in order to be accepted by someone or a group. Encourage sharing.

Working Time (½ session time)

1. Define sexual harassment as words or behaviors of a sexual nature that cause the receiver to feel uncomfortable.

2. Restate the following in your own words:

   Have you ever been in a situation where one or more girls were hanging out and one or more guys came by and started teasing and commenting about their being cool, funny, sexy, great bods, and so on? Suppose the girls just loved it and kept teasing the guys, too, making them laugh and hang around more. Would that be sexual harassment? (The answer is no.)

   Now suppose one of the guys in this group starts pressuring one of the girls in the group to come for a ride in his car and smoke some joints and get something going. The girl doesn't want to, but he keeps pressuring her and teasing her in front of the other girls, and she feels angry and embarrassed by what he is saying he wants to do. Would that be sexual harassment? (The answer is yes.)

3. Hand out copies of the Flirting or Harassment Situations (Handout 2) and have the group form dyads to discuss what is going on in and how they might handle the situations. Assign two or three situations to each dyad and give them a time limit for discussion and brainstorming.

4. Reassemble the group. Ask the dyads to share their situations and what they think is going on. Encourage the others in the group to comment; let them work through their thoughts and feelings.

5. Ask: "What do you think about these situations—are they ones you might find yourself in? What would you do if you found yourself in a situation where you know what's going on is harassment and not flirting?" Let the group explore ways to deal with such a situation and discuss how to follow up by reporting it to an adult who could intervene.

6. Discuss the following questions:

What if you are with a group of friends and they start harassing some other guys or girls? What would you do? How would you handle it if they began teasing you for being a wuss because you won't go along with them?

What if you find yourself in a situation where you think you are just teasing, flirting, and having fun because the other person is laughing, too? Then later you hear from friends or even the principal that the person didn't like it and is accusing you of harassment. How can you prevent this situation from happening?

What are some of the negative consequences of harassing someone else? (You could be suspended or expelled from school, or a lawsuit could be brought against you, your family, or your school by another youth's parents.)

What can you do in the future to be more aware of others' rights and your own rights in this area?

How can you help your friends and have your friends look out for you when sexual harassment might be the issue?

Processing Time (¼ session time)

1. Ask and discuss at least one question from each of the four processing levels:

INTRAPERSONAL

What feelings came over you as we discussed harassing others and being harassed yourself?

INTERPERSONAL

On a scale of 1 to 10—1 means low and 10 means high—how do you feel you are working together and helping one another in this group?

NEW LEARNING

What did you learn today about flirting and harassment that was surprising to you?

APPLICATION

Before our last session, what would you be willing to make a commitment to doing to help yourself and your friends deal with harassment in better ways?

2. Thank the girls generously for coming to group and give them a hope statement. Ask what special thing they would like to do or have next time to celebrate their achievements (for example, a pizza or popcorn party). Try to schedule a longer period of time for the last session so you can review *and* celebrate!

Flirting or Harassment Situations

SITUATION 1

Sherone, age 13, is sitting on the front steps of her apartment waiting for her friend Anya to come so they can go to the mall. Three guys Sherone knows from school are approaching her along the sidewalk. One of them, Raul, starts whistling and hollering, "What a babe!" as the three keep walking closer. Sherone rolls her eyes and looks away. The other guys laugh among themselves—they know Raul likes Sherone, and they don't want to make him mad. Raul keeps making eyes at Sherone, saying, "Man, she's a hot mama" and dancing along the street. Sherone giggles and says, "You want one up-side the head?" She likes Raul, too, and thinks it is cool that he is paying attention to her in front of the other guys. The guys pass by Sherone, laughing and joking with each other, and Raul keeps on shouting, "Cool Mama, ya wanna come wi' me?" to Sherone as they go around the corner. Is this flirting or harassment?

SITUATION 2

Wang and his girlfriend, Kwan, are sitting on the grass in the park drinking milkshakes. They have been going together since sixth grade and are now ninth graders. Wang leaves to find a restroom. Jeremy, a senior from the high school, comes along and starts talking to Kwan. Kwan is very friendly and outgoing, and she participates in several sports, is cheerleading squad leader, and is in honors classes, so she knows a lot of other guys and girls. Jeremy is telling Kwan her hair is gorgeous and she is the best cheerleader he's ever seen. He asks her if she would ever like to go to the varsity kick-off parties because he would love to have her company. She is laughing and feeling flattered and delighted. Wang comes back and gets very angry when he sees her laughing and joking with Jeremy. He tells Jeremy to quit harassing Kwan and get out of there. Is the situation between Kwan and Jeremy flirting or harassment?

SITUATION 3

The hall is packed with kids between classes. Krissi is at her locker trying to put her books away and get her gym things out. Paul comes along and starts talking to Krissi, saying that he would like to take her out after the game Saturday afternoon. She is excited and says, "Sure, but I'll have to ask my mom if we're going in cars and tell her where I'll be." Paul says that Krissi's mom just doesn't trust him and that Krissi should go anyway without asking. He pinches Krissi's backside and smears her lipstick with his fingers, then hurries off. Krissi is ticked because of what he said and irritated about the pinching. Is this flirting or harassment?

SITUATION 4

Five fifth- and sixth-grade boys are kicking a soccer ball around on the blacktop behind the school. They come into the school to get drinks of water, passing by the girls' restroom. Janika and Rashell are coming out of the restroom, and Janika is crying. The boys start saying, "Ya get on the rag, girl? Bet ya got the cramps real bad! Ha, ha!" One of the boys starts bending over at the waist, holding his abdomen and moaning, "Oh, I got it bad," then laughing and pointing at Janika. They won't let the girls out of the restroom and keep laughing at them. Is this flirting or harassment?

SITUATION 5

Make up your own situation and discuss. It can be a real situation one of you has been in recently, or it can be completely made up.

That's a Wrap

GOALS

Affective

To experience feelings associated with the group's ending

To relax and have fun reinforcing and encouraging one another for the group's work

Behavioral

To review what new thoughts, feelings, behaviors, ideas, or attitudes were gleaned from participating in the group experience

To celebrate the group's work together and say good-bye

To share goals for continued work after the group is over

Cognitive

To evaluate progress toward individual and group goals

MATERIALS

Treats decided on during the last session for the celebration

GROUP SESSION

Opening Time (¼ session time)

1. Welcome the girls to group and ask if, at this last session, they have any concerns about confidentiality. What about the ground rules? Remind them that confidentiality extends even after the group is over.

2. Ask, "Were any of you able to help yourselves or a friend who might have a problem about flirting or harassment?" Encourage sharing.

Working Time (½ session time)

1. Say, "Let's go through the topics and issues we dealt with during this group experience and have some fun and maybe a tear remembering them and sharing what we learned from them." Let all share who want to about what they have noticed or learned since these concepts were first presented.

> Session 1—Getting Started
>
> Getting acquainted and learning how thinking, feeling, and behaving are different
>
> Session 2—Sorting Things Out
>
> How friends help define us and other kids and adults can tell what we are like by the people we hang out with
>
> Session 3—Aliens
>
> Choosing friends carefully, not just ones who are "cool" but ones who are good for us, not bad influences
>
> Session 4—The Guys
>
> Pressures we experience because of dating: deciding to date or not date, to get involved with guys or not, or how much to be involved

Session 5—The Green Gossip Monster

How gossip affects us negatively (once it's out, you can't get it back)

Session 6—My True Colors

Feeling good about some of our chosen values and not changing them like a chameleon changes its colors just to have certain friends or belong to an in-group

Session 7—Flirting or Harassment?

How to tell the difference between flirting and harassment and what choices you can make to help keep yourself and others safe

Processing Time (¼ session time)

1. Discuss the following questions:

   What did you learn from coming to the group that really has made a big change in your attitude about being a girl?

   What have you learned from the group that has resulted in some behavior changes that you are going to keep in place, some ways of acting that work better for you now?

   On a scale of 1 to 10—1 being nothing at all and 10 meaning a lot of new ideas and behaviors—how much did you learn from coming to the group?

2. Have a share-around and invite each girl to say what she learned during the group from each of the other girls, then share one goal she would like to continue working on.

3. Thank group members for participating. Explain any plans for follow up you may have for the group and give the group a hope statement. For example:

   Sometimes it is very hard to say good-bye, especially when the person or persons mean a lot to you at that time. During the last several weeks we have shared many personal, private, and painful things about ourselves, and this makes us feel really close. The closer you feel, the harder it is to say good-bye. But this isn't good-bye forever! It is good-bye for the time being. We can get together in (1 month, 2 months—whatever is appropriate) to reconnect with one another and encourage one another on our self-change projects. It is good-bye for the group meeting each week as we know it. Sometimes it feels a little lonely when group ends. You might have just gotten started on some of your personal growth and have lots more wonderful things to discover and improve about yourself. This is good. Maybe you can work on them by yourself, and maybe you need more help. Please come see me if you need more counseling, because maybe I can refer you to another counselor or another place where you can get more help.

   I feel so excited and enthusiastic about how far each of you has come during the group experience, and I know you have some special skills and talents to keep improving yourself and continue being a support to your new friends.

4. Share the party treats and celebrate!

Jugglers: Middle School Transition Issues

Early adolescence is characterized by heightened arousal in nearly every area of development. Youth are experiencing bursts of energy, confusion of values, uncertainty in their identity, cognitive processing changes, and unprecedented physiological growth spurts. The middle school and junior high years have change and instability as major characteristics; therefore, these years are the most fertile for guidance and counseling activities to facilitate transitions from childhood to young adulthood. A major developmental task is learning to "juggle" many different activities at once: many teachers instead of one, a wide choice of extracurricular activities, physical changes that sometimes occur so fast youth hardly know what size clothes they wear, opposite-sex activities like dances and dating, huge increases in homework and school expectations, the transition from elementary to middle school and middle to high school. Every day, more objects to juggle are added!

Nationwide, the middle school movement appears to be taking a foothold, as educators and parents search for ways to meet the unique needs of today's preadolescents and young adolescents. The typical middle school ranges from grades 5 through 8, working with youth ages 9 through 13, with the goal of arranging educational and social programs to meet their unique developmental needs (Stone & Bradley, 1994). Group work with young adolescents is a natural—they are mesmerized by the group phenomenon, drawn to belonging to clubs, cliques, gangs, squads, and teams that "hang out" together. Peers are everything: their major source of influence, reinforcement, and emotional support. It seems obvious, then, to pursue working with groups of youth who have similar issues and concerns and to take advantage of their affinity for peer influence. Group counseling geared toward their transition issues can provide a forum for youngsters to learn new ways of thinking about overwhelming issues, acquire skills and techniques for handling difficult encounters, and develop a support system they can trust during times of turmoil. Youngsters this age desperately seek a forum for gripes and aggravations. They want answers and fairness but frequently don't want to be fair in return.

This topical group is especially suited to adding "freebie" sessions, where group members choose their own topic, identify their own goals, and determine their own reinforcement. Added to the existing series of eight, free sessions are contingent upon group members' "working" during previous sessions and are not to be used for group members to gripe or whine about things they can't do anything about. We are not trying to give youth total control of the group's direction, just take advantage of group members' natural curiosity and desire to take center stage, to be listened to respectfully and heard, and to have control of their own environment. Free topics could be added after the third and sixth sessions, resulting in a total of 10 sessions—whatever works well for your population and environment.

The session sequence is as follows:

Session 1—Getting Started

Session 2—You Gotta Have BIG Ears!

Session 3—Who Am I?

Session 4—My Power, Their Power

Session 5—My Middle Name Is "Flexible"

Session 6—Truth or Consequences

Session 7—Roller-Coaster Feelings

Session 8—That's a Wrap

GROUP GOALS

1. To develop an environment where the youth can relax, meet others who are experiencing difficulties like their own, and identify some major issues that divert energies in negative ways

2. To promote the group norms of becoming a supportive, encouraging person

3. To ensure that members can discriminate thinking, feeling, and behaving

4. To provide a secure, caring adult role model for youth to use as an anchor throughout their middle school experience

5. To model encouragement, support, positive communication skills, and hope to a group of youth who otherwise might not survive the negative influences they experience in middle school

6. To explore some of the realistic responsibilities and privileges youth are faced with as they rapidly mature

7. To identify some of the serious decisions that will face these youngsters very soon and explore how their decision making can affect them for many years to come

8. To develop awareness of and sensitivity toward adults' expectations and encourage realistic ways of responding

9. To explore the world of feelings, how group members are affected by extremes at this point in their lives, and how they can recognize their own and others' emotional reactions

10. To examine issues relating to self-respect and learn how respect for self and others helps one reach goals

11. Through free topics (if you choose), to give youth the chance to exercise choice, identify goals, and carry out plans for what they would like to do with their time

12. To review the group experience and set goals for future personal work

SELECTION AND OTHER GUIDELINES

This group is geared toward younger middle school students who are having a difficult time adjusting, fitting in, and "juggling" their new roles and responsibilities. It can be a very diverse group, with some members having difficulty because they are new to the school and some (perhaps because of AD/HD) who are more rigid and less able to "roll with the punches" in terms of changing classes, having many teachers, and meeting new friends. Other candidates might be bright youth who feel disconnected from peers and don't know how to go about developing a support system in a new place or youth who are shy, have few friends, and seem overwhelmed by the changes and demands of the new setting.

This group might be conducted each fall and spring for incoming sixth graders, sometimes preidentified as needing help adjusting. The group might be enhanced by one or two coping role models from seventh grade, "graduates" of the group from the year before, who can be supportive and help the younger kids while still working on issues of their own. One or two group members from this latter population could be selected if they have some positive behaviors to model for other members.

Also, be sure to have at least two youths, preferably one boy and one girl, of high social status in that grade or age group—that is, kids other kids like and are influenced by. Especially if you will have members who have had trouble with the school administration or the law, it is very important to role balance so you avoid creating a group of youth others see as undesirable. You want to be sure to have a "cool" name for the group, not something clinical. Examples include "Fresh Start Club," "Yagottawanna Team" (Thompson, 1987), "Go for It Club," "Movers and Groovers," and so forth.

REFERENCES AND SUGGESTED RESOURCES FOR PROFESSIONALS

American School Counselor Association. (1990, July). *Role statement: The school counselor.* Alexandria, VA: Author.

Berndt, T. J. (1996). Transitions in friendship and friends' influence. In J. A. Graber, J. Brooks-Gunn, & A. C. Petersen (Eds.), *Transitions through adolescence.* Mahwah, NJ: Erlbaum.

Davis, L., & Stewart, R. (1997, July). *Building capacity for working with lesbian, gay, bisexual, and transgender youth.* Paper presented at the conference "Working with America's Youth," Pittsburgh.

Dupper, O. R., & Krishef, C. H. (1993). School-based social-cognitive skills training for middle school students with school behavior problems. *Children and Youth Services Review, 15*(2), 132–142.

LaBreche, L. (1995, March). Switching schools can hurt self-esteem. *APA Monitor,* pp. 40–41.

Stone, L. A., & Bradley, F. O. (1994). *Foundations of elementary and middle school counseling.* White Plains, NY: Longman.

Strother, J., & Harville, R. (1986). Support groups for relocated adolescent students: A model for school counselors. *Journal for Specialists in Group Work, 11,* 114–120.

Thompson, E. C. III. (1987). The "Yagottawanna" group: Improving student self-perceptions through motivational teaching of study skills. *School Counselor, 35,* 134–142.

Yeaworth, R. C., McNamee, M. J., & Pozehl, B. (1992). The Adolescent Life Change Event Scale: Its development and use. *Adolescence, 27,* 783–802.

Getting Started

GOALS

Affective

To reduce tension and anxiety about the group

To develop an accepting atmosphere where the boys and girls can get to know one another

Behavioral

To develop ground rules that are acceptable and "owned" by all members

To participate in a getting-acquainted activity

Cognitive

To understand the purpose and the overall goals of the group

To learn what confidentiality is and understand its importance

To clarify how thinking, feeling, and behaving are different

To help members begin to identify what they want to get out of the group

MATERIALS

Limits of Confidentiality sign (see Appendix A, page 270)

Easel pad or posterboard and marker

Thinking-Feeling-Behaving Gears (see Appendix A, page 271)

Two large sheets of newsprint

Colored markers

A bag of individually wrapped candies

Healthy snacks (such as fruit, crackers, juice, raisins)

GROUP SESSION

Opening Time

For sessions after this first one, Opening Time will take up about one-fourth of the typical 40- to 50-minute session time, or about 10 minutes. For this session, however, you will need to plan on more time to discuss confidentiality, develop ground rules, and conduct a getting-acquainted activity. See the book's introduction for some ideas on how to schedule this extra time.

1. Welcome the girls and guys to group and discuss why the group is called "Jugglers" and what the general goals are for the group. Tell them that this is going to be a fun experience where they are going to have the opportunity to get some relief from some of their stresses with the new school format and learn how to cope better with both school and friendships. If you have chosen to have free topics, let them know that there are some set topics to deal with and that because they are at an age where they have lots of good ideas about what they need for themselves there can be some sessions where they vote for their own topic and choose for themselves. Members can even run these sessions, provided they are not used just to gripe.

2. Thoroughly discuss confidentiality (the "no-blab" rule): What is said and done in the group stays in the group. Be sure to give some examples of things adults or peers outside the group might say to pressure group members to share what happens in group. For example:

> How come you're in the group? You were in that last year.

> Do you guys tell on other kids in that group?

> I know Brandon went to the mental hospital this summer. What does he say?

After members are clear on what confidentiality is, share the Limits of Confidentiality sign (either as a handout or poster) and discuss: Let group members know you are bound by the confidentiality rule but that as the leader you are required to tell about what goes on in the group if you think someone will do harm to self or others, if someone says anything about child abuse or criminal activity going on, or if a judge orders you to turn over information.

3. Discuss the basic ground rules you have decided on for your group and request the group's input in developing a few more that would enhance their comfort in sharing with one another. For example:

> Take turns.

> Everyone has the right to "pass" (not share unless that's comfortable).

> Agree to disagree (no put-downs).

> Come on time.

Don't move on until the group agrees on the ground rules. Write or have the group write the rules on an easel pad or piece of posterboard and have each member sign the document to show agreement. You can then post these rules every session.

---

4. Invite the group to do an activity to get acquainted. Ask that they pair up with someone next to them and share their names, what they like best and least about middle school, and their all-time favorite pizza or sundae toppings. They can also choose, if they want, a "personal secret name" for group. For example, if Jenna wants to be called "The Cool One," she can request this. (No one has to have a special name.) Give them a time limit so they can share equally and tell them they will be introducing their partners to the group.

5. After they have shared, reassemble in the group circle and invite the pairs to introduce each other.

Working Time

Working Time will take half of a typical session, or about 20 to 25 minutes.

---

1. Introduce the idea that we have three things going on with us all of the time: thinking, feeling, and behaving. Show the group a copy of the Thinking-Feeling-Behaving Gears, then explain the following ideas in your own words:

> *Thinking, feeling, and behaving are linked together like gears on a clock or a machine. If you move or change one of the gears, the other two also move. You can't change one without having a change in the others. If you change your thinking, you are also going to have a change in feelings and what you do. If you change what you do, your feelings and what you think are going to change. For example, if you start doing your homework regularly, you feel better about yourself, you start thinking better of yourself, and other people start to think better of you, too. If you feel very angry, your behavior changes—sometimes you do things you*

wouldn't if you weren't angry, and then you think more angry thoughts. If you think positive thoughts, like "I can deal with this," then your behavior changes and you deal with it and feel better about yourself because of it. All three are connected. During this group we are going to be talking a lot about thoughts, feelings, and behaviors. Just so we all know exactly what we're talking about when we ask "How do you feel?" let's take a few minutes to check out this picture of the three connected gears that represent thinking-feeling-behaving.

2. Divide the group in half. Give each "minigroup" some colored markers and one sheet of newsprint. Invite them to come up with as many thinking, feeling, and behaving words as they can in 4 minutes. Tell them they can all write words, or they can select a recorder to do the writing. Examples of each type are as follows:

   Thinking: Brainstorming, dreaming, calculating, wondering

   Feeling: Angry, loving, smoochy, irritated, excited, attracted

   Behaving: Studying, skateboarding, driving, eating, burping

3. At the end of 4 minutes, tell the groups to stop and get back into the larger group to share the words. Give each group member a piece of candy (or give recorders enough to hand out to each minigroup member). Group members are allowed to eat the candy now.

4. Summarize:

   Now that you are aware of some feeling words and some words to represent how you think, would you be willing to share with us some of the ways you are feeling about changes going on in your life that are difficult for you, either related to friendships at school, subjects and teachers, or whatever is bugging you the most that you want to work on changing in the group?

5. Have a share-around and give all group members time to contribute. You could use the following sentence to get the group started and to help members relate the idea of thinking, feeling, and behaving to their personal goals:

   I feel _____ and _____ about _____ ,

   and one goal is to work on changing myself is to

   _____ (be) _____ (think) or _____ (do).

6. After group members have shared their feelings and goals, thank them for participating and tell them that you are going to wind down the session for today. Explain that the next part of the session is Processing Time, where there is an opportunity to go over what happened and say what they got out of the session.

Processing Time

Processing Time will take one-quarter of a typical session, or about 10 minutes.

---

1. Explain: "Today was our first time together. This was different from other things you do at school, where you have to finish some chapter or produce paperwork like math problems." Ask at least one question from each of the four processing levels:

   INTRAPERSONAL

   What kinds of thoughts and feelings were you having as we talked about what bugs you with friends and school and home?

   INTERPERSONAL

   What was it like for you to be a member of a group that talks about feelings and problems?

NEW LEARNING

On a scale of 1 to 10, 1 meaning no hope or confidence at all and 10 meaning a lot, how much hope and confidence do you have that we can help one another through some rough times ahead, that you don't have to go through this tough time alone? (Just allow responses. If the numbers are low, don't try to "solve" or "fix" it.)

APPLICATION

What tiny steps do you think you might be willing to take to inch a little closer to your goal?

2. Tell them that you have a great deal of hope and energy and enthusiasm for working with them over the next several weeks to make some changes and get things going in a positive direction. Using a few of their names, tell them directly that you think they are already making some positive steps to get through and learn to juggle things smoothly and feel good about themselves.

3. Thank group members for coming, remind them of the next session's day and time, then share the snacks.

You Gotta Have BIG Ears!

For this one, you will need a sense of humor and willingness to let the kids laugh and poke fun at your "big ears."

GOALS

Affective

To recognize feelings associated with being listened to and affirmed and not being listened to and rejected

Behavioral

To practice, in a humorous format, skills that will enhance interpersonal communication

Cognitive

To become aware of listening skills as essential in communication, whether with friends and other peers, teachers, parents, or other adults

To become aware that if you want others to listen to you, you need to be willing to listen to them

MATERIALS

One or more pairs of big ears from a toy or novelty store

Healthy snacks

GROUP SESSION

Opening Time (¼ session time)

1. Welcome members back to group. Ask what concerns they might have about confidentiality. Discuss any concerns about the ground rules or changes that might make it more comfortable for them in group.

2. Say, "At the last session, I asked what step you might be willing to take to get a tiny bit closer to your goals for the group. Where are you with that?"

Working Time (½ session time)

1. Ask group members: "On a scale of 1 to 10, 1 meaning not at all upset and 10 meaning extremely angry, how do you feel when you try to tell someone something you think is very important, and the other person is not paying a bit of attention?" Group members frequently say 8 to 10—very angry because they aren't listened to or respected. Respond as follows:

   So, let me see . . . it sounds like you are really ticked off if you are trying to tell your mom something, or your best friend something, and the person isn't even looking at you or acting concerned. Today I'd like to invite you to learn and practice "big-ears skills"! This is a humorous way to say listening skills. Listening is the other half of talking. If you want to be listened to and respected when you talk, you need to model to other people what you want. This actually teaches them how you want to be listened to and gives them the idea that this is the way they can expect you to listen to them. If you are willing to change your behavior and use big-ears skills, other people will notice, and perhaps they will catch on and "give you their ear," so to speak, when you want to be heard. Think about how you'd feel if while you were talking to a friend, your friend looked at you, gave you a nod and a smile and perhaps an "um-hum," and did not butt in on your story.

2. Take out your big ears and put them on. Let group members laugh and giggle and get it out of their systems. You can take it! If it takes a little humor to get their attention—small price to pay. Say, "I'm going to tell you a few of the big-ears skills, and then we'll do a little experiment to see how it works." Tell them the BIG EARS/GOOD LISTENER'S SKILLS:

   Skill 1: Make eye contact with the person who is talking to you but not more than 5 seconds at a time because after 5 seconds a person feels stared at.

   Skill 2: If you are walking along beside someone, turn and look at the person sometimes, not always away at other people or things.

   Skill 3: Don't butt in—let the person tell his or her story.

   Skill 4: Say something to reinforce the person to let the person know you are listening and paying attention, such as "um-hum," "OK," "all right," "I see." These are called *minimal prompts*—they encourage the other person to go on because you are listening.

   Skill 5: If you are sitting across from someone, smile and nod sometimes as well as using verbal reinforcers.

   Skill 6: Do not start talking about what you want to talk about until the person completely finishes his or her part of the conversation.

3. Ask the group members to form dyads and decide who is going to be the Talker and who is going to be the Listener. The Talker then tries very hard for 3 minutes to tell the Listener something really important.

   In this conversation, the Listeners will use TERRIBLE LISTENING SKILLS! We are going to exaggerate a bit, but in reality it really is like this sometimes. The Listeners do not watch the Talkers. Instead, they look away, take things out of their wallets or purses and start fiddling with them, clean their fingernails, look out the window, watch the clock, yawn, or do other distracting things. (As you are explaining, pretend to do these things.) These Listeners do not say anything to the Talkers. All this time the Talkers are trying hard to get the Listeners to pay attention and hear the neat things the Talkers are saying!

4. Tell the dyads that they will have 3 minutes to do this experiment. The Talkers will laugh and giggle and try to get the Listeners' attention, and some will even get mad! When the time is up, say:

   OK, Switcheroonie. Talkers, you now become Listeners. New Talkers will try for 3 minutes to tell something very interesting and important to the Listeners, who use TERRIBLE LISTENING SKILLS. Listeners, do not say anything to the Talkers, just do other things and act like the Talkers are not even there or not saying anything you want to hear.

5. Call time after 3 minutes. Ask, "When you were in the role of Talkers, what was it like for you to try to get your important message across to Listeners who were sending you the message that they didn't care about what you were saying and who were using terrible listening skills?" Encourage all group members to say how they felt.

6. Explain that now the group has used terrible listening skills, you will switch to the BIG-EARS SKILLS, or good listening skills. Have group members pair up with someone different in the group, then choose a Talker and a Listener. The Talkers will try for 3 minutes to tell the Listeners something really neat and special they want to share. This time the Listeners will use good listening skills, with eye contact, a nod and smile sometimes, no butting in, and an "um-hum" or some other way of telling the Talkers that they are getting the message.

7. After 3 minutes, Switcheroonie! Follow the same directions as before.

8. Call time again after 3 minutes. Ask, "As Talkers, what was it like when the Listeners were using good listening skills? How did you feel?" (They will likely say they felt important, cared about, like the listener really was a friend, like what they had to say was interesting, and so forth.)

9. Follow up by asking:

   Are there some people in your life who bug you that maybe you aren't using good listening skills with, and maybe if you changed a little, they would, too? Who might that be? (Common responses are coach, dad, girlfriend/boyfriend, sister.) *If you want other people to listen to you, then you are going to have to do the changing first to show them what you want. It doesn't work the other way around. They aren't going to change first—you have to change.*

Processing Time (¼ session time)

1. Ask at least one question from each of the four processing levels:

   INTRAPERSONAL

   We did some silly things today to make a serious point. What were you thinking and feeling when we were practicing the different listening skills?

   INTERPERSONAL

   What is it like for you to practice sharing and learning in a small-group situation?

   NEW LEARNING

   What new ideas or skills have you learned today that you can use before the next session?

   APPLICATION

   What would you be willing to practice, even one time, that could bring you a little closer to your goal of making this transition time of your life a little easier?

   Reinforce any and all offers to practice!

2. Give group members a hope statement, remind them of the day and time for the next session, and share the snacks.

Who Am I?

GOALS

Affective

To focus on how emotions are part of the growing process and get in touch with the fact that emotional mood swings are a painful but normal part of the process

To increase the comfort level in the group in sharing about more difficult issues

Behavioral

To observe a model and metaphor from nature to get in touch with issues about growing and maturing

Cognitive

To realize "I am not alone"—everyone this age is experiencing similar issues

To become aware that growth is a process and that all one's friends are at different stages of that process

MATERIALS

Pictures of the four stages of frog development: egg, hatched tadpole, tadpole with legs, frog. (You could also use plastic models, frequently available at nature or toy stores.)

Individually wrapped candies or sticks of gum

Healthy snacks

GROUP SESSION

Opening Time (¼ session time)

1. Welcome members back to group. Ask what concerns about confidentiality they might have. How are the ground rules working at this point? Encourage them to air their thoughts and feelings.

2. Ask, "Who would like to share what you did with your listening skills and how it turned out during the past week?" Listen carefully to each one who shares. Encourage them to share their successes and attempts at using the skills. After all who have worked on using the skills have spoken, give each one who shared a small piece of candy or stick of gum as reward for their efforts.

Working Time (½ session time)

1. Show the egg-to-frog metamorphosis materials, describing that the frog goes through a complete change of form from the beginning to the end stage:

   You can't even begin to imagine what the adult form would be if you just saw the egg, yet all of the genetic materials are in the tiny package that will develop into one species of frog . . . perhaps a colorful poison dart frog, a big green bullfrog, or a brown, warty toad. Even though human beings don't go through this complete change, we do have major physical changes from birth through old age. We also grow up "emotionally" during the time of adolescence. Adolescence is one of those times when our bodies make changes so fast that our emotions often can't keep up with what is happening to us. Observe the frog: the egg, hatchling tadpole, tadpole with legs and growing lungs, and mature frog. Suppose the egg represents a child about 10, who is still thinking, feeling, and acting like a child, then think of the frog as representing the emotionally mature and responsible 18- to 20-year-old who has some self-understanding, direction in life, and career goals—in other words, has the ability to understand his or her emotions and control them in positive ways. Who and where are you now?

2. Let whoever wishes to speak do so: Let the person who is speaking hold the frog pictures or models. Encourage and reinforce each group member for sharing about where he or she is in the process.

3. After everyone has shared, ask:

> What is most painful and aggravating about going through a "metamorphosis" of body and feelings?
>
> What is fun and exciting about going through major life changes? What is scary and painful?
>
> What kind of help do you need to get through this time of your life in a less bumpy and painful way? (Responses: More help from teachers, ways to get parents to be more flexible, information on boy/girl relationships, and so forth.)
>
> What skills could we focus on in group in some special sessions that would help you in concrete ways? Are you willing to try some new skills and ways of thinking?

Processing Time (¼ session time)

1. Ask at least one question from each of the four processing levels:

INTRAPERSONAL

What were you thinking and feeling today during our discussion and sharing about the physical and emotional changes going on in you?

INTERPERSONAL

Who in the group helped you by saying something you connected with? Tell her or him.

NEW LEARNING

What did you like best about this topic today?

Was anything new or surprising about the topic?

APPLICATION

What would you be willing to do this week to make a change in your behavior that might affect some of your feelings about the changes in you? Would you be willing to try something and come back next week to share that with us?

2. Remind group members of the time and place for the next session, give them a hope statement, and share the snacks.

My Power, Their Power

GOALS

Affective

To recognize positive and negative feelings about social and personal power

Behavioral

To select a relationship problem that would be helped by developing personal power and control

Cognitive

To identify what power means and understand who does and doesn't have it

To explore the idea of group power and personal power in relationships

MATERIALS

Easel pad or posterboard and markers

Healthy snacks

GROUP SESSION

Opening Time (¼ session time)

1. Welcome members back to group. Ask what concerns about confidentiality they might have at this point. What comments do they have about the current ground rules? Encourage questions and discussion.

2. Ask what behavioral practice anyone has tried since the last session—what did they notice that would make the road through adolescent emotional changes less bumpy?

Working Time (½ session time)

1. Discuss the idea that power and control are part of relationships and that some people in our society have more power/control than others. Invite group members to brainstorm groups of people who seem to have more power and groups that have less power. As they identify those who appear to have more power, have a member write these groups down on the easel pad or posterboard under a column headed "ONE UP/HIGH." (For example: Men, white people, rich people, supervisors/bosses, heterosexual people, able-bodied people, adults, elected leaders, medical doctors, school officials.) Have another group member itemize the groups under a second column headed "ONE DOWN/LOW." (For example: Students, women, persons of color, gay/lesbian/bisexual people, people with disabilities, elderly citizens, children, prisoners, mentally ill people.) Then ask, "What gives these groups power or keeps them from having power?" and invite discussion.

2. Explain that even though a person might be in a low power group in the society as a whole, individually that person can have a lot of power in relationships. Some of this power comes from making good choices—selecting appropriate friends, avoiding situations and people who are negative influences, and learning new social, interpersonal, coping, and communication skills to become "empowered."

3. Next ask some questions about how group members see their own power in relationships. Explain:

If you don't want to respond, you don't have to, or you can respond only to the questions you are comfortable with. This is a quick share-around so we can hear from everyone, then we'll process it later. Just respond with the number that best represents how you feel right now. On a scale of 1 to 10, where 1 means low power/no power at all and 10 means high power/very powerful:

How much power do you feel you have as a person?

How much power do you feel you have as a student?

How much power do you feel you have as a family member?

How much power do you feel you have to attract positive friends (friends who have the values and behaviors that will help you be a good person)?

How much power do you have to get out of friendships that you know are a negative influence on you?

4. Inquire, "On a scale of 1 to 10, where 1 means little or none and 10 means a great deal":

How effective are you at getting your ideas across to others?

What is your skill level in handling negative emotions like anger and fear without doing something hurtful or that you will regret later?

5. Go through the questions, one at a time, and ask the members what they believe they need to have or do to increase their feelings from low to high power in that area so they can get their life needs met. Try to encourage each member to identify one positive step, such as learning a skill, that will increase his or her feelings of positive power as a person. As you do so, prompt group members to use the linking and connecting skill with one another to help them realize that their peers are also struggling with feelings of confusion and lack of personal control.

Processing Time (¼ session time)

1. Ask at least one question from each of the four processing levels:

INTRAPERSONAL

What kinds of feelings were you having today while we were talking about being in power or nonpower groups?

INTERPERSONAL

What was going on with the group today as we discussed personal power and control?

What other group members helped you today to understand that to have some control over your life takes a lot of work?

NEW LEARNING

What surprised you about the power issue today?

APPLICATION

What are you willing to do to become more in control of your life? (Invite members to make one small change before the next session.)

2. Give group members a hope statement, remind them of the time and place for the next session, and share the snacks.

My Middle Name Is "Flexible"

GOALS

Affective

To recognize that feelings can change if we change our thinking and behaving

Behavioral

To participate in an activity to demonstrate the concepts of "rigid" and "flexible"

Cognitive

To brainstorm new, alternative solutions for problem situations

MATERIALS

Two types of drinking straws, the rigid kind and the bendable, flexible kind

About 20 large rubber bands

Paper cups and some kind of drink, such as juice or water

Napkins or paper towels

Several large sheets of newsprint

Markers

Healthy snacks

GROUP SESSION

Opening Time (¼ session time)

1. Welcome members back to group. Ask what concerns about confidentiality they have at this point and encourage them to air their thoughts and feelings. How are the current ground rules for them—any changes or additions needed?

2. Ask for sharing about any behavior-change projects—on recognizing power in relationships/groups or about other issues.

Working Time (½ session time)

1. Ask group members whether they would be willing to participate in an activity to help get in touch with how it might feel to be in a situation where they would be physically limited—for example, being in a hospital bed and not being able to get a drink of water when thirsty. The purpose is to explore the idea of being flexible in situations, using our heads to think of options rather than behaving in one "stuck" way each time a situation occurs. Explain that there is no pain involved, just a sense of being limited in what you can do, and it will be fun! This activity should take about 5 to 8 minutes, no more. Those who want to "pass" may do so.

2. Ask for a volunteer to be your helper. Those who want to participate are to move around the room to a place where they have enough space to lie down on the floor comfortably. The helper then gives each participant two large rubber bands.

3. While sitting in place, each member places one rubber band around his or her ankles so the ankles are banded together. You and the helper place the second rubber band around the wrists so that these are also bound. Participants then lie back down on the floor. The helper

pours some water or juice into the paper cups and places a cup beside each group member on the floor.

4. Read the following instructions to the group members on the floor:

   Imagine that you take a tumble off your back steps and sprain your ankle and one wrist, and break your other arm. You have to go to the emergency room and have them all taped up. In fact, they tape your ankles and wrists together and tell you to rest in bed for 3 days, until the swelling goes down, then come back and they will take off the bandages. So you are lying in bed the first night, and your mom brings you some juice because you are so thirsty. She asks if you need anything else. You say, "No thanks," and she leaves. Then you get really thirsty and lean over to your bedside table to get a drink. But, unfortunately, the straw in the juice is the RIGID kind, which doesn't bend! You try and try to get the straw in your mouth, but you can't move your arms and legs.

5. Have all of the group members lean over and try to get the rigid straws in their mouths to drink. They are not allowed to use hands or feet to get up or hold the cup. After they struggle for a minute, laughing and giggling, tell them to stop and lie back down. Then the helper goes to each cup, removes the rigid straw, replaces it with a flexible straw, and bends the flexible straw over.

6. Give group members instructions now to try to drink the liquid from the bent straw. Usually, they will be much more successful! Instruct them to end the exercise, take the rubber bands off, and bring their drinks back to the group circle.

7. Discuss the concepts "rigid" and "flexible" in terms of how group members solve problems. Give some examples of being rigid, such as not being willing to try some new foods, using the same excuses to avoid finishing chores at home, calling people the same names everyone else uses instead of trying to find some other way to deal with the situation, and waiting to do school projects until the last minute because they are boring, difficult, or unpleasant. Examples of being flexible, on the other hand, include being willing to wear a new color or style, taking the risk to try playing a musical instrument or a new instrument, volunteering to help at a local soup kitchen on a holiday, trying out for a new club, thinking of new ways to solve problem situations, and being willing to ask for what you need.

8. Ask the group for volunteers to have the rest of the group brainstorm suggestions for approaching some situation in a more flexible manner. Explain that the sharing members must feel comfortable disclosing the situation and that the brainstormers must remember the confidentiality rule and respect the sharers' privacy. The sharer gives a situation in which he or she feels "stuck" and can't figure out any alternatives. Thinking carefully and not responding with quick fixes, the brainstormers give "flexible" solutions to the problem. Have a recorder (or recorders) write each volunteer's "rigid" way of dealing with the situation on one side of a sheet of newsprint and several new, "flexible" ways of dealing with the situation on the other side. Allow as many group members as want to participate to do so.

9. Ask the group to participate in a quick, fun activity about the term *flexible*. Say, "We are going to pretend our middle name is 'Flexible,' and say our first name, our middle name, and our last name. I will say it, too." Say your own first name and have group members go around the circle saying their first names, one at a time. Have the whole group go around and say their first names one or two more times. Next have them say their new middle name, "Flexible," along with their first names—for example, Maria Flexible, Willie Flexible. Finally, ask the group to say their first names, new middle name, and last names—for example: Maria Flexible Hernandez, Willie Flexible Lee. Complete the procedure by saying, "Now you have named yourself flexible and have the flexibility skills to get out of behavioral ruts in the road!"

Processing Time (¼ session time)

1. Ask at least one question from each of the four processing levels:

   INTRAPERSONAL

   What were you thinking and feeling during group today, about behaving in rigid and flexible ways and about making some changes in your life that would allow you to use some new skills to get out of old, negative behavior patterns?

   INTERPERSONAL

   How are you feeling about being a group member at this point—what is it like for you?

   What did you notice about how the group is working and coming along?

   NEW LEARNING

   What new thoughts or feelings or behaviors do you have now that you didn't have before coming to group today?

   APPLICATION

   What do you think you would be willing to change between now and the next session to be more flexible in situations that you have been dealing with in ineffective ways?

2. Thank members for coming to the group and give them a hope statement. Remind them of the time and place for the next session, then share the snacks.

Truth or Consequences

GOALS

Affective

To recognize feelings (such as tension, anxiety about outcomes, frustration) associated with making decisions based on values

Behavioral

To learn and practice behaviors associated with consequential thinking

Cognitive

To anticipate short- and long-term consequences of alternative behaviors

MATERIALS

Easel pad or several large sheets of newsprint and marker

Truth or Consequences Situations (Handout 3)

Healthy snacks

GROUP SESSION

Opening Time (¼ session time)

1. Welcome members back to group and ask what concerns they might have about confidentiality. Talk about any issues. Next ask about the ground rules—are any changes or additions necessary?

2. Summarize:

   Last session we discussed the advantages of being flexible in situations rather than rigidly sticking with old, ineffective behaviors. What did you notice since then about your own behavior or others' behavior as concerns being rigid or flexible? What changes have you tried or are you thinking about trying? How did any changes work for you?

Working Time (½ session time)

1. Explain the idea that sometimes we make decisions about what to do in a situation without thinking about what the consequences might be—just do what is quick or convenient at the time, not taking time to weigh the consequences:

   Decisions have consequences in friendships, when you get a job, with your family, and in boy/girl relationships. Making quick decisions frequently leads to unpleasant negative things happening rather than positive things happening. Many times if you would just stop and consider what the consequences are likely to be, or could be, you could make a better decision. Even brief planning may not only help you avoid negative consequences, it may also help make many positive things occur. We might call this the "emotional truth"—that is, if you THINK about the situation and are honest about what is likely to happen if you act foolishly or hurtfully, you will be able to deal with the situation in perhaps a harder but better way for you in the long run.

2. Read a few of the following examples and ask group members to comment generally on the consequences in each.

> You decide not to do homework and watch TV instead, resulting in a lowered test grade because the homework topic was on a test.

> You wait until the last 2 days before beginning a project that was assigned a month ago, resulting in stressing, angering, and inconveniencing parent(s), friends, and/or siblings to help you get it finished so you don't fail.

> You horse around with the girls/boys and say things that are considered sexual harassment, resulting in your parents' being notified of possible legal action by the recipient and the recipient's parents, as well as possible expulsion from school.

> You stay up too late watching TV, resulting in your being exhausted and not having the energy to try out for (cheerleading, team, band, and so on).

> You yell names like "wuss" and "bitch" at someone because the kids around you are doing it, even though you really don't know the other student and it is not acceptable language in the halls, resulting in your getting an after-school detention.

3. Invite members to participate in an activity to think about short- and long-term consequences of their choices. Pass out the Truth or Consequences Situations (Handout 3). Invite a group member to lead the first situation. That member reads the situation and asks the rest to volunteer short-term and long-term consequences. As members suggest their ideas, the leader writes them on the easel pad or sheet of newsprint under the heading "Short-Term Consequences" or "Long-Term Consequences," as appropriate. The group can help identify the correct category.

4. Invite a second member to lead the second situation. Follow the same pattern; do as many as you have time for, leaving time for the group's own situations. Balance between sample situations and their own—whatever works for your particular group.

5. End the brainstorming of responses with process questions:

> What particular behaviors of yours would improve greatly if you used the "emotional truth" to deal with things rather than allowed negative consequences to happen?

> What would it be like for you if you took responsibility for thinking things through better and didn't have so many negative consequences occur?

> What surprised you about talking so openly about making better decisions as a result of thinking about short- and long-term consequences?

Processing Time (¼ session time)

1. Ask at least one question from each of the four processing levels:

INTRAPERSONAL

While we were talking about short- and long-term consequences, looking at possible ways to respond and what can happen if you avoid making good decisions, what were you thinking about or feeling?

INTERPERSONAL

What have you noticed is happening with our group?

If there is another group member who has particularly helped you get some new ideas today, would you please link with and tell that person?

NEW LEARNING

What new insights into your own behavior have you gained today?

APPLICATION

What kind of situations do you think might come up for you between now and the next session where you might have the opportunity to stop and think about the short- and long-term consequences of your behavior? Would you be willing to come and share some of your attempts and successes with the group?

2. Give a strong hope statement regarding the group's progress, attendance, disclosures, and efforts. If there are only going to be eight sessions (in other words, no "freebie sessions"), remind them that there will be only one more working session, then the last session will be a looking-back activity and celebration, with no new business. Remind them of the time and place for the next session, then share the treats.

Truth or Consequences Situations

SITUATION 1

You are invited to a sleepover with some friends. Your parents say it is OK, and you are excited because it will be with your best friends and there will be lots of pizza, a swimming pool, your favorite music on LOUD, and so on. You find out there is one person invited you don't like and decide to try to get this person "uninvited" from the party by telling lies about him/her so the host friend will not let this person come. You know this is the wrong thing to do and feel a little guilty about it. You go ahead and spread the lies.

SHORT-TERM CONSEQUENCES?   LONG-TERM CONSEQUENCES?

SITUATION 2

Your whole science class has been working on a big project, and your girlfriend/boyfriend is on your team for the project. He/she hasn't done any work on it and wants you to give him/her your work so it will look like he/she did part of it. You really don't want to because you spent a lot of computer time and library time getting all the information, but he/she pressures you, saying if you really care you will share part of the project so he/she won't get an F. You decide to list the short-term and long-term consequences of giving the information before you do it.

SHORT-TERM CONSEQUENCES?   LONG-TERM CONSEQUENCES?

SITUATION 3

Your best friend wants you to help take some 12-packs of sodas, bags of chips, and boxes of candy bars left over from a field trip. He is in charge of organizing things after the trip, and no one else knows exactly how much is left over. He asks you to help hide the drinks, chips, and candy in the lockers and come back for it later after everyone leaves. There are several big boxes of really cool candy, chips, and drinks, and it would be easy to take. You are a total junk-food hound and love the idea. Then you think of the short- and long-term consequences of stealing the goodies.

SHORT-TERM CONSEQUENCES?   LONG-TERM CONSEQUENCES?

YOUR OWN SITUATION

_____

_____

_____

_____

_____

_____

SHORT-TERM CONSEQUENCES?   LONG-TERM CONSEQUENCES?

Roller-Coaster Feelings

GOALS

Affective

To feel more comfortable with feelings that are often intense

Behavioral

To practice selecting levels of feelings rather than just reacting at a high level

Cognitive

To understand that part of a teenager's life is dealing with strong emotions

To work with the concept that feelings occur along a continuum

MATERIALS

Low-Medium-High Feeling Situations (Handout 4)

Picture, poster, or photo of a roller coaster

Healthy snacks

GROUP SESSION

Opening Time (¼ session time)

1. Welcome members back to group. Ask how they are feeling about the ground rules at this point—do any changes need to be made? Are there any concerns about confidentiality?

2. Review the last session's topic—short- and long-term consequences of decisions. Invite members to share any changes or attempts to change decisions because they thought about the short- and long-term consequences of their behavior.

Working Time (½ session time)

1. Begin a discussion about the idea that there are certain "developmental tasks" of adolescence, "jobs" that group members are taking care of just by going through the growing-up process. These tasks include the following:

   Developing a consistent identity (answering the question "Who am I?")

   Developing a value system that is relatively stable

   "Individuation" (separating from parents and becoming one's own person)

   Developing a sexual identity

   Developing an identity among peers

2. Explain, in your own words:

   It is normal while going through the teenage years to experience extreme highs and extreme lows of emotion as these developmental tasks are being worked on. Adolescence is a time of stress as well as great joy and happiness. Life sometimes seems like the roller coaster you rode on last summer, piercing the clouds going up and crashing to the ground coming down, with your head spinning in delight and wonder. These high and low feelings are difficult for you to experience and difficult for people around you to go through with you. Sometimes other people don't understand where you are coming from and get irritated with your strong emo-

tional reaction to something that doesn't seem that big of a deal to them. But to you it is very, very important! How do you deal with your feelings, and how do you deal with others, especially adults, who are not at the same place you are?

3. Give group members a chance to respond, then continue:

   Although you think that your feelings just happen, and that you "can't help it" if you are furious, thrilled, outraged, ecstatic, disgusted, delighted, or hateful, the fact is you have a great deal of control over how you feel. Feelings occur on a "continuum"—that is, from a low level to a high level, and you can choose whether you want to experience more or less intensity of a feeling.

4. Explain that there are about six major ways to feel: angry, sad, glad, guilty, scared, and lonely:

   Each of these feelings has a low, medium, and high level. You can experience just a little of each of them, a medium amount, or a very high level of them. When you have feelings at their low level, sometimes you hardly know what you're feeling. Your body can tell you that you are experiencing high emotion if you can "tune in" to your body's messages. For example, when you feel really angry, your face might get red, your fists clench, your palms begin to sweat, or you might get a headache or stomachache.

5. Pass out copies of the Low-Medium-High Feeling Situations (Handout 4). Read (or ask volunteers to read) each of the situations aloud. After all the situations have been read, ask, "How would you rank these situations in intensity? Which one seems to be the least serious and which the most serious?" (Situation 1 is the least, Situation 3 the most.)

6. Referring to the handout, ask group members to think where their level of feeling might be on each of the situations: "On a scale of 1 to 10, if 1 means very low-level feeling and 10 means the very most you can possibly feel, where are you?" Let as many as wish to respond share the intensity level of their feelings in one or more situations. Emphasize the ideas that it is possible to raise or lower your emotional response to a situation and that by making conscious choices to be more or less disturbed over a situation, you can use your energies to respond in better ways.

Processing Time (¼ session time)

1. Ask at least one question from each of the four processing levels:

   INTRAPERSONAL

   Maybe no one has ever talked to you about emotions having levels or told you that you have a right to choose how you feel instead of having an emotional response that "just happens." What have you been thinking and feeling as we talked about having power over our emotions?

   INTERPERSONAL

   How have other group members helped you today to get some new ideas about managing feelings that seem to be on a roller coaster and not controllable?

   What have you noticed about our group today—what seems to be happening as we work on our emotional "business"?

   NEW LEARNING

   What new information will you take away from today's session that can have a direct impact on how you will deal with emotional situations?

APPLICATION

What situation is coming up between now and the next session where you might be able to stop and think of what level feelings this situation really deserves and maybe not get so upset over it—or maybe be upset enough to take appropriate action?

2. Ask group members what special thing they would like to do for the last session to celebrate their work and progress. You might suggest that, since the name of the last session is "That's a Wrap," the group might like to have soft flour tortillas filled with something good. If so, ask what they would like to have as fillings for their "wrap."

3. Thank group members for coming and give them a hope statement. Remind them of the date and time for the next session, then share the snacks.

Low-Medium-High Feeling Situations

SITUATION 1

Suppose you are eating an ice-cream cone, and someone comes along and bumps you from behind. The ice cream flies off the cone and splats onto the sidewalk. Now it's hot, and you really wanted that ice-cream cone, and now it's gone and you don't have any more money to get another one. What are some feelings you might have?

1–3   Low: Peeved, bugged, disappointed, glum

4–7   Medium: Mad, bummed out, disgusted, aggravated

8–10   High: Enraged, miserable, furious, horrified, panicked

SITUATION 2

Your friend begs to borrow a CD you got from the library. You don't want to lend it out because you know you are responsible for returning it and don't want anything to happen to it. Sure enough, your friend tells you his little brother stepped on the CD and broke it. Now you will owe the library 19 dollars to replace it, and you will have to pay it out of your baby-sitting and chores money. What are some feelings you might have?

1–3   Low: Distressed, gloomy, cross, resentful, uneasy, anxious

4–7   Medium: Irritated, riled, alarmed, disgusted, burdened

8–10   High: Fuming, burned up, desperate, at the end of your rope, outraged, panicked

SITUATION 3

Your very special grandma has gone to the hospital. She is very sick, and your mom tells you your grandma has to have a triple-bypass heart surgery. You can't even talk to your grandma right now because she is in cardiac intensive care and can't have visitors until after her surgery. What are some feelings you might have?

1–3   Low: Interested, upset, bothered, blue, glum

4–7   Medium: Troubled, worried, anxious, distressed

8–10   High: Depressed, desolate, tormented, afflicted, grieved

That's a Wrap

GOALS

Affective

To get in touch with the major emotional points of the group experience

To have an opportunity to deal with feelings associated with the group's ending

Behavioral

To disclose what behaviors were most changed by the group experience

To celebrate with others who have worked hard and modeled behavior and attitude changes

To say good-bye

Cognitive

To have a sense of accomplishment for having set goals and attempted to make changes

To review "magic moments" of the group experience, events that made an impact

To plan ways to continue to work toward goals in the future

MATERIALS

A "magic wand" of some kind, such as a star wand from a novelty store or Halloween costume. (I use a floral decorating stick covered with glitter.)

Ingredients to make a "wrap" of some kind, such as large flour tortillas, seasoned ground beef or chicken, cut up lettuce and tomatoes, grated cheese, salsa, and refried beans

Sodas or drinks of some kind

Paper plates, napkins or paper towels

GROUP SESSION

Opening Time (¼ session time)

1. Welcome members back to group and ask if, at this last session, they have any concerns about the ground rules or confidentiality. Remind them that confidentiality extends even after the group is over.

2. Invite the group to share any experiences they had about choosing the intensity of feelings:

    What situations did you have where you could or did use the "1 to 10 technique" to raise or lower your emotional response to better suit the situation?

    Sometimes when you choose a higher level emotion than a situation calls for, you also respond with actions that are not appropriate, and you risk getting in some kind of trouble. How did you feel about using your thinking to take control of emotions that might have been out of control if you had chosen a higher level response?

Working Time (½ session time)

1. In your own words, say, "Our time together has come to a close, and it is our delight to review the ups and downs of the experiences we have had together." Tell them that the "magic wand" represents the special feelings of togetherness and helpfulness that they have had. Explain that you will go through the topics of the sessions and invite them to share if they had a "magic moment" during or after that session because of what they learned from other group members or their own experience. If the magic moment was because of another

group member, encourage them to "tell that person directly" (in other words, link with that person). For example, Susan might say to Ashley, about the last session: "My magic moment was when you said you had decided not to blow up at your step-dad and not talk to anyone in the family for 2 days, because I learned that I don't have to have a big fit over everything my 18-year-old sister says to me, and I can let some of it go sometimes."

2. Go through the major topics of each session. Pass the "magic wand" around to any group members who want to share a magic moment from that session.

> Session 1—Getting Started
>
> Learning about thinking, feeling, and behaving, and connecting these ideas to the topic of the difficult transitions going on in your lives
>
> Session 2—You Gotta Have BIG Ears!
>
> Understanding that if you want to be listened to, you need to listen to others
>
> Session 3—Who Am I?
>
> Thinking about how changes in you physically, emotionally, cognitively, and socially are all going on at this time of your life
>
> *Freebie session, if you had one.*
>
> Session 4—My Power, Their Power
>
> Recognizing power in relationships
>
> Session 5—My Middle Name Is "Flexible"
>
> Using rigid and bendable straws to show how choosing to be flexible in some situations often results in less stress and more positive outcomes
>
> Session 6—Truth or Consequences
>
> Learning that thinking ahead can help you evaluate the short- and long-term consequences of your behaviors—and make better choices and decisions as a result
>
> *Freebie session, if you had one.*
>
> Session 7—Roller-Coaster Feelings
>
> Talking about how by making a decision about how much or how little we want to experience feelings, we can have a more balanced emotional life and not feel so confused about highs and lows

Processing Time (¼ session time)

1. Ask the following questions:

> How was it for you today when we reviewed all the sessions and you shared magic moments and talked about how events were changing for you? What were you thinking and feeling as this sharing was going on?
>
> At this point, how does our group seem to you? In what ways has it changed since the beginning?
>
> What important new ideas have you learned about being in a group counseling experience with others who have problems and issues just like you?

2. Ask what each group member would like to keep working on in the future, and have a share-around so everyone has a chance to tell about their goals and receive encouragement from the group.

3. Explain any arrangements for follow-up. For example, you might have two follow-up sessions, one in a month and a second one in 2 months, as "brown bag" lunches in your office. Thank all for participating and give a hope statement:

> *Sometimes it is very hard to say good-bye. But this isn't good-bye forever! It is good-bye for the time being. You might feel that you have just gotten started on your personal growth and have lots more wonderful things to discover and improve about yourself. Maybe you can work on them by yourself, and maybe you need more help. Please come see me if you think you do, because maybe I can refer you to another counselor or place where you can get more help. You have taken some big steps toward improving your lives, and I believe in each one of you. You have shown me you have the ability to make changes for the better in your life. I have a great deal of hope and confidence that each of you will continue to take the risks to grow as a beautiful, kind, and loving person.*

4. Use the phrase "That's a wrap!" and invite all to make their own rolled-up wrap with the ingredients available. Celebrate!

Dating and Relating: Male/Female Relationship Issues

"Power and personal agency are important expressions of many other factors: individuality, freedom, responsibility, and viability" (Mahoney, 1991, p. 183). The past four decades give resonating voice to the issues of human rights in many arenas: for women, minorities, seniors, people with disabilities, and others. Issues relating to freedom, peace, ecology, health, and power have come into focus for nearly everyone in a "one-down" position in our society. We are a nation committed to pursuing voice for our issues and choice in the political and economic marketplace. Youth, however, are at the bottom of the power heap—discriminated against by adultism, sexism, heterosexism, classism, ableism, youthism, and poverty (Finkelhor, Hotaling, Lewis, & Smith, 1990). The powerlessness of youth is frequently expressed in premature, inappropriate, or violent relationships among them, through both friendships and sexual relationships. Abuse, neglect, and violence toward children appear to be creating youth with little or no motivation to behave in more appropriate ways toward themselves or their peers (Babcock, Waltz, Jacobson, & Gottman, 1993).

Even when adult supervision is caring and consistent, youth begin their journey to adulthood with their peers as their major compass for their behavior. They are drawn to the experience and expression of their sexual selves as an adolescent developmental task. As they mature, their sexuality expresses itself in whatever ways they have learned previously to meet their basic needs. Youth who have learned a modicum of self-control and values from a caring family are more likely to express their sexual needs and desires in a controlled manner than are youth whose families have provided little structure and modeling for social skills and little personal motivation to control hurtful behaviors. The relationship issues that spring from serious dating are heated and often very cloudy for young people, and they can be observed to be extremely conflicted about their own behavior.

It is apparent that even very young adolescents are often sexually active and that they have even less sexual knowledge than high school youth, who attend classes on such topics as biology and psychology, where they have the opportunity to receive sexuality education. Youth of middle and junior high school age frequently have no opportunities to learn about physical, emotional, and social issues related to the expression of their sexuality. Thus, their issues often are not addressed either at home or at school, and their erratic and often hurtful behaviors continue. This group experience, then, is intended for youth who appear to be in serious dating relationships and at risk for becoming involved in engaging in dangerous sexual behaviors.

In this group experience, you may choose to encourage responsible leadership skills on the part of group members. The opening activity sets the stage for this by developing a number of humorous methods for selecting a leader. Leadership is a serious responsibility, though, and you should assign responsibilities at your discretion and after applying your best professional judgment. If the topic needs further discussion or members are uncomfortable with a peer at the helm, an adult should remain the leader. Leadership is its own reward, but you will need to encourage applause or other positive recognition of members' leadership efforts. Remember to encourage members to "pass" if they don't want the responsibilities. Members can assume responsibilities for conducting Opening Time, Processing Time, or both. If both segments will be member led, it is best to choose two different leaders. You will want to retain responsibility for Session 6 (due to its sensitive content) and Session 8 (because it is the group's final meeting).

The sessions in the agenda are as follows:

Session 1—Getting Started

Session 2—Knowing Your Dating Values

Session 3—Dating Rights and Responsibilities

Session 4—Expressing Feelings to Your Girlfriend/Boyfriend

Session 5—Power in Relationships

Session 6—Date Abuse: Violence in Relationships

Session 7—Boomerang Behaviors

Session 8—Ending Relationships: When and How

Session 9—That's a Wrap

GROUP GOALS

1. To develop a safe environment where ideas and feelings about relationships can be explored and exchanged

2. To promote the group norms of becoming a supportive, encouraging person

3. To ensure that members can discriminate thinking, feeling, and behaving

4. To explore values and behaviors important to successful relationships

5. To discriminate passive, assertive, and aggressive behavior

6. To recognize that power is the basis for most relationship struggles

7. To become aware of behaviors that indicate a dating partner is not good for you

8. To explore benefits and risks of early sexual relationships

9. To raise awareness of abuse of power in relationships resulting in physical and psychological victimization

10. To learn skills to end relationships responsibly instead of using the "hit and run" approach

11. To encourage positive communication with knowledgeable adults when youth need new ideas about how to deal with problems in relationships

12. To review the group experience and set goals for future personal work

SELECTION AND OTHER GUIDELINES

Choose high, medium, and low self-disclosers, and be sure to role-balance. You will want to select a heterogeneous mix of youth, some who are known to be dating and sexually active, some who are dating and not sexually active, and some who may have been sexually active but have decided to abstain for some reason. Do not select best friends or worst enemies, dating partners, or previous dating partners.

It is highly recommended that male and female co-leaders be involved with this group, the co-leader preferably being someone having both group experience and some specialized knowledge and training in human sexuality (for example, a school nurse, social worker with previous sexuality group experience, or a biology, psychology, or life-skills instructor). If it is not possible to have such a co-leader for *all* of the sessions, it is absolutely essential to obtain the consent of members for someone with *expert knowledge* to participate in the session on the topic of date abuse/violence in relationships (Session 6). This topic draws heated feelings, and a knowledgeable co-leader will help keep balance and perspective.

REFERENCES AND SUGGESTED RESOURCES FOR PROFESSIONALS

Alfieri, T., Ruble, D. N., & Higgins, E. T. (1996). Gender stereotypes during adolescence: Developmental changes and the transition to junior high school. *Developmental Psychology, 32,* 1129–1137.

Babcock, J., Waltz, J., Jacobson, N., & Gottman, J. (1993). Power and violence: The relation between communication patterns, power discrepancies, and family violence. *Journal of Consulting and Clinical Psychology, 61,* 40–50.

Berkowitz, L. (1993). *Aggression: Its causes, consequences, and control.* New York: McGraw-Hill.

Bussy, K., & Bandura, A. (1992). Self-regulatory systems governing gender development. *Child Development, 63,* 1236–1250.

Carroll, M. R., Bates, M., & Johnson, C. (1997). *Group leadership* (3rd ed.). Denver: Love.

Deffenbacher, J. L., Lynch, R. S., & Oetting, E. R. (1996). Anger reduction in early adolescents. *Journal of Counseling Psychology, 43,* 149–157.

Finkelhor, D., Hotaling, G., Lewis, I. A., & Smith, C. (1990). Sexual abuse in a national survey of adult men and women: Prevalence, characteristics, and risk factors. *Child Abuse and Neglect, 14,* 19–28.

Firpo-Triplett, R. (1997, July). *Is it flirting or sexual harassment?* Paper presented at the conference entitled "Working with America's Youth," Pittsburgh.

Flanagan, A. S. (1996, March). *Romantic behavior of sexually victimized and nonvictimized girls.* Paper presented at the meeting of the Society for Research on Adolescence, Boston.

Mahoney, M. J. (1991). *Human change processes.* New York: Basic.

McMurray, D. (1992). When it doesn't work: Small group work in adolescent sexuality education. *School Counselor, 39,* 385–389.

Schechtman, Z., Vurembrand, N., & Hertz-Lazarowitz, R. (1994). A dyadic and gender-specific analysis of close friendships of preadolescents receiving group psychotherapy. *Journal of Social and Personal Relationships, 11,* 443–448.

Wolfe, D. A., Wekerle, C., Gough, R., & Reitzel, D. (1993, August). Promoting healthy, non-violent relationships: A prevention program for youth. In D. A. Wolfe (Chair), *Violence in adolescent relationships: Identifying risk factors and prevention methods.* Symposium conducted at the 101st annual meeting of the American Psychological Association, Toronto.

Wolfe, D. A., Wekerle, C., Gough, R., Reitzel-Jaffe, D., Grasley, C., Pittman, A., Lefebre, L., & Stumpf, J. (1996). *The youth relationships manual: A group approach with adolescents for the prevention of woman abuse and the promotion of healthy relationships.* Thousand Oaks, CA: Sage.

Wolfe, D. A., Wekerle, C., Reitzel-Jaffe, D., & Gough, R. (1995). Strategies to address violence in the lives of youth. In E. Peled, P. G. Jaffe, & J. L. Edleson (Eds.), *Ending the cycle of violence: Community responses to children of battered women.* Thousand Oaks, CA: Sage.

Getting Started

GOALS

Affective

To reduce initial tension and begin to relax with one other

Behavioral

To work with other members to develop ground rules necessary for feeling safe in the group

To experience a fun get-acquainted activity

Cognitive

To understand the purpose and general goals of the group

To understand confidentiality and its limits

To clarify the concepts of thinking, feeling, and behaving

MATERIALS

Limits of Confidentiality sign (see Appendix A, page 270)

Easel pad or posterboard and marker

A large, red paper heart (16 to 20 inches wide)

Smaller pink construction paper hearts, one for each member

Red markers

Transparent tape

Paper and pencils

Healthy snacks (such as fruit, crackers, juice, raisins)

GROUP SESSION

Opening Time

> For sessions after this first one, Opening Time will take up about one-fourth of the typical 40- to 50-minute session time, or about 10 minutes. For this session, however, you will need to plan on more time to discuss confidentiality, develop ground rules, and conduct a getting-acquainted activity. See the book's introduction for some ideas on how to schedule this extra time.

1. Welcome the girls and guys to group, and go over the name of the group, purpose, and major goals. Tell them this is going to be a fun experience but also intense and that there will be differences of opinion that might be very strong. Explain that each session follows a similar format: After this first session, Opening Time is for review and discussion of concerns left over from the previous session. Members will be invited to share how between-session behavior change projects are going and to participate in a "brag time" to give reinforcement to those who are making changes.

2. Explain that there will be opportunities to share things that are definitely not for the ears of anyone outside the group's ears, and that a strong commitment to confidentiality is expected from everyone. Thoroughly discuss confidentiality (the "no-blab" rule): What is said and

done in the group stays in the group. Be sure to give some examples of things adults or peers outside the group might say to pressure group members to share what happens in group. For example:

Hey, I heard you guys brag about sex stuff in that group—do you?

What does Letisha say in that group you go to?

Why can't you tell me? I'm your best friend—don't you trust me?

After members are clear on what confidentiality is, share the Limits of Confidentiality sign (either as a handout or poster) and discuss: Let group members know you are bound by the confidentiality rule but that as the leader you are required to tell about what goes on in the group if you think someone will do harm to self or others, if someone says anything about child abuse or criminal activity going on, or if a judge orders you to turn over information.

3. Discuss the basic ground rules you have decided on for your group and request the group's input in developing a few more that would enhance their comfort in sharing with one another. For example:

Take turns.

Everyone has the right to "pass" (not share unless that's comfortable).

Agree to disagree (no put-downs).

Come on time.

Don't move on until the group agrees on the ground rules. Write or have the group write the rules on an easel pad or piece of posterboard and have each member sign the document to show agreement. You can then post these rules every session.

---

4. Explain:

During this group experience we are going to share some of the leadership responsibilities. Sometimes I will do the leading activities, and sometimes group members will lead. I will usually conduct the Working Time activity. We will rotate the Opening Time and Processing Time leadership among members. No one will be required to lead unless he or she wants to. But we do need some novel and nifty ways to select leaders.

Ask the group to break up into two minigroups and go to different areas of the room. Their task is to take 3 minutes to brainstorm ways to select members who could be the leader that day. Explain that after the time is up, you will reassemble the larger group and each minigroup will present its list of possible qualifications for leaders. Tell members of each minigroup to be sure to learn one another's names before reassembling.

5. When you call time and members return to the group circle, encourage each minigroup to present its ideas briefly and let members know you appreciate their efforts. Then present your own, humorous list of leader qualifications. For example:

Person with the fewest buttons on that day

Person with a birthday closest to December 25

Person with the largest shoe size

Person with the smallest shoe size

Person born in the most distant place

> Make a chart of your qualifications to display during each group session. During future sessions, use these qualifications and not those dependent on member skills to determine who will be invited to assume leadership responsibilities.

Working Time

> Working Time will take half of a typical session, or about 20 to 25 minutes.

1. Distribute the individual heart cutouts and the markers. In your own words, explain the following ideas:

   Because our thoughts, feelings, and behaviors in this group experience are related to dating and members of the opposite sex, let's use the symbol of love to help us understand how these three parts of ourselves are different. Please take your marker, and on one side of your pink heart write FEELINGS you have when you are in love, like passion or jealousy. Next turn your heart over and draw a zig-zag line down the middle to divide the heart into two parts. On one side write THOUGHTS you might have while in love, such as "Does she love me?" "Is this the right person for me?" or "Am I in love?" On the other side write BEHAVIORS you might engage in, such as kissing, dancing, fighting, teasing, and so on. Share if you dare! (This usually results in lots of laughter.)

2. Encourage group members to come up and tape their individual hearts on the larger heart. As they do so, they may share one or two of the thoughts, feelings, or behaviors they have written.

3. Explain, then conduct a share-around:

   Now that you have greatly expanded your knowledge and vocabulary of love, let's get serious and pinpoint some goals you would like to work on during our group sessions. Let's hear at least one goal in the area of dating and relating that you would like to accomplish by the end of the group.

   For example:

   I want to be able to ask girls out and not be terribly hurt or mad if they say no.

   For me, I'd like to know how to say no to my boyfriend—not back down.

   I want to know what to say to girls and have them like me.

Processing Time

> Processing Time takes one-quarter of a typical session, or about 10 minutes.

1. Ask at least one questions from each of the four processing levels:

   INTRAPERSONAL

   While we were getting to know one another better and making sure we are all able to see how thinking, feeling, and behaving are different, what were you thinking or feeling inside yourself?

INTERPERSONAL

What was it like to be a group member today?

What did you notice about other members?

NEW LEARNING

What new idea or insight did you experience today?

APPLICATION

During the time before the next session, would you be willing to notice two or three feelings you have that keep happening in your relationships with friends, either the same or opposite sex?

2. Remind group members of the day and time for the next session and give them a hope statement like the following example:

I'm sensing that all of you are really motivated to make some changes toward better relationships, and I believe in your ability to make it so for yourself by all of us working together.

Enjoy the snacks!

Knowing Your Dating Values

If you choose, when you get to Processing Time explain that today you will start sharing the responsibilities for leading and learning. At that time you can display the chart of leader selection characteristics from Session 1 and let the group choose one characteristic—for example, the person wearing the most buttons today. If that person accepts the responsibility, give him or her the questions, written on a sheet of paper or separate index cards.

GOALS

Affective

To increase comfort level in discussing feelings and ideas about dating

Behavioral

To learn to be accepting of a range of dating values

Cognitive

To become aware of what dating values are important to members of the same and opposite sex

MATERIALS

Small paper cups, three for each group member

A roll of nickels, about 2 dollars worth of pennies, and a roll of dimes. (These belong to and are returned to the leader!)

Colored markers, three different colors

Healthy snacks

GROUP SESSION

Opening Time (¼ session time)

1. Welcome members back to group and ask about confidentiality. Encourage them to share their ideas, feelings, and concerns about keeping things confidential. How do they see the ground rules at this point—are any changes or additions necessary?

2. Review the topic of the last session (getting acquainted and thinking-feeling-behaving) and ask who would be willing to share their insights about recurring relationship feelings. Are these feelings a problem or a pleasure?

Working Time (½ session time)

1. Invite the group members to participate in an activity for the purpose of clarifying one's own values about what is important in a dating relationship and also to learn what other members of the group value. You might want to sit on the floor for this one, or on pillows or cushions of some type. Pass out the paper cups and instruct group members to take three each. They are to place the paper cups in front of them on the floor. Pass around the three marking pens, together, and have each member mark his or her cups with an H, M, and L (one letter per cup).

2. Tell the group members in a joking way that you had to take out a major loan to get the change you have there . . . so you need it back! No keeping your coins! Say that you are

going to invite them to share what they think is really of value in a dating relationship. Place all the coins in a pile in the middle of the group—a pile of pennies, nickels, and dimes.

3. Invite them each to share at least one thing they value in someone they are dating or would date. When one group member says a value, that member decides whether it is a high-, medium-, or low-ranked value in his or her value system. The group member takes a dime, nickel, or penny and places it in the cup marked H (for high value), M (for medium level value), or L (for low value). After the member shares the value, all the other group members can choose a coin and rank that same value for themselves, if indeed it is one of their values. Other members don't have to have the same ranking or the same value. Sample values include honesty, trust, humor, friendliness, helps me, likes kids, wants to get a college education, drives responsibly, doesn't put people down, is a smart student, is fun to be with and makes me laugh, respects what I think and want to do, doesn't take drugs or drink too much, takes care of himself/herself (neat, clean, well groomed), and so on.

4. After the first member has shared a value, another member can have a chance to share a different value. Keep on until the coins are gone and/or group members can't think of any more values.

5. Ask what comments they have about hearing their own and group members of the opposite sex's views on values in dating relationships. Let everyone share. (The girls are generally more animated than the boys. They are less likely to make a joke of the activity, as they are generally more mature. They serve as role models for the boys, who might have less well-developed skills in talking about relationships.)

6. Ask the following questions:

    What surprised you about the opposite sex's ideas about dating values?

    What values did nearly everyone have in common? What are the top two or three values?

    What new ideas about things to value do you have as a result of listening to other members' values?

    What happens when you begin to date someone and find out the person has different values from you? How do you deal with it?

    What values are so important to you that you would stop dating someone when you found out for sure that person did not have the same views?

    What do you think happens if you stay in a relationship where you both have very different major values?

7. Ask members to count their high, medium, and low coins and find out how many values they assigned to each area, then have fun sharing the amounts.

Processing Time (¼ session time)

1. Ask at least one question from each of the four processing levels:

    INTRAPERSONAL

    Today we started our journey together. While we were getting acquainted and doing the activity, what were you thinking or feeling?

    INTERPERSONAL

    We are a new group but are beginning to have a sense of us as a group, not just individuals. What did you notice about us as a group today?

    NEW LEARNING

    What new thoughts or ideas have you become aware of today from our activity—or from discussing confidentiality and our ground rules?

APPLICATION

Would you be willing to ask a parent or another adult you respect to name his or her three most important relationship values, then ask that person if it would be OK if you shared this information with the group?

2. Give a hope statement that the group is already working together to make a difference in their relationships. Remind them of confidentiality, especially with regard to someone they are dating. Confidentiality means *no one,* not even dating partners, is to share in the disclosures of the group members.

3. Remind them of the day and time for the next session, then share the snacks.

Dating Rights and Responsibilities

For this and following sessions, except for Sessions 6 and 8, you can invite group members to ask the questions for Opening Time, Processing Time, or both. Have group members select the leader(s) according to the characteristics presented in Session 1, then give the leader(s) the questions, written on a sheet of paper or on separate index cards.

GOALS

Affective

To relax and further develop cohesion as a group

Behavioral

To participate in an activity to help define a set of personal rights and responsibilities that apply to dating and all other types of relationships

Cognitive

To understand how passive, aggressive, and assertive responses are different

MATERIALS

My Bill of Rights (Handout 5)

Three empty chairs, in addition to group chairs or cushions

Signs for chairs: *PASSIVE, AGGRESSIVE, ASSERTIVE*

Small index cards, on which you have written the Dating and Relating Situations

Healthy snacks

GROUP SESSION

Opening Time (¼ session time)

1. Welcome the group members and invite them to discuss any situations they might have encountered since the last session regarding confidentiality. How are the ground rules working at this point for them? Are any changes needed?

2. Inquire if anyone has any comments or questions about the last session, on dating values, or if anyone asked about and is able to share some of a significant adult's relationship values. Ask how those values are the same or different from this generation's values. (No names of persons outside the group!)

Working Time (½ session time)

1. Pass out My Bill of Rights (Handout 5) and ask group members to read it silently first. Then ask if they would take turns reading aloud one of the rights that means something special to them.

2. Ask what they think about these rights—if they sound like rights they would like to claim for themselves. Discuss the idea that these rights are based on the concepts of fairness, equality, and respect. (They probably mentioned these during the last session when talking about their values.)

3. Explain the following ideas in your own words:

When you do not respect and value yourself, you tend to behave and communicate in ways that are called PASSIVE. This means you respect the other person's ideas, feelings, values, and opinions more than your own and don't respect yourself. When you are passive in a lot of situations you begin to feel taken advantage of and angry at the other person(s), and you have low self-esteem.

Sample passive behaviors:

Letting someone take your homework away from you or easily talk you into letting the person copy it

Allowing your boyfriend or girlfriend to pressure you into doing things you are not comfortable with

Not speaking up for yourself when someone calls you a name

Not asking for help from a teacher because you think he or she will think you are dumb

Allowing your boyfriend or girlfriend to make all the decisions about what to do, where to go, what movie to see, and so on

Telling yourself you really aren't that upset when someone steals your belongings

4. Summarize the following:

Another way of behaving is called AGGRESSIVE. This is when you do not respect other people's rights—the same rights you want. You may want to get your point, idea, or feeling across, but you do so in a way that is disrespectful and hurtful to others. When you behave in aggressive ways, you feel temporarily powerful and in control, but the end result is that people don't like you because you don't respect them, and you usually end up feeling guilty for behaving badly and not handling the situation in a better way.

Sample aggressive behaviors:

Calling people names like *dork, geek, weirdo,* or *queer*

Taking something from a younger child, like money or food

Being disrespectful to a teacher—for example, calling the teacher names

Getting mad at your boyfriend or girlfriend for changing his or her mind about going out with you or wanting to go to a different place

Expressing your anger in ways that hurt others, such as breaking things at home or yelling disrespectfully back at your mom

5. In your own words, explain:

Instead of respecting others more than yourself (passive), or disrespecting others to get your point across (aggressive), you can take more positive approach—being ASSERTIVE. This approach means respecting yourself and respecting the other person also. You can just plain ask in a straightforward way, or share your ideas, feelings, or opinions without the intent to hurt someone else.

Sample assertive behaviors and statements:

I want you to give me my book back. *(request)*

I believe in helping people when they need my help. *(opinion)*

No, I can't go to the store for you today. *(self-affirmation)*

I feel really angry when you hit your little sister, and I want you to stop it right now. *(I-message)*

6. Explain that the three empty chairs have signs for passive, assertive, and aggressive actions and that you will be inviting a group member to read the first of the Dating and Relating Situations. When another group member believes he or she knows if it is a passive, assertive, or aggressive behavior, feeling, or belief, that person goes and sits in the chair labeled as such. The person sitting in the chair gets to read the next situation. (Each situation is identified by type to help you guide discussion.)

Dating and Relating Situations

Maria said to Juan, "I feel irritated when you bug me to drink a beer when we go on a date, and I want you to stop it or I won't go out with you." *(assertive expression of feelings)*

Chelsea told her boyfriend to go to hell when he came late to see her. *(aggressive handling of situation)*

Marcus called Shawnay a bitch because she wouldn't pay for them to go to the Burger Queen to eat. *(aggressive, hurtful put-down)*

Selina wouldn't say no to her boyfriend when he wanted her to take some money from her mom because Selina was afraid he would leave her and go with her girlfriend. *(Passive reaction)*

7. Now ask the group members to come up with a couple of situations that they think are passive, aggressive, or assertive.

8. Ask, "Which of the rights do you want to work toward taking control of in your life by being more assertive instead of passive or aggressive?" After group members have responded: "If you were more assertive, say after you practiced this for a few weeks, what do you think the result would be in your relationships?"

Processing Time (¼ session time)

1. Ask (or have the group select a member to ask) at least one question from each of the four processing levels:

INTRAPERSONAL

During our session today, what were you thinking and feeling about this idea of rights and being assertive rather than passive or aggressive?

INTERPERSONAL

What did you notice about being a member of the group today? Is it any different than at our last session?

NEW LEARNING

What new ideas did you learn today that made an impression on you?

What changes have you noticed in your relationship with your boyfriend/girlfriend since you started the group?

APPLICATION

How do you think this information might help you in your dating and relating during the time between now and the next session?

What problems might the information you learned today help you solve?

2. Thank group members for coming and give them a hope statement. Remind them of the time and day for the next session, then enjoy the snacks.

My Bill of Rights

YOU HAVE A RIGHT TO . . .

Be treated with respect.

Have and express your own opinions and feelings.

Set your own priorities.

Say no without feeling guilty or giving explanations.

Ask for what you want and need.

Get what you pay for.

Ask for information from professionals.

Make mistakes.

Choose not to assert yourself.

Be independent.

Have your needs met (including by yourself).

Do less than you are humanly capable of.

Act only in ways that promote your dignity and self-respect as long as others' rights are not violated in the process.

If you know what your rights are,
you will be less hesitant about asserting them.

Expressing Feelings to Your Girlfriend/Boyfriend

GOALS

Affective

To get in touch with the major feelings that occur in relationships

Behavioral

To learn the skill of and practice using I-messages as a method of honest communication in relationships

Cognitive

To raise awareness of alternatives to blaming and verbal and physical abuse in anger situations in relationships

To learn that everyone in close relationships experiences strong emotions such as anger, guilt, and joy, and that everyone needs healthy ways to express these feelings

MATERIALS

I-Message Formula (Handout 6)

I-Message Examples (Handout 7)

Bag of candy, about 40 to 50 pieces

Healthy snacks

GROUP SESSION

Opening Time (¼ session time)

1. Welcome group members and give them some special verbal reinforcement for attending and participating in the group. Inquire what concerns they might have regarding confidentiality. How about the ground rules? Are they needing any changes?

2. Ask what passive, aggressive, and assertive behaviors they noticed in themselves after the last session and what they did about these behaviors. (Don't let them bring up other people's behaviors outside the group—keep them focused on their own.)

Working Time (½ session time)

1. Express the following ideas in your own words:

   Every relationship where people share close personal ideas, beliefs, fun experiences, and a lot of time together very soon runs into differences of opinion on many issues. How these differences are handled affects whether it's a good working relationship or a negative, hurtful one. The attitude that "we can work this out because we value equality and respect each other" is the basis for being willing to give and take, and to negotiate problems, issues, and differences.

   Some relationships are based on one person's trying to control the other person most of the time. This works for a while because the passive person usually gives in rather than have a fight or express his or her own opinions or ideas and be put down, or even physically hurt, by the other person. Eventually, though, the relationship breaks down and will end in some way, either by the passive person's getting out some way, or sometimes by violence. Either path is hurtful to both the passive and aggressive partner because the relationship is unequal and will continue to spin in this destructive cycle until it ends, usually in an unpleasant situation and with hurtful feelings for both.

Today we are going to learn and practice a healthy way to deal with negative emotions so that neither person is assaulted verbally and both have an equal chance of getting their needs met.

2. Explain that when we are angry with someone, we frequently go in to the "blaming mode," saying things like the following:

   You didn't bring my CD back again.

   You're lazy.

   You were supposed to buy me a soda.

   Why don't you ever do things right?

   You always insist on your way.

3. Discuss the fact that if you are angry you have the right to express your anger, but only in ways that are not aggressive and hurtful to others. I-messages are a way to express your anger without blaming or accusing, and they are more likely to result in the person's listening to you. The person might not do what you want, but you have given yourself the opportunity to express your legitimate anger and done so in a way that is not hurtful.

4. Display or pass out copies of the I-Message Formula (Handout 6). Go through the formula, explaining that it is important to say each section of it for the other person to get the message. In other words, you can't just stop with "I FEEL _____ WHEN _____." The BECAUSE and I WANT or I NEED part has to be there, too, so the other person gets the whole picture. People can't change if you don't tell them what you want.

5. Discuss what might happen if someone is used to your being passive and doesn't like your I-message. Stress that you have a right to express your feelings:

   You may have to use I-messages several times before other people get used to your being more assertive and expressing anger this way rather than blaming. They could ridicule you for talking funny or being "gritchy." If they do, they probably don't know how to deal with your new way of communicating and are afraid you are going to change too much. Try to be patient and accepting and stand your ground. If they respect you and are not trying to control you, most other people will eventually begin to understand that you will stand up for yourself and express yourself in positive ways.

6. Pass out copies of the I-Message Examples (Handout 7) and ask group members to take turns reading the examples aloud. Ask what questions they might have about the formula, what it means, results of using it, and so on.

7. Ask the group to form dyads and have each member share a situation in which he or she could use the I-message formula to express anger to someone. Dyads can then help each other come up with an I-message that fits the situation. Give a time limit so both people may share equally and explain that after they have worked together you will ask if anyone wants to share an I-message with the group.

8. After about 10 minutes, have members return to the group circle; ask for examples of I-messages. Each person who shares gets a piece of candy . . . they usually all share!

9. If you have time, ask the group to think of other situations and I-messages that could be used, rewarding each idea with a piece of candy.

Processing Time (¼ session time)

1. Ask (or have the group select a member to ask) at least one question from each of the four processing levels:

   INTRAPERSONAL

   What were you thinking and feeling today while we learned and practiced I-messages?

   INTERPERSONAL

   We've been together four times now. What is it like for you to be a group member and work on these important matters?

   NEW LEARNING

   What new ideas or feelings did you have today about expressing anger and keeping the lines of communication open in relationships?

   APPLICATION

   What situations do you have coming up this week with a girlfriend/boyfriend (or someone else you feel safer with) that might be a good time to use an I-message to get your anger or aggravation out in an assertive way?

2. Thank group members for coming and give them a hope statement. Remind them of the day and time for the next session, then share the snacks.

I-Message Formula

I FEEL . . .

_____

_____

WHEN . . .

_____

_____

BECAUSE . . .

_____

_____

AND I WANT/NEED . . .

_____

_____

I-Message Examples

MESSAGE 1

I feel irritated
when you take a book from my locker without telling me
because I don't know where it is and worry about it,
and I want you to ask me first.

MESSAGE 2

I'm really steamed
when you don't come at the time you say you are going to
because I feel worried about you and scared to wait alone,
and I want you to respect my time (come on time).

MESSAGE 3

I feel furious
when you make remarks about my hair
because I spend a lot of time trying to make it look the way I want,
and I want you to keep quiet if you don't like it.

MESSAGE 4

I feel resentful
when you always want me to spend my money on sodas and food
because I work very hard for my money,
and I want you to share equally in snack expenses.

MESSAGE 5

I feel confused and jealous
when you tell me I am your only girlfriend/boyfriend
because you flirt with other girls/boys when we are together,
and I want you to stop it or find another girlfriend/boyfriend.

MESSAGE 6

I feel embarrassed
when you wear those tiny little tank tops that show everything
because the other guys/girls are leering and snickering at you,
and I want you not to wear those when we are on a date.

MESSAGE 7

I feel humiliated
when you horse around like a 10-year-old
because my friends think I am going on a date with a kid,
and I want you to act like a grown-up, not a child.

Power in Relationships

GOALS

Affective

To get in touch with the same and opposite sex's feelings about abuse of power in relationships

Behavioral

To explore some ways of dealing with anger rather than through physical abuse or manipulation

Cognitive

To develop an understanding of the bases of social power in relationships

To become aware of power balances, negative power, and positive power

MATERIALS

Easel pad or posterboard and marker

A large bag of M & M's or individually wrapped candy (approximately eight pieces per group member)

Container for the M & M's or candy

Dish and spoon (if you are using unwrapped candy)

Healthy snacks

GROUP SESSION

Opening Time (¼ session time)

1. Welcome the members back to group. Ask what concerns there might be regarding confidentiality. How are the ground rules working at this point? Are any changes needed?

2. Ask the following questions about the last session's topic:

    What experiences have you had since the last session in practicing I-messages? (Reinforce any and all attempts or uses.)

    How has this changed things in your relationship with your girlfriend/boyfriend?

    What do you need to improve in your use of I-messages?

Working Time (½ session time)

1. Discuss the idea that when people are angry, they often respond in an aggressive rather than a passive or assertive way. Aggression as an expression of anger can easily turn into violence in relationships, especially when the person does not have any other skills to deal with anger. Explain:

    Relationship and family violence causes children and adults great physical and emotional
    pain. This can be avoided by learning how to deal with your own anger and other people's

---

The discussion of social power in this session is based generally on information in *The Youth Relationships Manual: A Group Approach with Adolescents for the Prevention of Woman Abuse and the Promotion of Healthy Relationships,* by D. A. Wolfe and colleagues (Thousand Oaks, CA: Sage, 1996).

anger toward you. You can't stop other people from being angry, but you can control your reaction to their anger.

2. Write (or refer to, if you have previously written) the following on the easel pad or posterboard.

    Power bases: Personal assets and resources, such as knowledge, skills, or money, that form the basis of one partner's control over another

    Power processes: Interpersonal techniques to gain control, such as one person's being more assertive, aggressive, passive, or persuasive

    Power outcomes: Who makes the final choices, decisions—who "wins" in the situation

3. Place the M & M's in their container in the middle of the group. Invite group members to participate in recognizing power bases, processes, and outcomes as you read the following relationship situations aloud. Each situation can have several kinds of power elements. When a group member recognizes a power element, he or she raises a hand and tells the power element and what behavior in the situation matches it. When correct, the member gets a piece of candy. Only one identification of power element per member is allowed for any given situation. Next ask the whole group if they recognize any *other* power elements in the situation, and let them respond. When all elements are recognized in that situation, move on to the next one. Do as many as time allows, reserving time for processing.

Situation 1

Jeremy is dating Latonda, who is from a wealthy family. Her mom and dad are both doctors, and they live in a huge, expensive house. Latonda talks a lot about getting her own sports car when she turns 16, and Jeremy knows she will get it. He really likes Latonda but wants to have a more equal relationship because she is always buying expensive gifts for him, and he can't afford to do the same. He feels pressured to let her have her own way when they go on dates because he is afraid she will drop him if he doesn't agree with what she wants/says. What kinds of power elements are present in this situation?

Situation 2

Ahmed likes to go out with his girlfriend, Leah. Ahmed's family comes from India, and his family values women's being passive and accepting of what men want. Ahmed thinks this is a good idea for American girls also and wants the girls he dates to be like Indian girls. Leah is from an American family, but she is quiet and shy by nature and doesn't know how to be assertive, even though she gets mad when Ahmed seems so bossy and pushy. He can always talk Leah into doing whatever he wants. What kinds of power elements are present in this situation?

Situation 3

Mañuela is dating José. She is very aggressive and uses put-downs to get people to give in to her. She pressures José by using put-downs and name-calling, and José does what she wants. He likes Mañuela but does not know how to deal with her aggressive tactics. He is getting very angry with her. What kinds of power elements are present in this situation?

Situation 4

Tyler's girlfriend, Sarah, is angry with him. Tyler is constantly nagging her to have sex with him, telling her things like "You won't get pregnant until you're 15 or 16," "I don't have any STD's or AIDS, do you?" and "If you want to be my girlfriend you have to, or I'll drop you and date so-and-so, who will." Sarah continues to say no but is feeling like something is going to happen soon about this issue because she can't deal with his pressure and doesn't know what to do. What kinds of power elements are present in this situation?

Processing Time (¼ session time)

1. Ask at least one question from each of the four processing areas:

    INTRAPERSONAL

    While you were listening to the situations and responding to them, and hearing about the bases of power in relationships and how people express their anger and needs to others, what were you thinking and feeling?

    INTERPERSONAL

    What kinds of feelings are you having about being a group member at this time? What do you notice about our becoming a group in here instead of just individuals?

    NEW LEARNING

    What new ideas or feelings have you experienced today that have made an impression on you?

    APPLICATION

    How do you think you could use this information and learning experience to help you in your relationships between now and the next session?

2. Indicate that the next session's topic is date abuse and relationship violence and that you would like group members' permission to invite a co-leader with some special knowledge and skills who would be able to help them. Discuss any concerns, especially regarding your guest's ability to keep information confidential.

3. Thank group members for coming and give a hope statement. Remind them of the day and time for the next session, then share the snacks.

Date Abuse: Violence in Relationships

Stop! Before proceeding, it is very important to read the comments to the leader on page 108. Because of the nature of this session, it is best if you and/or your co-leader(s) conduct the Opening Time and Processing Time activities. Group members can take on leadership responsibilities during the next session, if you wish.

GOALS

Affective

To get in touch with the same and opposite sex's feelings about violence and abuse of power in relationships

Behavioral

To develop a guideline that everyone in the group can agree on (and that can be shared with others outside the group, if the group decides to do this) for understanding which behaviors are appropriate and which are not on a date or in a dating relationship

Cognitive

To learn the definitions of sexual assault

To gain a perspective on how both sexes view pressures in relationships that can allow violence to occur

MATERIALS

Definitions of Sexual Assault (Handout 8)

Myths and Facts about Sexual Assault (Handout 9)

Easel pad or posterboard and marker

Healthy snacks

GROUP SESSION

Opening Time (¼ session time)

1. Welcome the members back to group and introduce the guest co-leader. Ask the guest to share some things about himself or herself, and ask the group members to introduce themselves.

2. Briefly review the last session's topic (power in relationships) and ask the group for any comments.

3. Remind members of the importance of confidentiality and thoroughly discuss any concerns. Review the ground rules established at the beginning of the group, focusing especially on

---

"Definitions of Sexual Assault" (Handout 8) has been reprinted by permission from D. A. Wolfe and colleagues, *The Youth Relationships Manual: A Group Approach with Adolescents for the Prevention of Woman Abuse and the Promotion of Healthy Relationships* (Thousand Oaks, CA: Sage, 1996). "Myths and Facts about Sexual Abuse" (Handout 9) has been adapted from information provided by the Ontario Women's Directorate, Sixth Floor, Mowat Block, 900 Bay Street, Toronto, Ontario M7A 1L2 (Telephone: 416–314–0247; Website: www.gov.on.ca/owd).

everyone's right to respect. Say that sometimes when we feel angry or blamed it is easy to try to blame someone else and be aggressive, which disrespects the other person's right to respect. State that you will make your very best effort to support *every* group member's right to respect.

Working Time (½ session time)

1. Ask group members what they have heard from their friends, siblings, television, and TV and other sources about the topic of date rape and dating violence, and let them share their perceptions. (Beginning with this kind of discussion starts the session on a positive note and helps members realize they will not be lectured at or blamed.)

2. Pass out copies of the Definitions of Sexual Assault (Handout 8). Introduce the definitions as an opportunity to clarify the meanings of the terms. Emphasize that these violent acts are illegal and that the terms have specific meanings in society. Invite group members to choose one of the terms and read it to the group, until all have been read.

3. Pass out the Myths and Facts about Sexual Assault (Handout 9). Ask the group members to read a myth and then invite discussion. Go through each of the myths, allowing members to voice their opinions, question, make appropriate comments, disagree, or whatever. (Refer as needed to the comments and responses on page 108.)

4. When finished with the myths, ask:

   What is it about these myths that gets under our skin and causes us to feel irritated at boys, at girls, or at our society?

   How can we get rid of ideas that we might have that we now discover are hurtful to others and keep us from growing personally?

5. Use the easel pad or posterboard to record what group members agree should be responsibilities each sex has to avoid getting into situations where violence can or does occur. Examples include the following.

Girls' Dating Responsibilities

   Be smart—make it your rule not to go out with boys who have a reputation for physical or emotional abuse.

   Be assertive—about what you will and won't allow physically, and stick to your beliefs. No waffling!

   Don't go in a car or on a date with someone who is drinking or using drugs, boy or girl.

   Get out of situations immediately when you sense trouble.

   Have an "escape plan"—always have a way to get home besides your date.

   Know your own limits with sex; realize guys get turned on faster and farther, so absolutely no teasing. Stop sooner rather than later.

   Know all the types of sexual assault and be able to explain them to anyone.

Guys' Dating Responsibilities

   Work to rid yourself of male stereotypes, such as thinking girls are for sex and don't really mean no.

   Be aware that drugs and alcohol impair judgment and visual-motor coordination and increase the likelihood that you will do something you will regret later.

   If you don't know EXACTLY what a girl wants or means, ASK.

   If a girl says one thing and does something to indicate she does not mean it, she is confused, too, so don't have sex if the message is mixed.

Know the definitions of assault, sexual assault, date rape, aggravated sexual assault, sexual assault causing bodily harm, and sexual assault with a weapon.

If there is time later on, group members can copy the dating responsibilities for girls and dating responsibilities for boys on a small index card to keep and carry. However, the focus of this session is discussion, sharing of feelings and opinions, and clarification of facts and ideas related to date violence and only secondarily production of a guidelines-for-relationships card that everyone can take away from the group.

Processing Time (¼ session time)

1. Ask at least one question from each of the four processing levels:

   INTRAPERSONAL

   Today we discussed a really heavy topic. What were some of the thoughts and feelings that kept running through your mind when we talked about these issues?

   INTERPERSONAL

   What did you notice about our group today—what was going on silently between you and other group members or between other members?

   NEW LEARNING

   What new ideas or experiences have you had today that might change the way you think about these topics?

   APPLICATION

   How might you change your behavior as a result of having this frank discussion today?

2. Ask if anyone has anything else they would like to add on the topic. Thank the co-leader for coming and for sharing the special knowledge he or she provided.

3. Remind group members of the day and time for the next session and give them a hope statement. Share the snacks.

Date Abuse: Violence in Relationships

This session can pull very strong emotions and reactions from participants. The topics in the group so far have built up to this one, providing some insights and skills for group members to understand underlying concepts and deal with negative feelings that the session topic or after-session situations bring.

It is essential that there be a co-leader for this session, if not for all of the sessions in this group. The co-leader can be a school nurse, a school social worker or psychologist, or a community mental health counselor. The co-leader should possess group counseling training and experience, as well as a thorough knowledge of, commitment to, and skills in addressing the issues of abuse of women, sexism, control, and power.

It is also important to be aware of the type of comments, gestures, and behaviors that are likely to come from group members when this issue is addressed. Female group members' safety is essential in a situation debating the causes and effects of violence against women; do not underestimate the strength of the negative reactions of the young males in your group.

Be certain to readdress the issue of ground rules at the beginning of this group, reminding group members that they agreed and signed a commitment to respect everyone—and remind the group again as joking, minimizing, and belittling comments come up. It is very likely that some group members have experienced physical, sexual, and/or emotional abuse already and will self-disclose in this situation. It is essential that their disclosures be treated with respect. For this reason, the leader(s) should do this session's Opening Time and Processing Time.

Male defensiveness surfaces almost immediately in the form of an attitude or behaviors that deny the significance of the abuse of women in society. Both males and females feel uneasy and blamed because of the prevalence of male relationship violence, so this attitude may arise from either sex. Defensiveness can have many faces, from laughing and snickering to snide comments to others in the group (for example, comments about the topic's being "dumb"), lack of participation, boredom, irritation, petty comments to female members, and so on. Defensiveness MUST be addressed openly and in a supportive manner, or it will sabotage the group experience. Do not get entangled in being defensive back! Answer defensive comments or questions straightforwardly rather than trying to control the acting out directly.

Usual comments and possible responses include the following:

Comment: Women and girls deserve what they get. (This is a victim-blaming tactic.)
Response: Violence is never justified.

Comment: Violence is caused by druggies and alcohol drinkers, not sober guys.
Response: Alcohol makes abuse worse, but without alcohol the abuse still happens.

Comment: Girls like guys who abuse them—they keep going back for more and don't leave.
Response: Many women can't leave due to poverty or having nowhere to go, children to support, and no one to help them. The abuse cycle contains a promise to reform and some positive behavior, so the woman frequently believes the man and stays for the small amount of good in the relationship. Most women who are killed by their partners are killed after leaving.

Comment: Men are abused, too, not just women and girls.
Response: Men are abused also, but the overwhelming majority of victims of relationship abuse are women. Men usually have more resources: They are physically bigger and more powerful, have more money and places to go, and are more likely to have a secure job.

Comment: Guys always get blamed for abuse.
Response: Most relationship violence is committed by males, who are socialized to be aggressive in our society. (Focus on the issue of what needs to change in relationships, not on who is to blame.)

Definitions of Sexual Assault

ASSAULT

The intentional use of force on another person against his or her will. Touching, slapping, kicking, punching, or pushing are all examples of assault. It is also assault to THREATEN to use force. For instance, if someone threatens to beat you up, this can be an assault even if the threat is not carried out.

SEXUAL ASSAULT

Any unwanted sexual act imposed on one person by another. A person may be charged if you were forced to kiss, fondle, or have sexual intercourse with the person or you were kissed or touched in a sexual way without your consent (with no sign of physical injury or abuse).

SEXUAL ASSAULT WITH A WEAPON

Sexual assault with the use of a weapon (either an imitation or a real weapon) or with the threat to use a weapon.

SEXUAL ASSAULT CAUSING BODILY HARM

The victim was physically hurt during the sexual assault. A person could also be charged if he or she threatened to hurt a third party (such as a victim's child) or if he or she was with someone who sexually assaulted another.

AGGRAVATED SEXUAL ASSAULT

The victim was wounded, crippled, disfigured, or brutally beaten during the sexual assault. The victim's life was endangered.

DATE RAPE

Sexual assault that occurs in a dating or social situation.

Myths and Facts about Sexual Assault

Myth: Sexual assault is most often committed by strangers.

Fact: Women face the greater risk of sexual assault from men they know, not strangers. Of the women who are sexually assaulted, most are sexually assaulted by men known to them—dates, boyfriends, marital partners, friends, family members, or neighbors.

Myth: The best way for a woman to protect herself from a sexual assault is to avoid being alone at night in dark, deserted places, such as alleys or parking lots.

Fact: Most sexual assaults occur in a private home, and the large percentage of these occur in the victim's home.

Myth: Women who are sexually assaulted "ask for it" by the way they dress or act.

Fact: Victims of sexual assault report a wide range of dress and actions at the time of the assault. Any woman of any age and physical type, in almost any situation, can be sexually assaulted. No woman ever asks or deserves to be sexually assaulted. Whatever a woman wears, wherever she goes, whomever she talks to, "no" means "no."

Myth: Men of certain races and backgrounds are more likely to sexually assault women.

Fact: Men who commit sexual assault come from every economic, ethnic, racial, age, and social group. The belief that women are more often sexually assaulted by men of color or working-class men is a stereotype rooted in racism and classism.

Myth: It's only sexual assault if physical violence or weapons are used.

Fact: Sexual assault is any unwanted act of a sexual nature imposed by one person on another. Most sexual assaults are committed by a man known to the victim and involve verbal pressure, tricks, and/or threats.

Myth: Unless she is physically harmed, a sexual assault victim will not suffer any long-term effects.

Fact: Sexual assault can have serious effects on a woman's health and well-being. Women who have been sexually assaulted feel anger and fear, and can become more cautious and less trusting.

Myth: Women cannot be sexually assaulted by their husbands or boyfriends.

Fact: Women have the right to say no to any form of sex, even in a marriage or dating relationship.

Boomerang Behaviors

GOALS

Affective

To increase sensitivity and empathy for the needs of others in a relationship

Behavioral

To present negative and positive aspects of sexual behavior that affect partners in a relationship

Cognitive

To explore the statement "what goes around, comes around"—that self-centered sexual behavior has far-reaching consequences for both partners

MATERIALS

A boomerang. If you have an opportunity, this session could be held outdoors so the group members can throw the boomerang. If not, get a soft plastic or Styrofoam one, and protect breakables, such as the lamp in your office!

Healthy snacks

GROUP SESSION

Opening Time (¼ session time)

1. Welcome members back to group. Ask what questions group members have about confidentiality, especially after the last session. Do any of the ground rules need to be changed?

2. Ask what ideas, feelings, or questions they might have left over from the previous session's topic, date abuse and violence. Ask if they encountered any situations in their own lives where they could use some of the information they learned. (Have them do this without sharing names of out-of-group members who might not want to be mentioned.)

Working Time (½ session time)

1. Explore some of the reasons young people get involved in sexual behavior at an early age by asking group members to share their ideas. Some common responses include the following:

> It's fun, feels good.
>
> It's exciting because adults don't want you to.
>
> Makes you feel grown up, in control of your own life.
>
> Fun to always have someone to go places with and be with.
>
> Like having someone who loves you.
>
> Want to have a boyfriend/girlfriend to make out with.
>
> The other kids are doing it, and I don't want to be left out or called a wuss, prude, geek, or gay.

Since everyone in the group is not sexually active, there will be some who say, "I am not involved, and I don't want to be now."

2. Share that even though group members sometimes think and say everyone is doing it, everyone is NOT doing it. There are a lot of kids who are not having sex and don't have any intention of getting involved. There are some who are thinking about it and some who were

active and have made the decision not to be for some time in the future. Stress that there are really a wide range of behaviors and ideas about being sexually active. Sometimes if their close circle of friends is active, it may seem that everyone is, but this isn't a fact.

3. Explain the following in your own words:

> *You are probably already aware of some of the negative consequences of early sexual activity, such as getting AIDS or other STD's, getting pregnant, having an abortion, adopting your baby out, trying to raise a baby and go to school and prepare for the world of work, and losing friends with other kids because of your situation. There is another issue—respecting yourself and respecting the other person. Without respect, relationships turn sour, and the stage is set for abuse and some of the other power issues we have already discussed. If self-centered decisions are made about sexuality, often other people are hurt in ways that affect them for many years.*

4. Ask the group if they have heard the saying "What goes around, comes around" and, if so, what they think it means. Let group members explore the idea that negative, hurtful deeds done to someone else have a way of coming back to us in the future. Say, "If you deliberately hurt someone else, some time you are going to get that hurt back on yourself. Do you think this is true or just a made-up idea?" Explain that you will stay with the idea for a little while that this is an accurate representation of what happens in life.

5. Show the group the boomerang and invite them to imagine that it represents what you send out to others and what comes back to you. Ask them to think of a situation where someone says or does something negative to another person and a negative consequence could come back to the sender. Explain that whoever thinks of a situation gets to throw the boomerang out and catch it back. Some example situations follow. (Note that these may but do not necessarily have to deal with sexual behavior.)

> Suppose you have herpes and don't tell the girl or guy you have sex with—that is sending negative out. If the person you have sex with has an STD, too, and doesn't tell you, you could get one back!

> If you're always cussing out a teacher and get caught a bunch of times, the teacher or another teacher could get aggravated with you and not give you a break on a test or something.

> If you tease the guys and get a reputation for it, you might not get asked out by some new really cool guy because the other guys tell him and he won't get near you.

> If you call kids names like "geek" and "queer," some other kids might say other bad things about you, or those same names.

> If you get an attitude at home and say smart-mouth things to your mom, she might get aggravated with you and take away some privileges like staying up until midnight on weekends watching movies, so it comes back.

> If you don't do what you say you're going to do and your mom and dad can't trust you, you might not get to do something that needs a lot of trust, like going out of town with a friend's family.

6. After several have given examples and thrown the boomerang, discuss:

> What are you thinking at this point about how negative behaviors have lasting effects?

> How could you deal with a situation where you have the opportunity to get your way but know it is going to be hurtful to someone else, maybe someone who is less powerful, less aggressive, less knowledgeable, or less persuasive than you are?

> What do you think about the idea overall that if you violate and disrespect other people's rights, you are going to experience some of the same back? Would this deter you from doing it?

Processing Time (¼ session time)

1. Ask at least one question from each of the four processing levels:

   INTRAPERSONAL

   While we were playing with the boomerang and thinking of situations where negative behaviors toward others might, could, would result in negative actions coming back to you, what were you thinking and feeling?

   INTERPERSONAL

   What kinds of things did you notice going on in the group among other group members, even nonverbal behaviors that give you an idea of how people might be feeling about this topic?

   NEW LEARNING

   What did this topic cause you to think about that might be new or different from the way you have been thinking in the past about how your behavior affects others?

   APPLICATION

   Based on what you have learned, how might you change how you act toward your girl-friend/boyfriend or other friends?

2. Thank group members for participating and give them a hope statement. Explain that there will be only one more working session, then the final session. Remind them of the day and time; tell them that the final session is not for new business but for reviewing and celebrating, so to be thinking about what they would like to do.

Ending Relationships: When and How

GOALS

Affective

To get in touch with feelings before, during, and after a relationship comes to an end

Behavioral

To brainstorm assertive ways to end relationships, illustrate them, and share them with the group

Cognitive

To explore reasons we have difficulty dealing with ending relationships

MATERIALS

Drawing paper

Colored markers, crayons, or watercolors

Healthy snacks

GROUP SESSION

Opening Time (¼ session time)

1. Welcome members back to group and inquire about any concerns they might have about confidentiality. Invite discussion of any concerns relating to the ground rules.

2. Ask what group members noticed since the last session about negative behaviors returning to the sender in some way. What changes might they have made in their relationship behaviors as a result of thinking about this idea?

Working Time (½ session time)

1. Discuss the idea that in our society we have a very difficult time saying good-bye to people, especially when someone dies:

   Many adults don't want their children to go to the hospital to see a grandmother or relative who may die soon, or to the funeral home to say good-bye. The reason usually is that they are "protecting" the child from seeing or experiencing the realities of this life, that any one of us could get sick and that we all die sometime. Adults even say "She passed away" instead of "She died," which sounds harsher. We are really afraid of dealing with the negative feelings of grief, fear, guilt, anger, depression, and personal failure that occur after the death of a loved one.

2. Point out that we also have a difficult time ending love relationships:

   Many times people just leave, move away, run away, or somehow don't face it at all. It's hard to say you don't love someone anymore, or that you have major differences in values and are incompatible. What are some of the hurtful ways you have noticed that people end relationships?

   Move away and not tell the person you are moving.

   Just start dating someone else.

Tell all your friends you don't like the person anymore and have them tell your boyfriend/girlfriend.

Start a big fight, pretend it is the other person's fault, and say good-bye.

Tell him you want to get pregnant so he'll leave you alone.

Start saying negative things about your boyfriend/girlfriend to other friends so the person will hear and get mad and leave you.

3. Point out that these hurtful examples are passive or aggressive, not assertive, ways to deal with the situation. Pass out the art materials and ask group members to pair up and think of a more creative, positive way to end a relationship than the ones just mentioned. Ask the pairs to draw the situation and be prepared to show it and explain it to the rest of the group. Give the group a time limit; let them move to different parts of the room to discuss and draw.

4. Have the group reassemble and ask each pair to share their picture. You can have a vote to determine the most positive, creative way—the way that is least hurtful to both parties.

5. Ask the following questions:

What did you learn from coming up with positive ways to deal with this touchy topic?

What would be the likely result if both persons felt less threatened and hurt from the break-up?

Could these ways take all of the pain of a break-up away? Why or why not?

Processing Time (¼ session time)

1. Ask at least one question from each of the four processing levels:

INTRAPERSONAL

As we were thinking and talking about ways to deal with ending relationships, what kinds of thoughts and feelings were you having?

INTERPERSONAL

What did you notice about the group today as we dealt with this touchy topic?

NEW LEARNING

What new ideas or behaviors did you learn from this activity that you could actually use in your relationships?

How would changing your behavior and doing something more positive the next time a relationship ends be helpful to you and to the other person in the relationship?

APPLICATION

Between now and the next session, would you be willing to observe how others might be ending a relationship and perhaps share with them a more positive, less hurtful way to do so? (For example, sometimes it hurts a great deal to face the other person. It could be done through an honest, kind letter rather than not doing so at all.)

2. Remind the group members that the next session is the last and decide what special goodies they would like to have at the end of the session to celebrate their successes and personal growth. Remind them of the day and time for the last session, then share the snacks.

That's a Wrap

The group's last session is best conducted by the leader. (You can explain to group members by saying that this session is very important as well as a little different, so you want to take on the responsibilities for Opening Time and Processing Time yourself.)

GOALS

Affective

To get in touch with major emotions experienced during the group process and at the group's ending

To enjoy a celebration for the learning experiences and progress made in the group

Behavioral

To reinforce one another for personal growth

To say good-bye

Cognitive

To recognize new ideas and concepts learned during the experience and recall turning points

To think about goals for future behavior change

MATERIALS

A stuffed toy of an octopus, preferably with different-colored tentacles

Party food for the celebration

GROUP SESSION

Opening Time (¼ session time)

1. Welcome members to group and inquire about any concerns relating to the ground rules. Discuss any issues concerning confidentiality; remind the group that confidentiality extends even after the group sessions are over.

2. Ask what comments, concerns, or questions they might have from the previous week's session. Invite them to say what they noticed about ending relationships among their peers and friends, without naming names of specific people/events that could possibly be hurtful. What changes have they noticed in their own ideas and behaviors about ending relationships of all kinds?

Working Time (½ session time)

1. Discuss the idea that each session brought new ideas, feelings, behaviors, and insights to group members, and that you noticed each session that some members really had a special experience when the topic "hit home" for them. Show them the octopus, with its eight "arms" or tentacles, and say that each tentacle has special suction cups that help the octopus grab and hold onto its food. Tell them you are going to go through the topics of all the sessions, one by one, and ask them to share what really "grabbed them" from that session—what made an impact and stuck with them as an idea or behavior or feeling that helped them deal with dating and other relationships in better ways. You will pass the octopus around, and whoever is speaking gets the critter.

Session 1—Getting Started

Getting acquainted, brainstorming ways to select leaders for Opening Time and Processing Time, and learning how thinking, feeling, and behaving are different

Session 2—Knowing Your Dating Values

Doing a "values audit" by using different coins to show how important various values are to you

Session 3—Dating Rights and Responsibilities

Choosing assertive behaviors instead of being passive or aggressive in relationships

Session 4—Expressing Feelings to Your Girlfriend/Boyfriend

Learning how to use I-messages as a powerful way to say what you want or need

Session 5—Power in Relationships

Talking about how each person in a relationship has more or less power to control what happens and about how severe abuse of power often occurs as violence

Session 6—Date Abuse: Violence in Relationships

Becoming aware of painful behaviors and consequences of abuse of power in relationships (a pretty heavy topic!)

Session 7—Boomerang Behaviors

"What goes around comes around": Thinking about how hurtful or self-centered behaviors, especially sexual behaviors, can come back and hurt you

Session 8—Ending Relationships: When and How

Talking about why it is difficult to end relationships and about more creative, healthy ways to deal with this situation

2. Use the Working Time to encourage group members to share their special thoughts, feelings, and behavior changes associated with each of the sessions.

Processing Time (¼ session time)

1. Ask and discuss the following questions:

Now that the group is over, what are your thoughts and feelings about being a member?

If we were starting the group all over again, what would you do differently than you did this time?

Who in the group do you have to thank the most for helping you gain some new insights and understand yourself better? (Tell that person and say thank-you.)

What did you learn from this group experience that has had or will have the greatest impact on your present or future way of behaving in boy/girl relationships?

What one thing do you want to keep working on the most?

2. Explain any follow-up plans and give the group a hope statement for the future. You might say, for example:

As we have learned, sometimes it is very hard to say good-bye. But this isn't good-bye forever! It is good-bye for the time being. We can get together in (1 month, 2 months—whatever is appropriate) to find out how we are doing on working toward our goals and to keep our connections going. You might feel that you have just gotten started on your personal growth and have lots more wonderful things to discover and improve about yourself. Maybe you can work on them by yourself, and maybe you need more help. Please come see me if you think you do, because maybe I can refer you to another counselor or place where you can get more help.

You have taken some big steps toward improving your lives, and I believe in each one of you. You have shown me you have the ability to make changes for the better in your relationships. I have a great deal of hope and confidence that each of you will continue to take the risks to grow.

3. Share the party snacks and celebrate!

"Teaching Tolerance": Understanding and Valuing Individual and Cultural Differences

In 1971, a young attorney named Morris Dees started an organization called The Southern Poverty Law Center (SPLC) in Montgomery, Alabama. The purpose of this organization was to provide legal services for persons who were discriminated against and could not afford attorneys for their defense. At the same time, I moved to Montgomery and started a clinic school for children with special needs, while pursuing doctoral studies at Auburn University. Our families became acquainted, as we were both professionals in the community who were mission driven, working toward enhancing opportunities for youth and families to make it through this life in peace and brother/sisterhood.

As the organization grew, other professionals and attorneys became involved, and their crusade to stop hate and violent crimes against the poor and people of color grew dramatically. In 1991, the SPLC launched a special project called Teaching Tolerance and a magazine by the same name. The magazine, then as now sent out free of charge, was designed to provide elementary and secondary educators all over the country with ideas and resources for promoting peace, justice, and racial harmony and understanding. *Teaching Tolerance* magazine includes articles by educators who have dealt successfully with issues of violence and disrespect in the classroom, sports, and social living, as well as interest articles exploring diversity through art, dance, psychodrama, field experiences, and innovative curricula. At this point project Teaching Tolerance provides a number of other resources to promote peace and embrace diversity, either free or at cost.

The title of this group agenda is used with the kind permission of The Southern Poverty Law Center. I hope that by sharing information about this organization and its work, and by using this group, school and mental health professionals will become more acquainted with this tremendous source of information, support, and materials to promote peace. I encourage interaction with the SPLC and the Teaching Tolerance staff. Supporting this organization's commitment to the education of youth about the values of peace, oneness, goodwill, and concordance in our multicultural society is a great opportunity to "put your money where your mouth is." For more information, contact:

Teaching Tolerance
400 Washington Avenue
Montgomery, Alabama 36104
Telephone: 334–264–0286
Fax: 334–264–3121
Internet: www.splcenter.org

The group counseling experience described in the following pages is designed to help mental health professionals who work with youth from diverse backgrounds—ethnic, racial, socioeconomic, and multicultural—whose problematic behaviors are caused, influenced, maintained, or exacerbated by the very diversity in which they live. To young adolescents, "differentness" is frequently viewed as "not cool" . . . "cool" being those who fit in, are valued, and are accepted. For example, those who do not have cool clothes, for whatever reason, are often ostracized from the in-group because they look different. Youth therefore try every way possible to assure that their parents will purchase them the right clothes so they can be seen as members of the in-group. Many cultures and ethnic groups have different dress and behavioral standards for their youth. Families from Vietnam, India, or Dubai, for example, may have standards of dress for their children that are acceptable in the parents' culture but that subject the children to ridicule and scapegoating at school.

Whatever the local reason, there are universal reasons for promoting acceptance, valuing diversity, and learning peacemaking skills. Frequently, the youth who need peacemaking skills the most live in a world of adults and other youth who have few positive values and who model violence, crime, hate, and egocentric behaviors of every kind. How can you teach these youth to be kind, accepting, love one another, and value diversity when they have absolutely no models in their surroundings for these values? The answer is unfortunate: There are many you cannot reach. Reach the ones who want out, who want help, who show some glimmer of interest in growing and improving. Work with youth by taking them places where they can see and experience other ways of doing things, other values, other models for success that they don't see outside of school. Spend time developing relationships because relationships last. It is my firm contention that people change people, not stories, books, programs, computers, or courses. People impacting on other people . . . the human spirit is touched and changed by contact with other positive human spirits, and this is what the group counselor provides in abundance for group members.

The sessions in this group are as follows:

Session 1—Getting Started

Session 2—M & M's: What's the
　　　　　Difference?

Session 3—Beautiful and Ugly Are Only
　　　　　Skin Deep

Session 4—Different Drummers

Session 5—Body Boundaries

Session 6—"It's Not Easy Being Green"

Session 7—Walk a Block in My Socks

Session 8—Frogs, Toads, and Other
　　　　　Survivors

Session 9—That's a Wrap

GROUP GOALS

1. To facilitate development of a trusting, supportive environment in which members feel secure to risk and share

2. To promote the group norms of becoming a supportive, encouraging person

3. To ensure that members can discriminate thinking, feeling, and behaving

4. To increase sense of belonging to a positive, diverse community and decrease sense of isolation and differentness

5. To improve self-image by enhancing communication and self-disclosure

6. To gain understanding of individual differences as a positive concept

7. To develop cohesion based on shared difficult situations

8. To get in touch with fear and anger associated with feeling different

9. To learn the concept and skill of empathy

10. To experience a bonding activity symbolic of unity in diversity

11. To review the group experience and set goals for future personal work

SELECTION AND OTHER GUIDELINES

The goals of this group are to promote understanding and acceptance of individual differences and to teach attitudes and behaviors of tolerance, respect, and adaptability in a world of differences. The group, then, should be composed of youth from a variety of cultural, ethnic, and social backgrounds, to add richness and diversity. If you have particular groups in a school setting that oppose each other, include members from each group. You might want to concentrate on two different groups only and split the membership between those two. Or if there are several groups within the setting and you want to make some inroads among them, choose two members from each group.

If you select several gang or group leaders, they will spend a great deal of the group time in a power struggle, defining their territory, control, and ownership—so if you choose to do this, be aware that you will need a longer group experience than eight sessions to develop cohesion and a working atmosphere. If you select all members from a single gang or group, you are more likely to be able to develop understanding and problem-solving skills among them than if you have sub-group leaders who will spend their personal energy in verbal posturing, and perhaps aggression, establishing and reestablishing their power. Members from different groups need sufficient time to develop a working relationship.

Keep in mind the regular selection guidelines given in this book's introduction, and look at a possible mix of six to eight youth from diverse backgrounds. Depending on your location and circumstances, such backgrounds could include the following:

Youth who are "out" as gay or lesbian

Youth of African American, Native American, Mexican American, Asian American, other non-European descent, as well as youth of European background

Youth from other countries (first generation)

Youth from a region of the United States distant from your location

Youth who have a parent in prison

Youth from Orthodox Jewish homes, migrant farm worker families, or Appalachia

Youth who have serious medical problems/illnesses, or who have an emotional problem such as depression (but who are receiving treatment and are stable)

Youth who are homeless

Youth who are HIV-positive or who have AIDS

Session 3, "Beautiful and Ugly Are Only Skin Deep," talks frankly about values, and you must be flexible and accepting, and avoid challenging members in such a way that they spend their time being defensive and protecting their turf/values. Your goal is for them to be exposed to, hear, and see modeled appropriate values that will enhance them as human beings and to let them challenge one another regarding values. Be sure some of the members you select have values you want modeled and the skills to challenge others appropriately so this doesn't degenerate into a "me against them" situation.

Another issue regarding this group is that the Working Time activities are heavily dependent on props, objects used to stimulate discussion that function as metaphors or cues for something else, such as M & M candies (used to illustrate differences outside but sameness inside); spiders (to represent fears); Kermit the Frog video/song (about individual differences that cause us pain); moccasins (to represent empathy); and frogs and toads (as a metaphor for surviving difficulties). Please read through all of the materials sections of the groups before you start so you can get your frogs and toads in order!

REFERENCES AND SUGGESTED RESOURCES FOR PROFESSIONALS

Anderson, J. D. (1994, March-April). Breaking the silence: Creating safe schools for gay youth. *Student Assistance Journal*, pp. 21–23.

Carnegie Council on Adolescent Development. (1995). *Great transitions*. New York: Carnegie Corporation.

Colman, S. A., & Merta, R. J. (1999). Using the sweat lodge ceremony as group therapy for Navajo youth. *Journal for Specialists in Group Work, 24*(1), 55–73.

Copeland, N. D. (1989). *Managing conflict: A curriculum for adolescents* (Grades 9–12). Albuquerque: New Mexico Center for Dispute Resolution.

Drew, N. (1994). *Learning the skills of peacemaking* (Grades K–8). King of Prussia, PA: Childswork/Childsplay.

Ferrara, M. L. (1991). *Group counseling with juvenile delinquents: The limit and lead approach*. Thousand Oaks, CA: Sage.

Goldstein, A. P., & Huff, C. R. (Eds.). (1993). *The gang intervention handbook*. Champaign, IL: Research Press.

Henriques, M., Holmberg, M., & Sadalla, G. (1987). *Conflict resolution: A secondary school curriculum* (Grades 7–12). San Francisco: Community Board Program, Inc.

Hyppo, M. H., & Hastings, J. M. (1984). *An elephant in the living room*. Minneapolis: Compcare Publishers.

Johnson, D. W., & Johnson, R. T. (1991). *Teaching students to be peacemakers.* (Grades K–6). Edina, MN: Interaction.

Jones, R. B., & Jones, G. (1995a). *The healing drum*. Salt Lake City: Commune-a-Key Publishing.

Jones, R. B., & Jones, G. (1995b). *Listen to the drum: Blackwolf shares his medicine.* Salt Lake City: Commune-a-Key Publishing.

Jones, R. B., & Jones, G. (1996). *Earth dance drum: A celebration of life.* Salt Lake City: Commune-a-Key Publishing.

Karns, M. (1995). *How to create positive relationships with students: A handbook of group activities and teaching strategies.* Champaign, IL: Research Press.

Kirk, G. K. (1992). The developmental process of asserting a biracial, bicultural "identity." In M. P. P. Root (Ed.), *Racially mixed people in America.* Thousand Oaks, CA: Sage

Lane, P. (1995). *Conflict resolution for kids: A group facilitator's guide* (Grades K–6). Muncie, IN: Accelerated Development.

Little Soldier, L. (1997, April). Is there an "Indian" in your classroom? Working successfully with urban Native American students. *Phi Delta Kappan,* pp. 650–653.

Lovett, S. (1997). *The encyclopedia of extremely weird animals.* Santa Fe: John Muir Publications.

McGinnis, K. (1993). *Educating for a just society* (Grades 7–12). Wilmington, OH: Wilmington College Peace Resource Center, Institute for Peace and Justice.

Pang, V. O. (1995). Asian Pacific American students: A diverse and complex population. In J. Banks & C. M. Banks (Eds.), *Handbook of resources on multicultural education.* New York: Simon & Schuster.

Ponterotto, J. G., & Petersen, P. B. (1993). *Preventing prejudice: A guide for counselors and educators.* Thousand Oaks, CA: Sage.

Ryder, L. (1990). *Being free: Prevention curriculum for American Indian youth.* St. Paul: Children Are People, Inc.

Schrumpf, F., Crawford, D. K., & Bodine, R. J. (1997). *Peer mediation: Conflict resolution in schools* (rev. ed.). Champaign, IL.: Research Press.

Shakeshaft, C., Barber, E., Mergenrother, M. A., Johnson, Y., Mandel, L., & Sawyer, J. (1995, April). *Peer harassment and the culture of caring in schools.* Paper presented at the annual meeting of the American Educational Research Association, San Francisco.

Sue, D. W., & Sue, D. (1990). *Counseling the culturally different.* New York: Wiley.

Tatum, B. D. (1997). *"Why are all the black kids sitting together in the cafeteria?" and other conversations about race.* New York: Basic.

Getting Started

GOALS

Affective

To begin to develop a sense of universality by learning things about each group member

To relax and begin to develop cohesion and comfort in the group

Behavioral

To collaborate with other members to develop ground rules for the group

To participate in a fun activity to help members get to know one another

To practice one social custom when meeting someone new (shaking hands)

Cognitive

To understand the purpose and general goals of the group

To understand the concept of confidentiality and its importance

To differentiate thinking, feeling, and behaving

MATERIALS

Limits of Confidentiality sign (see Appendix A, page 270)

Easel pad or posterboard and marker

Get-Acquainted List (Handout 10)

Thinking-Feeling-Behaving Gears (see Appendix A, page 271)

A large sheet of newsprint

Colored markers

Healthy snacks (such as fruit, crackers, juice, raisins)

GROUP SESSION

Opening Time

For sessions after this first one, Opening Time will take up about one-fourth of the typical 40- to 50-minute session time, or about 10 minutes. For this session, however, you will need to plan on more time to discuss confidentiality, develop ground rules, and conduct a getting-acquainted activity. See the book's introduction for some ideas on how to schedule this extra time.

---

1. Welcome group members and go over the name, purpose, and general goals of the group. Stress that the main purpose of this group is to get to know one another and learn to find things to appreciate about everyone—individual differences and diversity. In your own words, say:

   We are all on this earth together trying to make it through life the best we can, and we need all of the help, support, and encouragement we can get. Everyone has something positive to contribute, and each of you has been selected for this group because of the rich background of ideas and culture that you can bring and share.

2. Thoroughly discuss confidentiality (the "no-blab" rule): What is said and done in the group stays in the group. Be sure to give examples of things adults or peers outside the group might say to pressure group members to share what happens in group. For example:

> Just tell me what she said—I won't say a thing!

> Sara told me you group guys make fun of your parents and teachers. Is that true?

> Jaime said the counselor only picks weird kids for the group. Why are you in there?

After members are clear on what confidentiality is, share the Limits of Confidentiality sign (either as a handout or poster) and discuss: Let group members know you are bound by the confidentiality rule but that as the leader you are required to tell about what goes on in the group if you think someone will do harm to self or others, if someone says anything about child abuse or criminal activity going on, or if a judge orders you to turn over information.

3. Discuss the basic ground rules you have decided on for your group and request the group's input in developing a few more that would enhance their comfort in sharing with one another. For example:

> Take turns.

> Everyone has the right to "pass" (not share unless that's comfortable).

> Agree to disagree (no put-downs).

> Come on time.

Don't move on until the group agrees on the ground rules. Write or have the group write the rules on an easel pad or piece of posterboard and have each member sign the document to show agreement. You can then post these rules every session.

---

4. Hand out copies of the Get-Acquainted List (Handout 10) and invite each member to participate in an activity for the purpose of getting to know one another. Tell them that they can work in dyads, which will be more comfortable for them to begin with, and that they will then share some things they learned about their partners when they return to the group circle. (They don't have to memorize a lot of things about each person, but they should try to remember at least one thing besides the person's name.) In dyads, they are to choose any items from the list and share that information with their partners for 1 to 2 minutes. Then the other partner does the same.

5. After the time is up, instruct partners to shake hands and say, "See you later, *(name)*" or "Nice to meet you, *(name)*." They then move on to another partner until they have all shared with each other person in the group. You might want to use a clicker, bell, whistle, or signal that they are to end the conversation, shake hands, and move on.

6. After all have participated, have them return to the group circle. Invite them to share at least one thing they remember about each other group member in addition to that person's name.

Working Time

Working Time will take half of a typical session, or about 20 to 25 minutes.

---

1. Introduce the idea that we have three special parts to us that are happening at the same time: thinking, feeling, and behaving. These three parts are going on constantly, like the gears in a car's transmission. Share the Thinking-Feeling-Behaving Gears. Explain that if we change any one of these parts of us, the other two parts also must change:

If you change how you think about something, then your feelings about it will change also, and you will start doing different things, too. For example, say you have been thinking about having to go to the dentist to have a tooth filled and have been worrying (a feeling) about how painful it is when the dentist gives you a shot to numb your gums. You have thought about it so much you begin to get scared (another feeling) about what will happen. So you tell your mom that your tooth doesn't hurt so much now (a behavior) so maybe you can avoid having to go to the dentist. Your mom tells you she got some information in the mail from your dentist about a new medicine that can be rubbed on your gums with a cotton swab to numb your gums so you won't feel a thing. Now you start thinking about this as a much better way to numb your gums than being stuck with a needle, so you change how you feel about the situation by stopping the worrying and feeling more relaxed (a different feeling). You tell your mom that now you don't mind going to get it over with (a changed behavior). So, when you change one thing, all of them change: thinking, feeling, behaving.

2. Lay out a large sheet of newsprint on the floor in the middle of the group, pass out the colored markers, and invite group members to think of something they could draw that would represent the three related parts: thinking, feeling, and behaving. For example, on a train, thinking might be represented as the engine; feelings, the wheels; and behaviors, the train cars. Or a volcano could represent feelings boiling up inside; the bursting-out hot lava, behaviors; and the mountain's base, thoughts. Whatever they would like to draw must show three ideas, aspects, or parts that are connected and working together. Encourage each member to get down and participate.

3. When they have finished, have them all stand up and invite them to describe their drawing. Ask the following types of questions (you are trying to get at the group's process):

   How did you agree on what you were going to draw?

   How did you deal with members' ideas that the majority didn't like? (Were they acknowledged before being rejected, or were put-downs involved?)

   Make positive reinforcing statements about their picture.

4. Regroup in a circle. Say:

   Since you have done a spectacular job understanding thoughts, feelings, and behaviors, and have lots of interesting ways to describe them, please share how you would like to be thinking, feeling, and behaving differently at the end of this group experience.

   Give a brief, one- to two-sentence example of a member's goals. For example: "Ylena, it sounds like you are wanting to learn to be patient with kids who don't understand your accent, as well as help them understand you are trying to understand them, too."

5. Clarify and reinforce group members' statements as they speak. After all members have shared how they would like to be thinking, feeling, and behaving as a result of working in the group, say:

   Let's be sure everyone is in touch with everyone else's goals. Because we are going to be a support, encouragement, and cheering system for one another, it is important to be able to know what other members' goals are.

   Ask who would share briefly what a couple of other members' goals are. (Your high self-disclosers will probably attempt this task first.) Reinforce and say thank-you. Ask another member to reiterate one or a couple of other members' goals. Continue until all members have had a chance to say/clarify some other member's goals.

Processing Time

Processing Time will take one-quarter of a typical session, or about 10 minutes.

---

1. Ask at least one question from each of the four processing levels:

   INTRAPERSONAL

   Today we met the first time together and talked about what you want to be thinking, feeling, and doing differently and working toward during the group. As you were doing the drawing activity, coming up with your goals, and listening to other members' goals, what kinds of thoughts and feelings were you experiencing? (You could self-disclose as an example: "I was thinking about how many creative ideas you came up with for your drawing, and I was feeling a little anxious about leading this session and doing a good job of it so you would really learn a lot.")

   INTERPERSONAL

   When you came in today, we were not a group, just eight individuals sitting down together. Now we have begun to do things together and get to know one another in different ways. How are you feeling right now about being a group member?

   NEW LEARNING

   What new ideas and feelings do you have now that you didn't have before this group session?

   APPLICATION

   What do you think you could do before the next session to start getting a little closer to the goals you described?

2. Thank group members for coming, then give them a hope statement like the following example:

   After our first session today, I feel joyful and hopeful that each person can reach his or her personal goals and that, as a whole group, we will develop into a strong support system for one another.

   Remind them of the day and time for the next session, then share the snacks.

Get-Acquainted List

1. My name is ——————————————— .

2. People who live in my house with me are ——————————— .

3. My pets are ————————————————— .

4. The best movie I've ever seen is ————————————— .

5. My favorite restaurant is ———————————————— .

6. My favorite place in the whole world is ————— because ————— .

7. The thing I do best is ————————————————— .

8. When I have some free time I like to ————————————— .

9. My earliest memory is ———————————————— .

10. A funny thing happened to me when ————————————— .

11. My favorite song is ————— because ————————— .

12. My favorite entertainer is ————— because ————————— .

13. My favorite animal is ————— because ————————— .

14. When I am 20 years old I would like to be doing ———————— .

15. The person I like best so far in this group is ————————— .

16. The person I think will help me the most is ———————————— .

17. What I would like to know about the leader is ————————— .

18. What I would like to tell the leader is ———————————— .

19. What I want most out of this group is ————————————— .

20. What I like best about my personality is ————————————— .

21. What I don't like about my personality is ————————————— .

22. I hate doing ——————————————————— .

23. I love doing ——————————————————— .

24. I really want to change ————————————————— .

25. My wish for this group is ————————————————— .

M & M's: What's the Difference?

GOALS

Affective

To develop a sense of universality by learning that group members have common problems and feelings

To feel motivated to become curious about and accept others' differences

Behavioral

To sharpen ability to recognize likenesses and differences

To take a step toward accepting and valuing people who are different

Cognitive

To identify a wide range of factors that can differ and be alike in the same item (the candy) and to apply this idea to human likenesses and differences

To explore the concept that many individual differences are external and not really important

MATERIALS

M & M candies. You can use any other candy that has obvious irregularities in size, shape, or color on the outside but has the exact same flavor or filling inside. Different-colored "Good 'n Plentys" work very well. Separate the candy into little zip-lock snack bags so each group member has an individual see-through bag of whatever candy you use; candy must be loose, not wrapped.

Healthy snacks

GROUP SESSION

Opening Time (¼ session time)

1. Welcome the members back to group. Ask what concerns, comments, or questions they might have about confidentiality. Ask how they think the ground rules are working for them at this time and if they would like to change or add to them.

2. Ask what ideas they might have had since the last session about their goals for the group, as well as about any actions anyone might have taken toward a goal.

Working Time (½ session time)

1. Pass out the plastic bags of candy, instructing group members that the candy is not for eating NOW, but that they can eat it later. Reiterate that the group focus is to help each group member develop new attitudes and behaviors toward others who appear different.

2. Invite the group to divide into pairs and, with a partner, try to come up with as many ways as they can that the candies are different: longer/shorter; fatter/skinnier; smooth/bumpy; cracks/breaks/splits/crevices; color/shades/mottling; texture; and so on. Give them a time limit to work.

3. Call time and have members come back to the group circle. Invite each dyad to share the differences they discovered.

4. Ask, "We have been talking about how the candy is DIFFERENT on the outside in so many ways. How is that like us? Like everyone else in the school?" Encourage group members to bring up differences of race, ethnicity, language, religion, socioeconomic status, educational

level, sexual preference, intellectual ability, food preference, creativity, athletic ability, and so forth.

5. Ask group members to open their bags and eat a few pieces of the candy, then ask the following questions:

> What do you think the differences are on the inside? (They are the same.)

> How is the candy like all of us, everyone in the school, and everyone in the world? (Same human nature: feelings, need to accomplish something, to love someone and be loved, to be capable of doing things, to express emotions and ideas, to have a family and make it through this world as best we can.)

Point out that where we are different shows up in external things like our environment, heritage, culture, and so on.

6. Encourage members to share personal ways they might be alike. For example, "I like/want _____." The responses will likely span a wide range: a cool haircut and clothes, computer games, a motorcycle, movies, success, a boyfriend/girlfriend for company, a fun job that pays a lot of money, free time, travel, to go to college or get other training, to be in a band.

7. Sum up by asking the following questions:

> What have you learned about likenesses and differences from doing this activity with the candy?

> What do you appreciate about other members of the group?

> What do you think we might do together to help other kids in the school begin to understand that we are really all very much alike inside and that the outside things can be things we grow to appreciate and accept, and sometimes agree to disagree on?

Processing Time (¼ session time)

1. Ask at least one question from each of the four processing levels:

INTRAPERSONAL

Today we talked about human likenesses and differences. You did a super job exploring this idea. While we were talking about this and sharing with one another, what kinds of things were you thinking and feeling about your own likenesses and differences?

INTERPERSONAL

What did you notice about other group members as we discussed our likenesses and differences?

NEW LEARNING

You came up with lots of great ideas about how we are alike as human beings. What idea did you connect with the most, or what new idea might help you be more patient and accepting of others?

APPLICATION

What are you willing to do before the next session to take some "baby steps," which means not big changes but little changes that are easier to accomplish, to help you get closer to your goals for the group?

2. Thank the group for their outstanding ideas and efforts, and give them a hope statement. Remind them of the time and day for the next session, then share the rest of the candy and other snacks if you have them.

Beautiful and Ugly Are Only Skin Deep

Before beginning, review the comments about this session in the introduction to this group agenda.

GOALS

Affective

To explore and enhance trust level among all members

Behavioral

To experience breaking open a geode and exploring the interior as a metaphor for differences between exterior and interior qualities

Cognitive

To deal with the concept that we often have to get past socially unacceptable exteriors to get to the beauty inside a person

To grapple with the idea that the beauty of life isn't about acquiring things such as money, property, cars, or degrees but about values such as honesty, integrity, trustworthiness, loyalty, and kindness

MATERIALS

An unopened geode. You can find geodes at a local rock shop, if you have one, or you can order them from the Oriental Trading Company (1–800–228–2269). You can have one large geode, two or three smaller ones, or a small one for each group member. A large one usually has more dramatically beautiful crystals inside. You could also buy an exquisite one, already broken, and put the two halves together with duct tape or rubber bands so it looks like a whole rock, but you will lose the experience of breaking it open.

An old sock that the geode will fit into (socks if you have more than one geode)

A hammer

Old newspapers

Healthy snacks

GROUP SESSION

Opening Time (¼ session time)

1. Welcome the members back to group. Ask what concerns, comments, or questions they might have about confidentiality. Ask how they think the ground rules are working for them at this time.

2. Invite ideas and comments left over from the last session, about external differences and similar feelings and goals inside. (Some similar internal goals to mention include finding a life partner and a meaningful way of making a living, and becoming the best we can.) Ask group members to share what they might have done since the last session to move closer to their personal goals.

Working Time (½ session time)

1. Pass around the geode, then place it in the center on the floor on some newspapers. Some of the group might know or guess what the rock is—if so, this is fine. In your own words, say:

   Suppose you were visiting some cousins who live out in the country where there are a lot of rocky places. You are walking along with your cousins by a stream and see a lot of really UGLY rocks, ones that look like this. Some of them are piled together and some are just around. Your cousin says, "Wow, look at these cool rocks—let's take a bunch back to the garage." You think your cousin has lost it because these are the UGLIEST rocks you have ever seen, dirty and bumpy and absolutely no neat colors or patterns on them—so why bother carrying them back? Your cousin insists, so you help carry a few small ones that don't weigh too much back to the garage.

2. Ask the group to describe everything they can about the rock, staying with external appearances only, then discuss whether they have met or experienced people in their lives who appear not to have beautiful external physical features or who look very different from others and are rejected by people almost immediately because of their appearance. Explore the concept that people are judged to "be" a certain way instead of "appearing" a certain way. For example, sometimes people will say, "Oh, he or she is (weird, ugly, dumb, a geek, jock, queer)." Sometimes people wear things that tell other people they belong to a certain group, and these are identifying appearances, but these appearances do not show anything about underlying character.

3. Ask members whether they have ever been misjudged by how they appear to others:

   For example, if you wear your hair and dress in a way you think is really cool, perhaps if you walk into a store, the store manager might think you look like someone who would rob the store and call the police. You could end up being embarrassed and really mad because you weren't doing anything illegal, just looking at magazines. The manager misjudged you by your appearance.

   Discuss ways group members might misjudge others by their appearances and not what's inside them.

4. In your own words, explain:

   All of us have things about our external appearance we don't like. Sometimes we don't like a part of us because it is not "in" or valued by our friends. For example, a long time ago, having extra weight—being what we would now call fat—was considered highly desirable because when food was scarce, only rich people had enough food to be fat. Now being fat is considered unhealthy and undesirable. People can control their weight to some extent by eating well and exercising, but not very many people will ever look like models in the magazines. We also have things about our appearance that we can't control at all—perhaps not without cosmetic surgery. We don't like being misjudged by something we can't help or change easily.

   This is an opportunity for you to model self-disclosure by describing something you don't like about yourself physically but have had to live with. Showing your own vulnerability can help the kids self-disclose, too. Discuss who decides what is beautiful and attractive and what isn't. Share that appearances valued by society change—for example, in some places a certain shade of red hair might be "in," so women dye their hair that color to match what is valued at that time.

5. Have a group member put the geode in a sock and hit it hard. Sometimes you have to hit it a couple times, but try not to smash it in too many pieces! Usually it will break in half with a direct hit.

6. Open the geode, then discuss the idea that the inside is completely opposite of the outside, that if you hadn't taken the time to break inside something as hard as a rock that you wouldn't have this opportunity to enjoy the beauty. Discuss:

> *What about someone who might appear unattractive on the outside, and you judge that person to be unattractive on the inside? What if you take the time to get to know the person and find out that he or she has a kind of beauty that you can really learn from and appreciate? Perhaps the person is kind and caring, honest and loyal as a friend, and has important life goals. This is the kind of person you would like to have for a friend . . . not someone who looks good on the outside but is dishonest and you can't trust, wouldn't stick with you if you needed help, or would take from you in any way. Sometimes you have to take time and trouble to get to know a person, and maybe your friends might ridicule you for talking to someone they misjudge, but you have the right to choose your own friends. If the "cool" friends who look good aren't working for you, perhaps they don't really understand you or have your best interests at heart. You always have the option of getting to know people who have other good qualities that might not be as acceptable to your current friends. Who needs friends that aren't for YOU?*

Processing Time (¼ session time)

1. Ask at least one question from each of the four processing levels:

   INTRAPERSONAL

   While we were talking about the geodes and external and internal beauty, what kinds of things were you thinking about and feeling?

   INTERPERSONAL

   This is the third session for us as a group. What is it like to be a group member at this time?

   What have you noticed about our group?

   Who seems to be willing to self-disclose in the group? Who seems not quite ready for sharing himself or herself with us yet?

   NEW LEARNING

   What new ideas and feelings do you have from doing this geode activity today?

   APPLICATION

   During the time before our next session, what would you be willing to do to notice the judgments people make about other people by looking only at their exteriors, not their internal character?

2. Thank group members for coming, give them a hope statement, and remind them of the day and time for the next session. Share the snacks!

Different Drummers

GOALS

Affective

To delight and enjoy rhythm as an expression of feelings

Behavioral

To learn the connection between feelings and physical expression of them

Cognitive

To explore thoughts related to experiencing rejection, discrimination, prejudice, and intolerance

MATERIALS

An assortment of simulated (or real, if you have access) percussion and other instruments, such as pots and pans, metal pie plates, different sizes of drinking glasses, wood and/or plastic cutting boards, hand bells, jingle bells (individual or on a strip), drums, harmonicas, recorders, tambourines, and so on

A sheet of newsprint or posterboard displayed so everyone can see it, with these words printed on it: *BIGOTRY, BIAS, PREJUDICE, HATE CRIMES, RACISM, SEXISM, AGEISM, INTOLERANCE, INEQUALITY, RELIGIOUS PERSECUTION, ANTIDISABILITY SENTIMENT, HOMOPHOBIA,* and *REPRESSION*

Healthy snacks

GROUP SESSION

Opening Time (¼ session time)

1. Welcome members back to group and invite them to share any concerns or questions about confidentiality. How are the ground rules working for them at this time?

2. Ask if they noticed any situations where they or someone else was misjudged or discriminated against because of something external that cannot be changed, such as race, family income, or ethnic background. What was it like to witness or be part of that situation?

Working Time (½ session time)

1. Explain that the focus of the group today is on ways people disrespect human rights—for example, bigotry, bias, prejudice, hate crimes, racism, sexism, ageism, intolerance, inequality, religious persecution, antidisability sentiment, homophobia, and repression. Refer to the sheet of newsprint or posterboard and briefly define these terms as you say them.

2. Ask group members if they have a story they can tell about a very hurtful time when they were directly involved in one of these types of disrespect. (Some will have many negative incidents to relate, and some will have fewer or more indirect situations to describe.) Give each group member a time limit—such as 2 minutes—otherwise, the whole working time will be spent telling the therapeutic tales.

3. Describe the instruments (display them in the center of the group) and say that today you are inviting the group to participate in a creative way to show how they felt when they experienced the bias or discrimination they previously described.

4. Have each member choose one instrument, then divide the group into two smaller groups. Select one of the situations a member of each minigroup related earlier. Discuss with each

group how their situation could be divided into three parts: what happened first, or before the main situation; what happened second, or the main situation; and what happened last, or the results of the situation. Then instruct the groups to go to different parts of the room, if it is big enough, and decide how they are going to use the instruments to act out the feelings of the person involved for each part of the scenario. For example:

Michele: (A biracial group member) I have taken dance lessons and gymnastics since I was 3 years old and know lots of cool steps and routines from dancing and gymnastics that I thought I could share with the JV cheer squad so they could be better. I have some friends on the squad, so I thought I had a good chance of getting on. When I heard they had made the decisions about the new members I was so excited and ran down to the gym to see if the names were posted or I could find out somehow. Two girls on the squad came out the doors just as I came in and said, "They don't want any queer half-breeds on the squad, Michele." I couldn't believe my ears and broke out crying!

Leader: It sounds to me like it went like this with these feelings: First, you were confident, excited, happy, and hopeful you'd be chosen. Second, you heard the horrible words "They don't want me." Third, you experienced a wave of disbelief, anger, and rejection. So with your instruments, how would you make rhythms to represent the three states of this experience: excited/hopeful, crushing/rejecting, and angry/disbelieving?

5. Let the groups practice and decide how to represent the three feeling states with their instruments. After they practice, it's performance time. One group does a whole musical rendition of the situation's feeling states on their instruments.

6. Thank the musicians and move on to the other group and situation. If you have time, group members may act out more of the scenes described, either with your assistance in dividing the scenes into three parts or dividing the scenes on their own. Leave time for questions.

Processing Time (¼ session time)

1. Ask at least one question from each of the four processing levels:

   INTRAPERSONAL

   While we were making music to represent the feelings you experienced when extremely painful things happened that violated your human rights, what kinds of things were you thinking and feeling?

   INTERPERSONAL

   What did you notice about the other group members while we were listening to the music?

   NEW LEARNING

   What new ideas, feelings, thoughts, daydreams, or connections happened for you during this experience?

   APPLICATION

   How could you use what you learned from this activity to help you deal with negative situations? For example, remembering the music of anger, of guilt, of rejection, of forgiveness—how could that help?

2. Thank group members for coming and participating in a new adventure into music. Remind them of the next session's day and time, and tell the group members that for this coming session they will need to wear comfortable clothes that will allow them to lie down on the floor. Give them a hope statement, then share the snacks!

Body Boundaries

In this activity, you will ask group members to move into different positions in order to explore relationships in space with an object and become aware of their comfort level in various positions. They will need to be wearing comfortable clothes; some will have remembered to do so, and some won't. If the girls come wearing skirts, have them select a place where they can lie down with their feet toward the wall and heads toward the middle of the room.

GOALS

Affective

To get in touch with feelings and thoughts about what it is like to have someone/something in one's personal space

Behavioral

To give and receive attention from peers about personal space

To practice being assertive about personal space needs

Cognitive

To understand the concept of personal space and comfort level

To develop an understanding of the importance of physical contact and become aware of one's own and others' needs and desires relating to this

To develop tolerance for others' personal space needs

MATERIALS

One object for each group member—for example, basketball, volleyball, cap, child's chair, camera, book, musical instrument, jacket or sweater, dish, cup, and so forth

A large room (classroom size). If there is furniture, move it to the side or one corner. (Members are going to sit, stand, lie down, and move about in relation to their objects, so there must be enough room for them to do so without bumping into one another.)

Tape measure (long enough to measure up to 15 feet)

Healthy snacks

GROUP SESSION

Opening Time (¼ session time)

1. Welcome the members back to group and invite them to share any concerns or comments about confidentiality. Now that the group has been together several times, how are the ground rules working? What changes might be needed?

2. Inquire if anyone has any comments or information they would like to share regarding the last session, where they used music to show painful situations related to violations of their human rights.

Working Time (½ session time)

1. Discuss the idea that every human being has what is called "personal space," which is that distance around one's body where a comfort zone is established. Explain, in your own words:

   Cultures, gender, and the nature of the relationship affect a person's comfort level when interacting with others, as does room size and amount/arrangement of furniture. If someone comes too close to us, we begin to feel very uncomfortable. For most people, this space is about 12 to 20 inches. It's as though we OWN that space around us, and other people are not invited there.

   We do allow people into our personal space who have a special relationship to us—for example, parents and children hug and kiss each other, we embrace friends we haven't seen in a while, or we might have a wrestling match with a friend or sibling. Boyfriends/girlfriends allow each other some time in each other's personal space, but they do so at each person's comfort level. Many crimes are defined by someone's invading someone else's personal space: assault, battery, rape, murder, theft of personal belongings, and so on. Since we "own" our space, we have the right to tell others to "bug off" if they are too close.

2. Explain that you will be asking each group member to select one of the objects and that he or she will be moving around the object—getting closer and farther away from it, sometimes thinking of it as what it is and sometimes pretending it is another person. The purpose of this is to help group members get in touch with feelings and thoughts about what it is like to have someone/something in their personal space. Explain that you will be asking them some questions about their objects and that they are to answer silently, in their minds, not aloud. They will have a chance to talk about what they think and feel later.

3. Have group members select an object and move to a place in the room where they are 6 to 8 feet from any other person. Ask them to place their objects on the floor and sit down. Pick up and move each member's object about 15 feet away from the person. (Depending on room size, one person's object might actually be close to someone else.)

4. Have them then lie down on the floor and look at their objects. Say the following:

   Think about your object and its distance and closeness to you.

   Think about the object and pretend that it is your best friend and you are trying to tell that person something. How do you feel about your best friend's being 15 feet away? (Wait and let them think and feel—no verbal responses.)

   Now think about the object as being your worst enemy—someone you don't even want to see, let alone be 15 feet from. How do you feel about this closeness? (Wait and let them think and feel.)

   Now sit up and look at your object. Think of it as your best friend. What is different about being sitting in relation to this person rather than lying down? (Wait.)

   Now think of your object as your worst enemy. How is it different facing your worst enemy sitting rather than lying down? What is it like with a person you feel so negatively about being at this distance? (Perhaps even 15 feet seems too close—or not close enough, if you choose to strike.)

5. Ask each member to move his or her object about half-way closer from where it was (7 to 8 feet away). Go through the same process:

Your object is much closer now. Think about your object as a person you have been waiting to meet all your life, the most wonderful person you can imagine. Any age, sex, and physical characteristics you want. And this person loves you so much! This person is loyal, trustworthy, and would do anything for you. You want so much to tell the person how much he or she means to you, how much that person's friendship is a special part of your life. You try and try, but the words won't come out of your mouth. What kinds of things are you thinking and feeling right now? (Wait.)

Now think about your object as someone you dislike very much. This person has been the source of a lot of pain for you. You don't even want to look at the person, but now you have to look at him or her right in the eye. You feel your blood starting to boil. You would like to run since you aren't allowed to say anything to the person right now, and you can't stand being this close. What are you thinking and feeling right now? (Wait, no verbal responses.)

What do you think this person might say or do? How do you feel being this close/far from this person?

6. Ask members to move their objects closer, to about 3 feet from them. Members lie down on the floor and face their objects:

What would you like to say to your object right now? Go ahead and say it silently. What does it feel like having your object just 3 feet from you? What kinds of things would you want to say if you thought your object was going to get really, really close to you in just a minute?

Think about the people in your life that it would be OK if they were in the object's place, 3 feet from you. What people would you NOT want 3 feet from you?

How do you feel about 3 feet as part of your personal space? Are you comfortable with most people's being here, but no closer? How much closer do they have to get for you to feel really uncomfortable?

Now reach out and move your object closer to you. (Some might need help.) *Place your object where your absolute personal space begins, where you would feel really uncomfortable for a friend or nonrelative to come any closer. I will measure this space and tell you what it is.*

7. Use the measuring tape to measure where each member indicates his or her personal space starts, then share this information privately by showing the member the tape and whispering if need be. After you measure, members may sit:

Now think of your object as your best friend or a trusted family member. What feelings do you have if such a person is in your personal space? (Wait, no verbal responses.)

What could you tell this person about your feelings and needs about your personal space? How do you think the person would respond? Feel?

Now your object has become someone you dislike very much. You don't even want to be in the room with this person, much less have him or her in your personal space. The person is close and steps right into your personal space. What are you thinking? What kind of feelings run through your body and mind? What would you like to do? What would you like to say? How would you handle this?

Now push your object away to where it is just an object in space again. Say good-bye to your object, thanking it for being part of your life during this experience.

Processing Time

Processing may take longer than usual because the activity didn't allow for expression of feelings and many of the feelings called up may be intense. This is really the only chance group members will have to interact with one another about the activity, so spend time and be sure to use linking and connecting so they will share and learn from one another.

---

1. Ask at least one question from each of the four processing levels:

    ### INTRAPERSONAL

    This has been a very unusual experience, trying to get in touch with thoughts and feelings about personal space and who is and isn't allowed there. What kinds of things were you thinking and feeling as I was asking these questions?

    ### INTERPERSONAL

    What was it like to watch the other members of the group observe and think about their objects? What did you notice about being a group member today?

    ### NEW LEARNING

    How was this experience new for you?

    What new ideas, thoughts, feelings, or behaviors do you have now that you didn't have before the exercise today?

    What have you learned about telling people about your comfort level regarding your personal space? What might you do differently now if someone gets too close to you? If someone stays too far away?

    ### APPLICATION

    Between now and the next session, how might this experience help you understand friends and family members?

2. Thank group members for participating in this very different kind of activity and give them a hope statement. Remind them of the day and time for the next session, then share the snacks.

"It's Not Easy Being Green"

GOALS

Affective

To get in touch with feelings related to painful situations that can't be changed

To enjoy the warm and positive aspects of Kermit the Frog's song "It's Not Easy Being Green"

Behavioral

To self-disclose personal information about difficult life issues

To exchange ways to help and support one another

Cognitive

To confront the concept of unchangeable life circumstances and the fact that we must take personal responsibility for learning to cope rather than being negative about the things we can't change

MATERIALS

Videotape *It's the Muppets! More Muppets, Please!* (Burbank, CA: Jim Henson Productions, Inc., 1993)

Healthy snacks

GROUP SESSION

Opening Time (¼ session time)

1. Welcome the members to group and inquire if there are any concerns regarding confidentiality. Ask how the ground rules are working.

2. Ask what comments or questions the group might have about last week's session, about personal space:

   What did you notice about your own personal space and how people respected it or didn't respect it?

   What did you notice about other people and their personal space?

   How did you deal with people too close or too far from you?

   What behavior changes might you have made because of learning about this idea?

Working Time (½ session time)

1. Start the session by forwarding the videotape to the part where Kermit the Frog sings "It's Not Easy Being Green." Play the song, then ask members to discuss what they think it means. Encourage each group member to share.

2. Invite each member to share something about himself or herself that:

   Cannot be changed (or changed easily at this time—say, for example, without cosmetic surgery)

   Has been the source of emotional and/or physical distress and pain or irritation for quite some time

   Has taken a special effort or special skills to deal with

   Have each group member start out saying, "It isn't easy being . . . " (for example, a person with asthma, someone with a dad in prison, a boy who is always the shortest one in the class, a

139

redhead, the child of a mom who is lesbian, always overweight, a girl whose mom and dad came from the Czech Republic, a guy who is blind in one eye, called "fag," called "mental" or "Special Ed").

These are very personal self-disclosures and require a group with trust and cohesion. Be sure to be very supportive and reinforcing of each group member as he or she shares. The experience is very moving and powerful in most groups.

---

3. After all have shared, have group members use the linking and connecting skill to help one another, as the example in the next step of this procedure shows. Then say:

   It sounds like each one of you has experienced a lot of pain over situations you didn't ask for and feel stuck and out of control because you can't change them. Kermit said positive things about being green, so he has turned lemons into lemonade in his color situation. What is something POSITIVE you have learned from your unique experience?

   Encourage each member to find something positive he or she has learned or experienced as a result of the situation.

4. Ask: "Since your situation has been going on for quite a while, what are some ways that you have learned to cope with your differentness that you could use as advice to help others cope with their situations?" Encourage members to share some way they have learned to deal with their own situation, using linking and connecting. For example:

   Josh, I linked with you when you said you are blind in one eye. Because my asthma is so bad sometimes I can't even focus on the blackboard and the teacher might think I am not paying attention and yell at me, and it's just because I am squinting and trying to get it, so I know how you feel. But I just make sure I tell her in a nice way that I didn't mean any bad things in her class—I just had a bad asthma day, so maybe you could just remind them that you can't see so well either with one eye, and they would be more kind.

Processing Time (¼ session time)

1. Ask at least one question from each of the four processing levels:

   INTRAPERSONAL

   Today you shared about very personal difficulties and circumstances that you can't change and that are often painful and angering. What were you thinking and feeling as you and the other group members were sharing this kind of personal stuff?

   INTERPERSONAL

   What was it like for you to be a group member today, listening to yourself and others sharing things that were very painful?

   NEW LEARNING

   What new ideas or behaviors have you learned today that will be a help to you as you continue to cope with your issue?

   APPLICATION

   What can you do before the next session to make your situation better, perhaps from something you learned today?

2. Thank group members for coming and give them a hope statement. Let them know that the next session will be the last "working" session and that the final one will be a review and celebration. Remind them of the day and time for the next session, then share the snacks.

Walk a Block in My Socks

This session makes use of the saying "Don't judge someone until you have walked a mile in his moccasins." Although it can't be attributed to any particular tribal group, the saying is part of the Native American oral tradition. According to some, the original saying was "until you have walked 2 miles in his moccasins," which white settlers changed to "1 mile."

GOALS

Affective
To enhance self-esteem by self-disclosing and getting positive feedback

Behavioral
To express more sensitivity to the feelings of others and to model to others how to be sensitive to our own feelings

Cognitive
To raise awareness of empathy as a skill to help understand others and help others understand us

MATERIALS

A pair of moccasins (size 12 men's, or the largest size you can find—I found some on clearance at the end of the season at a discount store for under 6 dollars!)

Big socks (optional)

Healthy snacks

GROUP SESSION

Opening Time (¼ session time)

1. Welcome the members back to group. Ask what concerns members have about confidentiality. What changes or additions might be necessary to the ground rules?

2. Connect back with the previous session's topic of "being green," or having an ongoing issue that is unchangeable but that you have learned some positive ways to cope with. Ask who would like to comment or describe any new behaviors or ideas related to this issue.

Working Time (½ session time)

1. Place the moccasins by your feet, take off your shoes, and ask group members whether they have heard the saying that you cannot judge a person until you have walked a mile in that person's moccasins. The meaning is, you don't have the right to judge anyone unless you really know what that person's life is like and what challenges he or she faces. Since you absolutely cannot ever have the same experiences as another person, you can really NEVER pass judgment. (If you like, you could work in the session title as well: "In other words, you can't judge me until you've walked a block in my socks.")

2. Ask group members if they would be willing to put on the moccasins and tell the group about a time when someone judged them harshly or incorrectly because that person didn't understand their actions or motivations. Place your feet on top of the moccasins and model by sharing an incident and related feelings. Then conduct a share-around with the other members.

3. When group members have finished, encourage them to use the linking and connecting skill to give support and feedback to one another.

4. Discuss the idea that their friends may often make negative, hurtful judgments about teachers, parents, and other friends and peers without really understanding what those people are going through:

> *No one can ever really understand what you are going through, and you can't understand all of anyone else's circumstances, behaviors, and feelings. What are some things that you can do when you are with a person or a group of kids who start saying judgmental things about someone else? For example:*

> She must be really dumb to fail that test twice.

> My dad just doesn't care about me at all.

> Ashley is a bad person because she always does _____ .

> Kiva likes classical music . . . what a stuck-up!

5. Encourage group members to brainstorm statements they could make to others to get them to stop and think before saying things that will be damaging to another person's feelings, self-esteem, or reputation. For example:

> I really don't know the person and don't want to make that judgment.

> I haven't walked a block in his socks, so I don't know that to be true.

> I'd rather not say something I can't really judge.

> I don't want to participate in hurting other people.

6. Group members may say they would be ridiculed if they said things like that. If so, ask, "How would you want your own best friend to act in a situation where someone said something negative and judging about you? Your friend would have the opportunity to either go along or stand up for you by making one of the statements we just discussed. If you wouldn't be willing to stand up for a friend, could you expect a friend to do so for you?"

Processing Time (¼ session time)

1. Ask at least one question from each of the four processing levels:

   INTRAPERSONAL

   What kinds of feelings and ideas did you have today while we were discussing making negative judgments about others?

   What did you think of the Native American saying that you shouldn't judge anyone until you have walked 2 miles in his moccasins? (If you have group members with Native American cultural heritage, encourage them to share more specific ideas that add to the feelings.)

   INTERPERSONAL

   What have you noticed about our group today—are any particular changes going on?

   NEW LEARNING

   What new ideas or feelings do you have as a result of our session today?

   What were you surprised about?

   APPLICATION

   What do you think you might be able to try between now and the next session as a result of dealing with this issue today?

2. Thank group members for coming, give them a hope statement, and remind them of the day and time for the next session. Share the snacks!

Frogs, Toads, and Other Survivors

GOALS

Affective

To develop self-confidence and encourage self-expression

Behavioral

To use drawing to facilitate expression of feelings related to situations where human rights have been violated

Cognitive

To raise awareness about coping skills group members already possess

To understand a metaphor for surviving difficult situations and learning to go on and cope even more effectively

MATERIALS

Pictures of many different species of frogs and toads, especially South American poison dart frogs (400 species). Frogs appear in many books, calendars, and other resources. One book I especially like is *The Encyclopedia of Extremely Weird Animals,* by Sarah Lovett (Santa Fe: John Muir Publications, 1997). This book has fabulous frogs as well as lots of other strange animals to use for other activities.

Drawing paper

Colored markers

Healthy snacks

GROUP SESSION

Opening Time (¼ session time)

1. Welcome members back to group. Invite comments about any confidentiality issues. Ask what concerns members might have about the ground rules. Let group members know that this is the last working session and that the next session will be the last time they will be together as a group. Tell them to be thinking about how they can celebrate at the next session—you will ask for their thoughts at the end of this one.

2. Connect with the last session about not making judgments about other people. What did group members notice about their own and others' behavior regarding talking negatively about situations they really couldn't have firsthand knowledge about? Repeat the idea that no one can really know exactly how you feel or why you behave in a certain way.

Working Time (½ session time)

1. Show group members the pictures of different kinds of frogs and toads, letting them look, ask questions, and make comments about all the strange colors, sizes, and shapes. Discuss the fact that frogs are amphibians, which means they can live on both land and water, and there are hundreds of kinds, not just the green pond frog and brown warty toad they are familiar with. (Some group members may have seen different frogs and toads at a zoo.)

2. Share that the frog has been around longer than human beings and has survived every type of weather and natural disaster that has ever occurred—ice ages, hurricanes and tornadoes, desert storms, floods, tidal waves, air and water pollution, even human beings who kill them for a meal or sport! Summarize:

Not only are frogs SURVIVORS, they have adapted to living on every continent except Antarctica. Creatures who survive in nature do so because they have special qualities that we also need to survive life's difficulties. Frogs are adaptable, persistent, flexible, patient, and go through a complete metamorphosis during their lifetimes. They change from an egg to a tad-pole and to a tadpole with legs. Then their tails drop off, they grow lungs, and they crawl out on the land! If the frog can change and survive through life's scariest and most threatening times, surely we humans, who have intelligence and the ability to learn new skills to deal with life, can also change.

3. Pass out the drawing materials and invite group members to draw a picture of a situation in which they experienced bias, rejection, or disrespect because of someone else's intolerance and how they dealt with that situation. They can draw some frogs on there, too! Tell them you will be asking them to share their pictures when finished. Give them a time limit (save about 10 minutes for sharing with the rest of the group).

4. When the time is up, encourage discussion about the drawings. Before they share, tell the group they need to answer the following questions about their drawings and that they can tell anything else they want:

   What type of human rights violation is happening in the drawing?

   What are your major feelings about the characters in the picture?

   What coping skills did you use?

   What could you share with others about what you learned in this situation that might help them?

Processing Time (¼ session time)

1. Ask at least one question from each of the four processing levels:

   INTRAPERSONAL

   What kinds of thoughts and feelings were you having as you were drawing a picture of a violation of your human rights?

   INTERPERSONAL

   What was it like for you to be a group member today?

   NEW LEARNING

   After drawing your picture and listening to the other members share about their situations, what new thoughts and feelings do you have about people doing hurtful things to one another because of their race, religious beliefs, gender, sexual preference, age, or any other difference?

   APPLICATION

   What can you take away from this session that will help you be a better person?

2. Remind group members that the next session will be the last and ask how they would like to celebrate—perhaps with ethnic foods group members could bring. Thank them for participating, give them a hope statement, and share the snacks.

That's a Wrap

GOALS

Affective

To have an opportunity to deal with feelings about the group's ending

To feel a sense of accomplishment for progress

Behavioral

To create and experience a ceremony to validate the idea that the group has learned to identify and deal with violations of human rights in more positive ways

To celebrate the group's work together and say good-bye

Cognitive

To solidify cohesion among the group and develop an understanding that group members can call on one another in the future for help

To review what has been learned in the group and reinforce understanding and acceptance of individual differences

MATERIALS

White candles, tapers about 12 inches long, one for each member and yourself

Easel pad or posterboard

Colored markers

Party goodies and/or ethnic foods

GROUP SESSION

Opening Time (¼ session time)

1. Welcome members to the last session. Ask them how they think the ground rules, including confidentiality, have worked for them during this group experience. Remind them that confidentiality extends even after the group is over.

2. Connect with the last group, on the topic of surviving difficult situations. Ask what group members noticed about their own behaviors since they have had a new awareness of their own individual differences and increased ability to accept one another and others outside the group with tolerance and understanding.

Working Time (½ session time)

1. Review and discuss the content of the previous sessions:

    Session 1—Getting Started

    Getting acquainted and learning how thoughts, feelings, and behaviors are different—a concept used throughout the sessions

    Session 2—M & M's: What's the Difference?

    Exploring likenesses and differences and how we might look different outside but have the same human needs

Session 3—Beautiful and Ugly Are Only Skin Deep

Breaking open a geode—finding out that we can misjudge others if we depend on appearances only

Session 4—Different Drummers

Creating a short musical representation of our feelings about a situation in which our human rights were disrespected in some way: bigotry, sexism, racism, prejudice, and so on

Session 5—Body Boundaries

Exploring our personal space and thinking about people we want and do not want close to us

Session 6—"It's Not Easy Being Green"

With the help of Kermit the Frog, getting in touch with a difficult situation we have had to learn to cope with

Session 7—Walk a Block in My Socks

Learning that making judgments about others isn't possible because we can never really know exactly why someone does something or feels a certain way

Session 8—Frogs, Toads, and Other Survivors

Finding out that if we want to survive and grow, we need to be able to adapt—maybe even go through a complete change of form, like the frog

Processing Time (¼ session time)

1. Give each group member a candle and explain, "These candles will serve as a symbol of your new knowledge and hope." Tell them that as a symbol of their brotherhood/sisterhood and bond as teachers of tolerance, you invite them to make up and write down their own official peacekeepers' statement, right now. The statement must include a tolerance statement, a hope statement, and a universal acceptance statement. For example:

   > We, the Peacekeepers Society of Jonathan Jennings Middle School, do hereby acclaim the nine of us to be official peacekeepers. We agree and promise to be tolerant of our peers' and adults' individual differences. We have a great deal of hope that we will be successful making a difference in our school to help stop violations of human rights of all kinds. And we will make an effort every day of our lives to try to accept and understand all peoples of the world in a more positive and loving way.

2. Once the group has developed and written their statement, all members sign it and practice saying it aloud a few times. Then invite everyone to stand in a circle, light the candles, and repeat the statement together. Blow out the candles!

3. Share with group members your pride and appreciation for their work during the group. Let group members know what the arrangements are for follow-up (meeting again, reconnecting, and giving one another support for continued efforts toward peace and understanding). Give the group a hope statement for the future, perhaps saying that you know they will carry "the light of understanding" to others and that they will help their friends, family members, and everyone they meet to become more tolerant and accepting of differences.

4. Have your treats or ethnic goodies and celebrate!

Give a Little, Take a Little: Relationships at Home _____

Relationships with parents and siblings are the source of both problems and opportunities for young adolescents. Developmentally, adolescents are trying with all their might to begin the individuation process that will end in their becoming their own adult persons. Academically, they are thrust into a whirlwind of pressure to complete more homework, change classes, make decisions about classes that have potential career importance, and select other activities that can enhance or compete with available time, energy, and resources. Physically, the genes are jumping and the hormones hopping, with new body changes occurring along with huge growth spurts. The physiological changes, accompanied by hormonal ups and downs, result in the moody, snappy, unpredictable, child-then-adult syndrome we are all familiar with at school and home.

Our society has changed so dramatically in the past 25 years that we are now faced with issues that were unimaginable a few decades ago. The issue of freedom has always been important, but with the availability of cars, jobs, and computers, technology has served parents and the education community a plate of indigestible problems and conflicts. Communication between parents and children is more critical than ever, but time and motivation to communicate seem to be at a premium. One of the essential ingredients for youth to be willing to listen and learn from adults is missing—a trusting relationship. Many parents are absent from the daily lives of their children. It is common practice for parents to shuttle their children around quickly from activity to activity until the children are exhausted and the parents are exasperated. Or the parents depend on others to get their children here and there to their many extracurricular activities and barely have time to talk to them at night or before running off to work and school in the morning. It takes a solid, meaningful, two-way relationship between parent and child to make it through the major power struggles of adolescence. Group counseling can provide a safe, trusting relationship with an adult who has clear values on major issues, who is willing to model for youth.

This group experience is focused on helping young adolescents get in touch with several issues that emerge during this time and that impact on family relationships. Parents are continually making efforts to help their children move from the egocentric thinking and behaving of childhood to a more balanced approach of understanding and acting on behalf of others as well as self. Egocentrism, appropriate in early childhood, interferes with mature relationships. Trust, respect, empathy, social skills, and other interpersonal dynamics require give-and-take and consideration of others' points of view. Group counseling can help provide experiences that promote and facilitate insight into one's own and others' behavior and feelings.

The sessions in this group are sequenced as follows:

Session 1—Getting Started
Session 2—Power Struggles
Session 3—My Freedoms and Responsibilities
Session 4—I'm Not the Only One Living Here
Session 5—Cutting Edge: Technology at Home
Session 6—Teeter-Totter: Balancing Family, Friends, School, and Other Responsibilities
Session 7—The Gifts I Bring
Session 8—That's a Wrap

GROUP GOALS

1. To facilitate development of a trusting, supportive environment in which members feel secure to risk and share

2. To promote the group norms of becoming a supportive, encouraging person

3. To ensure that members can discriminate thinking, feeling, and behaving

4. To develop a support system among group members for dealing with stress

5. To raise awareness about developmental processes occurring at this time of life

6. To encourage the view that desired freedom must be balanced with responsibility

7. To help group members get in touch with the needs and rights of other family members

8. To develop a forum and norm for expressing needs, feelings, and frustrations

9. To increase ability to tolerate and manage stress and frustration

10. To raise awareness of parents' needs and concerns, as well as of the power struggles between parents and adolescents

11. To offer assertion skills as a way to assist in negotiation and give-and-take within the family

12. To develop awareness of how group members' wants and needs impact family members

13. To encourage decision making for home situations, including empathy for self and others

14. To review the group experience and set goals for future personal work

SELECTION AND OTHER ISSUES

The primary goal of this group is to provide a forum for youth to explore and learn new skills related to being a balanced, contributing family member. This group, then, is broadly based and can be used to address a wide range of problematic issues that spill over into the school setting. You could select members with the following issues:

Youth whose problems getting along at home affect their grades

Youth who are overwhelmed by extracurricular activities that take up their time

Youth in conflict with parents over use of technology (television, computer, video games, and so forth)

Youth who feel their parents are too restricting and who argue about every issue that comes up

Youth who are in control at home, with parents who have given up

Youth who have the skills and ability to work with parents but who have sibling issues

Be sure to role-balance, including high, medium, and low self-disclosers. You definitely don't want a group of whiner/complainers with no motivation to learn give-and-take. Each potential group member needs to have a strong skill, ability, attitude, or coping mechanism that will be his or her gift to the group.

REFERENCES AND SELECTED RESOURCES FOR PROFESSIONALS

Berry, J. (1987). *Every kid's guide to understanding human rights.* Chicago: Children's Press.

Bosma, H. A., Jackson, S. E., Zijsling, D. H., Zani, B., Cicognani, E., Xerri, M. L., Honess, T. M., & Charman, L. (1996). Who has the final say? Decisions on adolescent behavior in the family. *Journal of Adolescence, 19,* 277–291.

Covey, S. (1997). *The seven habits of highly effective families: Building a beautiful family culture in a turbulent world.* New York: Golden Books.

Dorn, L. (1983). *Peace in the family: A workbook of ideas and actions.* New York: Pantheon.

Guerra, N. G., Moore, A., & Slaby, R. G. (1995). *Viewpoints: A guide to conflict resolution and decision making for adolescents.* Champaign, IL: Research Press.

Kurdek, L. A., Fine, M. A., & Sinclair, R. J. (1995). School adjustment in sixth graders: Parenting transitions, family climate, and peer norm effects. *Child Development, 66,* 430–445.

Larson, R. W., Richards, M. H., Moneta, G., Holmbeck, G., & Duckett, E. (1996). Changes in adolescents' daily interactions with their families from ages 10 to 18: Disengagement and transformation. *Developmental Psychology, 32,* 744–754.

Molina, B. S. G., & Chassin, L. (1996). The parent-adolescent relationship at puberty: Hispanic ethnicity and parent alcoholism as moderators. *Developmental Psychology, 132*, 675–686.

Orton, G. L. (1997). *Strategies for counseling children and their parents.* Pacific Grove, CA: Brooks/Cole.

Payne, L. (1997). *We can get along: A child's book of choices* (Grades 1–7). Minneapolis: Free Spirit.

Shaevitz, M. H. (1983). *The Superwoman syndrome* [Book/cassette]. Niles, IL: Nightingale/Conant.

Vernon, A. (1993). *Developmental assessment and intervention with children and adolescents.* Alexandria, VA: American Counseling Association.

Wolf, A. (1991). *Get out of my life, but first could you drive me and Cheryl to the mall? A parent's guide to the new teenager.* New York: Noonday Press.

Getting Started

GOALS

Affective

To reduce tension related to the new experience and expectations of the group

To begin developing a sense of "we-ness," or group cohesion

Behavioral

To participate in a getting-acquainted activity

To work with other group members to help develop ground rules

Cognitive

To understand the purpose and goals of the group

To learn what confidentiality is and how it applies to oneself and other group members

To learn how the thinking, feeling, and behaving processes are different and how they relate

MATERIALS

Limits of Confidentiality sign (see Appendix A, page 270)

Easel pad or posterboard and marker

Thinking-Feeling-Behaving Gears (see Appendix A, page 271)

A large sheet of newsprint

Healthy snacks (such as juice, raisins, nuts, crackers)

GROUP SESSION

Opening Time

For sessions after this first one, Opening Time will take up about one-fourth of the typical 40- to 50-minute session time, or about 10 minutes. For this session, however, you will need to plan on more time to discuss confidentiality, develop ground rules, and conduct a getting-acquainted activity. See the book's introduction for some ideas on how to schedule this extra time.

---

1. Welcome the members and go over the name and general goals of the group. Stress that the purpose of the group is to help each member select a problem situation he or she is having with parents or siblings and to learn new skills, ideas, and attitudes to deal with the problem in a more effective way.

2. Discuss the need for confidentiality (the "no-blab" rule): What is said and done in the group stays in the group. Be sure to give some examples of what people outside the group might say to pressure members to share what happens in group. For example:

   What do you talk about in group, anyway?

   Do you tell whether you do drugs in that group?

   What does Tina say about me?

After members are clear on the concept, share the Limits of Confidentiality sign (either as a handout or poster). Let group members know you are bound by the confidentiality rule but that as the leader you are required to tell if you think someone will do harm to self or another person, if someone says anything about child abuse or criminal activity going on, or if a judge orders you to turn over information.

3. Discuss the basic ground rules you have decided on for your group and request the group's input in developing a few more that would enhance their comfort in sharing with one another. For example:

    Take turns.

    Everyone has the right to "pass" (not share unless that's comfortable).

    Agree to disagree (no put-downs).

    Come on time.

    _____

    Don't move on until the group agrees on the ground rules. Write or have the group write the rules on an easel pad or piece of posterboard and have each member sign the document to show agreement. You can then post these rules every session.

    _____

4. To get acquainted, have group members pair up and share the following information about themselves:

    A hobby or activity I do very well

    My favorite meal

    The TV show I always try to watch

    Best game ever invented

    My favorite relative other than parents/siblings

    What I like to do best with a computer

    My biggest worry about being in this group

    What I hope to accomplish by being in this group

5. After a few minutes, have members come back to the group circle and introduce their partners, sharing everything they can remember.

Working Time

_____

Working Time will take half of a typical session, or about 20 to 25 minutes.

_____

1. Explain that before the group starts talking about any problems at home, it's important to learn how thinking, feeling, and behaving are different. During group, you will be asking members many times how they are feeling about something. Often people don't know how they feel or aren't in touch with their feelings, so they say what they are thinking rather than what they are feeling. They can even confuse what they are doing with what they are thinking!

2. To illustrate, share the Thinking-Feeling-Behaving Gears. Summarize, in your own words:

    Each of us has many "parts" to us, like gears in a machine. The gears all have to work together for the machine to work right. If one gear gets off, out of gear, then none of them works right. Thinking, feeling, and behaving are related in us like gears are in a machine. If your thinking isn't accurate, then your feelings aren't right either, and you also behave in ways that show your thinking is out of whack. Negative thinking makes negative behavior and negative feelings.

3. With the group, generate some thinking, feeling, and behaving words. For example:

   Thinking: Imagining, deciding, examining, learning, organizing, remembering, wondering

   Feeling: Annoyed, confused, doubtful, furious, jealous, joyful, weary

   Behaving: Arguing, eating, flirting, gossiping, imitating, smiling, yelling

   Divide the sheet of newsprint in three sections, one for each category, and write these words as group members come up with them.

4. Ask members to work as a group to decide how to illustrate the thinking-feeling-behaving relationship. They could draw a gear at the top of each column on the list, or perhaps a head (thinking), heart (feeling), and hand (behaving)—whatever metaphor they like. After they have finished the drawing, have them share their thoughts on how they depicted the idea.

5. Discuss the idea that they are going through rapid changes in every area of life and that these changes often bring them into conflict with adults. They are wanting more adult-like freedoms, such as going places with friends, choosing their own clothes, setting their own schedules, being involved in sports and social activities, and using family resources. Say, "Since you can't change people who are not present, we can't change your mom or dad or sisters/brothers directly, but we can work on changing you. What would you like to be thinking, feeling, and doing after you work on your project for the eight sessions of this group?" (Help each group member articulate exactly what it is he or she wants to be different at the end of the group.) For example:

   Alyssa: My problem is my mom and I fight all the time. She is so restrictive and won't let me do ANYTHING by myself with my friends. I can't stand it and we fight, fight, fight.

   Leader: OK, Alyssa, since we can't change your mom because she isn't here in the group, could we say that your target behavior is to reduce the number of times you fight with your mom and increase the number of times you ask her to sit down and the two of you come up with some kind of compromise that lets both of you win in this situation? (Check your summary out with Alyssa.)

   Dana: Well, my problem is my cousin. She lives across the street from me and is my friend also. We wear the same size, and she is always borrowing my clothes and messing them up. I can't tell her no because my mom and her mom are sisters and they would get all over us and tell us we had to be nice.

   Leader: Let me see if I understand what you're saying. You want to learn to say no to your cousin, who always wants to borrow your things and then doesn't return them or returns them in less than good condition. And you want to know how to deal with your mom's pressure to be nice to your cousin but don't want to have to lend your cousin your stuff. (Check with Dana.)

   Jiri: I can't get along with my dad. He wants me to like computers and science, and I like motorcycles and baseball. We never have gotten along since I was a baby. It's like we're from two different families. I love my dad, but he is hard on me because we don't do things together like he wants to. He won't go to the things I like, and I don't want to go to the things he likes, so we just don't talk anymore.

   Leader: Correct me, Jiri, if this isn't what you're wanting. It sounds like you want to be able to share some of your likes with your dad and have them accepted, and you want to spend some time with him on something that you both could enjoy and get along with. Maybe you would also like to try to understand why he likes the things he does, even if you don't like them. (Check with Jiri.)

6. After members share and you help clarify their individual target behaviors, thank them for being so open and willing to work on their issues. Tell them the next session you will begin to learn new ways to deal with the problematic things going on in their lives.

Processing Time

Processing Time will take one-quarter of a typical session, or about 10 minutes.

---

1. Ask at least one question from each of the four processing levels:

   INTRAPERSONAL

   Our first session together gave us the opportunity to clarify the important concepts of thinking, feeling, and behaving, which we will be using throughout the group. As we shared together and discussed our problem situations, what kinds of feelings were you having and what were you thinking?

   INTERPERSONAL

   We are here together in a special relationship. We have a chance to work together as a support system for one another and to become a team of sharing friends to help give direction, examples, encouragement, and energy for our work ahead. How was it for you to be a member of the group today?

   NEW LEARNING

   What new ideas, thoughts, or feelings do you have now that you didn't have when you came in here today?

   APPLICATION

   Between sessions, I'd like to invite you to think about and notice what kind of thoughts and feelings you have when your special problem situation comes up, so you are aware of what is going on. Who would be willing to try that?

2. Thank members for coming to the group, for participating to the best of their ability, and for supporting one another. Give a hope statement like the following example:

   You have shared some very personal ideas and feelings today, and set some goals to work toward. I have a great deal of hope and belief that each of you can reach your goals and can support and encourage other group members along the way.

   Remind them of the time and day for the next session, then share the snacks.

Power Struggles

This activity may take more time than you have for one session. Don't try to cram everything in and not have time to process what it means—rather, conduct this activity over two sessions, doing and processing half of the "sculpts" one day, then doing and processing the second half on another day. Group members need to process at the time of the sculpts to be able to remember the dynamics!

GOALS

Affective
To feel the tension and stress that family power positions create

Behavioral
To participate in "family sculpting" to demonstrate where the power is and isn't in each participant's family

Cognitive
To recognize conflict situations where power is the issue

To get in touch with who has the power in one's own family

MATERIALS

Objects that identify adult careers/jobs, such as a physician's bag, briefcase, hard hat, laptop computer, and so on

Healthy snacks

GROUP SESSION

Opening Time (¼ session time)

1. Welcome members back to group and ask what comments they might have regarding confidentiality. Do any of the ground rules need changing? Since it is early in the group, take time to encourage them to discuss any worries and concerns.

2. Ask:

> What thoughts, feelings, or actions have you noticed since the last session related to your target behavior?

> What were some of the feelings you noticed when a situation occurred? What kinds of things were you thinking when it occurred?

> Were there any differences in the way you responded/acted in the situation from the way you might have before?

Working Time (½ session time)

1. In your own words, explain the following:

> *Today I'd like to invite you to participate in what is called "family sculpting." Family sculpting is a way of acting out in a kind of frozen scene how family members seem to you, your perception of who has the power in most situations. The purpose of doing this is to identify from your point of view where the power is and how that power is used to control family members. This is very private stuff, so remember that what we say and do in here is confiden-*

tial, including everything we act out about our family relationships. It is not the business of anyone outside the group.

First, think of a situation when you and your parents and other family members got into a disagreement about something. We will call this "your point." You are trying to show your family in a disagreement situation, and you have a particular point or idea that you want all of us to get from your sculpting. When you think of your point, share it with me, and I will help you clarify and shorten it to a scene you can do.

Emma: My point is that my mom always wins arguments and gets her way, no matter who it is with, even my grandma. So most of us just let her have her way, except my brother, Lenny, who fights back with her sometimes.

Jake: My point is my little sister, Nella, has diabetes, and my mom is always giving her things and taking her places and making excuses for why Nella doesn't have to do chores or homework or anything, but me and my brothers have to do it all, even taking out the stinking garbage all the time. Nella makes fun of us and says she'll tell mom if we complain or hurt her, and me and my brothers can't stand her sometimes.

2. Each person takes a turn creating a scene with as many group members as he or she needs. The "sculptor" tells the players to sit, stand, lie down, or occupy whatever postures he or she wants to get the point across. When the group member whose family it is has everyone in place, then the group member takes the place of himself or herself. No one in the scene says anything aloud, but if, for example, a parent repeats a hurtful statement over and over to a small child, the sculptor could position one actor on a chair as the parent and another actor on his or her knees below to show how small and insignificant the child feels when this happens.

3. Advise group members to ask themselves these questions in creating their scenes:

   Where are my family members—parent(s), siblings, relatives—standing or sitting?

   What is their body language like? (Finger shaking, frowning, ignoring, walking out)

   What do their faces look like? How are they saying the words? (Mean, controlling, demeaning, loud, whispering)

   What am I doing? Saying or not saying? My face? Body language?

4. Begin with the first volunteer: Have that group member describe his or her point to you, select other group members, and make the sculpt. After everyone is in place, the sculptor describes what is going on, including who is saying what and what the power issue is all about.

5. Continue having members sculpt as time allows. Questions for each sculptor include the following:

   What is the main power issue going on?

   Are there one or two people who always seem to have the power struggles?

   What is your role in the scene?

   What are your main feelings when a scene like this really happens in your family?

   What are you usually thinking? What are you usually saying to yourself?

   Now, how would you like the scene to look—how would you change it?

If you have time, you could have each group member sculpt an ideal situation: how the scene would look if the issue were improved.

Processing Time (¼ session time)

1. Summarize the following, then ask at least one question from each of the four processing levels:

   This session brought up some serious feelings and issues that you have been dealing with for some time. It is painful and frustrating to be face to face with family situations you think you have no control over and can't change and that impact you in negative ways.

   INTRAPERSONAL

   What were some of the thoughts and feelings you had today as you were involved in your own family sculpt or as you observed or participated in other group members' sculpts?

   INTERPERSONAL

   What was it like for you to be a group member today, either as a sculptor or part of someone else's sculpt?

   NEW LEARNING

   Now that you have had this experience of showing and talking about a frustrating family situation, how are your ideas or feelings different from before?

   APPLICATION

   Who would be willing to observe how they deal with power situations in which it appears someone wants to "win" and someone is going to "lose"? How many would like to try to think of how their own power struggle could be turned into a "win-win" situation, with both people getting something positive out of it, even though no one gets everything he or she wants?

2. Thank group members for coming today. Ask if there are any really heavy feelings that anyone is experiencing that they might need to talk about further in order to be able to go back to class. If some members need to talk more, arrange a time to follow up.

3. Give the group a hope statement and remind them of the day and time for the next session. Share the snacks!

My Freedoms and Responsibilities

GOALS

Affective

To air feelings about parental control and the struggle to get one's needs and wants met

Behavioral

To use a reading about home responsibilities as a stimulus for discussion

To define *freedom* and *responsibility* and look at how they interact

Cognitive

To identify a technique to make progress on individual goals

To become aware of the cause-effect relationship between responsible behavior and acquiring more "adult-like" freedoms

MATERIALS

Home Rules (Handout 11)

Healthy snacks

GROUP SESSION

Opening Time (¼ session time)

1. Welcome members back to group and ask what concerns they might have regarding confidentiality. Then focus on the ground rules, asking if they seem to be working or if group members need any changes to feel comfortable to self-disclose.

2. Ask how the family sculpting impacted them since the last session:

    What did you notice about family power struggles?

    If you were involved, what were you feeling and thinking as the power struggle was going on and afterward?

    Are there any feelings left over that still need to be processed?

Working Time (½ session time)

1. Discuss the idea that as group members go through changes in adolescence, they want more freedom to do things adults do, such as have their own money, drive, work, have dating and love relationships, and choose their own careers. Summarize:

    These things are very different from childhood tasks and responsibilities, and the transition time is often difficult. (They readily agree!) The discussion today is focused on how to assess whether what you want and need is reasonable for your age and how to go about obtaining it without getting into arguments. Being angry and demanding turns parents off, and you end up getting trouble instead of the freedom you want.

The "Home Rules" have been reprinted with the kind permission of Marjorie Hansen Shaevitz from her book/cassette *The Superwoman Syndrome* (Niles, IL: Nightingale/Conant, 1983).

2. Distribute copies and invite members to take part in a reading of the Home Rules (Handout 11). Each person who wants to read a line may do so. After the reading, ask:

> What does this whole reading (not individual lines) mean to you?
>
> Why would someone like a parent think this would be important and want this kind of approach to be important to all family members?
>
> How could using this approach help things at your house?
>
> Which of these things do you do REGULARLY?
>
> Which do you NEVER or RARELY do?
>
> Which would be the easiest for you to start and keep doing to improve your mom's and dad's feelings about you?
>
> Which would be the hardest to start and keep doing?
>
> What do you think would be the result if you took this reading home and asked your mom, dad, and brothers and sisters to look at it, and everyone agreed to start doing these things as best as they could?
>
> What kind of family reward would your parents be willing to plan with you for making life easier for everyone?
>
> What additions do you think are needed at your house?

3. Discuss the idea of *negotiation,* a skill where both or all persons involved in a dispute about something sit down together and try to come up with a compromise:

> *A compromise means that there are no winners and losers—everyone gets to "win" something, but everyone must give up something of what he or she wants in order for everyone else to get a little. Give-and-take means giving up some of what you want and getting some of what you want. Sometimes we fight because we want ALL of what we want, but that isn't going to happen. So, SOME is better than NONE.*

4. Ask group members to bring up their target situations and, together, have the group work with each member to help come up with ideas that person could use to work out a compromise with the other person(s) in the situation. Spend the rest of the working time assisting one another in coming up with workable ideas for compromises.

5. Ask what group members would be willing to do before the next session in terms of using compromises and giving more at home—in other words, taking more personal responsibility for doing things in the ways the Home Rules suggest.

Processing Time (¼ session time)

1. Ask at least one question from each of the four processing levels:

   INTRAPERSONAL

   Today we discussed ideas to get your needs and wants met by being more responsible at home and making it easier for your parents to see you as a responsible young person who deserves more freedom. What were you thinking about and feeling as we read the Home Rules and shared how using negotiation and compromise might help?

   INTERPERSONAL

   What have you noticed about our group at this point, after three sessions together? What seems to be happening with us?

   NEW LEARNING

   What new ideas do you have now that you can use in your own situation?

APPLICATION

What would you be willing to do before the next session to make a big step forward in working on your target behavior?

2. Thank members for coming to group. Give them the hope statement that you believe they are making progress and improving their communication with one another. They are developing a support system and some new ways of thinking, feeling, and behaving in their problem situations. Remind them of the time and day of the next session, and share the snacks.

Home Rules

If you sleep on it . . . make it up.

If you wear it . . . hang it up.

If you drop it . . . pick it up.

If you lay it down . . . put it away.

If you eat out of it . . . wash it (or put it in the dishwasher).

If you make a mess . . . clean it up . . . NOW.

If you turn it on . . . turn it off.

If you empty it . . . fill it up.

If you lose it . . . find it yourself.

If you borrow it . . . put it back where it belongs.

If you move it . . . return it.

If you break it . . . replace it.

If it rings . . . answer it.

If it howls or meows . . . feed it or let it out.

If it cries . . . love it.

THANK YOU!

The Management

I'm Not the Only One Living Here

GOALS

Affective

To raise sensitivity to family members' needs

To get in touch with feelings about conflicting interests

Behavioral

To enhance communication with family members about needs

To practice cooperative behaviors

Cognitive

To develop awareness of how one's behaviors affect other family members

To explore changing perceptions about family life

To recognize one's own and others' needs when resources must be shared

MATERIALS

Drawing paper, one sheet per member

Colored markers or paint and paint brushes

Healthy snacks

GROUP SESSION

Opening Time (¼ session time)

1. Welcome the members back to group. Ask what concerns or issues they might have regarding confidentiality. Do the ground rules need revising, or are they working at this point?

2. Inquire what changes members might have made at home regarding being more responsible, according to the Home Rules discussed during the last session, and how that might have changed others' opinions of or behavior toward them.

Working Time (½ session time)

1. Discuss the idea that unless we live at home by ourselves, there are always other people to get along with and with whom we must share space:

   There are always ongoing conflicts between self-interest and the interests of family members. Each home/living space has personal space and shared space, and a need for sharing of other resources, such as parents' time, money, and family responsibilities. Sometimes there is one person you really have a problem with about a particular issue, and sometimes it is several people and an array of situations. We can't solve all of these problems at once, but we can look at one issue and try some group problem solving.

2. Invite group members to use the art materials to draw or paint a picture of the conflict that is bugging them the most at this point. At the bottom of the picture, have them write a title representative of the issue. For example: "The Big Bathroom Hassle," "Who Owns the Refrigerator?" "I Need Some Clean Clothes!" and "My Room Is My Room." Allow members to move around or lie on the floor to complete their pictures. They may talk to one another,

sing, or listen to music while drawing. You can circulate and serve as consultant, making sure they understand the task and draw a picture as instructed.

3. After a reasonable amount of time, have members bring their pictures to the group circle and explain their titles and situations. Invite members to give suggestions on how to solve each person's dilemma. Continue until all group members have shared and received support, encouragement, and ideas for how to tackle the situation. You may also give ideas about the situations, helping participants understand give-and-take. Emphasize that they aren't the only ones who live in the family and that their parents make decisions about certain issues that they may not agree with but that might be for the good of the whole family. For example, even though kids believe their bedrooms are their own private territory, parents usually see kids' rooms as part of the house, and house rules apply, such as not leaving food around.

4. Discuss the idea that sometimes parents make major changes in their own lives that affect everyone, and sometimes these decisions are not popular and may be misunderstood. For example:

A parent goes to graduate school, and that takes energy, money, and time from the children.

A parent's job requires moving to another area/state, uprooting teens from school, sports, and friends.

A parent decides that a child may not get involved in another sport or activity due to over-load—both the child's and the parent's.

Processing Time (¼ session time)

1. Ask at least one question from each of the four processing levels:

INTRAPERSONAL

Today we discussed situations that require give-and-take to get along with family members. What were you thinking and feeling as you drew your pictures and as you shared and helped other group members figure out how to deal with their situations?

INTERPERSONAL

What was it like for you to be a group member today as you shared and as you listened to and helped other group members?

What kinds of things are happening to our group? (Cohesion, sense of growing trust, helping one another)

NEW LEARNING

What new have you learned today, either from information and advice given to you or from what you heard given to someone else that might apply to you?

APPLICATION

What do you think, realistically, that you can do before the next session to improve your situation? Would you be willing to come back and share how your efforts went?

2. Thank group members for coming and give them a hope statement. Remind them of the day and time for the next session, then share the snacks.

Cutting Edge: Technology at Home

This session involves inviting group members to write editorials about their issues regarding technology use in their own homes. Writing the editorials could be one session, and then sharing and processing the writing and working out consensus-building approaches for group members to try at home could be another session. Another variation is to have them write a second editorial from their parents' perspective and then compare the two.

GOALS

Affective

To express feelings about having to share and be limited in using technological/electronic equipment at home

Behavioral

To experience writing out issues in editorial form

To listen to the experiences of other group members and be of help to them

Cognitive

To recognize personal issues as problems that affect other family members as well

To accept consensus building as a method of dealing with issues better than blaming, arguing, and constantly having to be in a "win-win" situation

MATERIALS

Notebook paper and pencils or pens

An editorial or two as a model of the type of writing expected. (You can get these from a newspaper or another published source, or write them yourself.)

Healthy snacks

GROUP SESSION

Opening Time (¼ session time)

1. Welcome the members back to group. Inquire what concerns they might have about the issue of confidentiality. Ask how the ground rules are holding up for them at this time and if anything needs to be added or changed.

2. Ask what members might have noticed about situations at home where they were faced with negotiating or making changes about use of space or other issues discussed during the last session. How did they deal with the situation, and how did they feel about it?

Working Time (½ session time)

1. Discuss the idea that because we have access to technology that wasn't even in existence a few decades or even years ago, technology is now a source of family conflict:

   Parents and children are faced with making decisions about the use of computer and Internet time, personal telephones and TVs for kids, surround-sound TVs, HDTV, WebTV, VCRs for family and individual use, boom-boxes for each child in the family, cell phones and beepers—and how all of this relates to "family time" issues. Major arguments arise when different family members want and/or need access when time and technology are limited. You may feel

very protective of your wants and needs, and develop strong negative feelings toward sib-
lings and parents who limit your use of these resources. At the same time, parents are
responsible for assisting ALL family members in sharing resources and getting their basic
needs met, and they must deal with the struggles between and among everyone.

2. Invite group members to participate in an activity for the purpose of getting in touch with the major issues going on regarding the use of technology in their homes. They are to pretend they have just been appointed the Editor-in-Chief of the *Teen Times,* a highly prestigious national newspaper that is read by both teens and their parents. In this position they have the opportunity to share their views in an editorial entitled "One Teen's Dilemma." The focus of the editorial is technology and whatever issue is bugging them the most. The article, no more than 200 words, must have a clear point and not be just a forum for griping and blaming.

3. Read a sample editorial or two to help members get an idea of what you expect, then give them a time limit and have them write their own. Circulate and help them work on their editorials if they want assistance.

4. After the writing period, reassemble the group and have them read their editorials aloud. After all have read, ask the following questions:

    What ideas, concepts, or issues did you hear running through all or almost all of the editorials? (Power struggles about wants/needs, alienation between/among two or more family members over the issues, ongoing hostility between/among family members, unresolved conflicts, and so forth)

    What feelings appeared to be present in all of the people involved in the editorials?

    What feelings appeared that were specific to a particular person?

5. Explain that, in a family as in any other group, disagreements need to be negotiated and the people involved should try to come to some kind of compromise. The people might have to give up some of what they want, but both also get some of what they want. This makes it a "win-win" situation instead of a "win-lose" situation, where one person gets everything and the other gives up everything. Discuss any positive, innovative ways parents or youth could resolve these sticky situations, share the resources, and so on.

Processing Time (¼ session time)

1. Ask at least one question from each of the four processing levels:

    INTRAPERSONAL

    What kinds of thoughts and feelings did you have as you wrote and listened to the editorials today about your and other members' problem situations?

    INTERPERSONAL

    How are you feeling about being a group member at this point—are there things about it that you are finding helpful?

    What have you noticed about the other group members today?

    NEW LEARNING

    What new ideas or behaviors have you learned today that you might be able to put in practice to get through some of your own problems?

    APPLICATION

    Which of these ideas would you be willing to try before the next session to take a risk and make a difference in your situation?

2. Thank members for coming to group and give them a hope statement. Remind them of the day and time for the next session, then share the snacks.

Teeter-Totter: Balancing Family, Friends, School, and Other Responsibilities

Many young people have not lived long enough to have experienced the negative effects of "overdoing it." When they are involved in reinforcing activities, it is difficult for them to believe in giving up something for the sake of balance. This activity uses physical laws of nature to illustrate that things, machines, and bodies need balance to "work right" and that if we overload ourselves we won't function well and can break down.

GOALS

Affective

To discuss feelings relating to balancing the increasing responsibilities of the teen years

To share a lighter moment during the group by having a fun activity

Behavioral

To work out and help others work out how to balance their stressful activities

Cognitive

To increase awareness of self and others as users of family resources and participants in family responsibilities

MATERIALS

For each group member, a dowel rod or section of quarter-round molding about 20 inches long. (I found rods of clear plastic for about 10 cents each at a plastics manufacturer.)

Yarn or string

Cardboard or posterboard

Marking pen and a pair of scissors for each group member

A paper punch

Clothespins (about 30)

Healthy snacks

GROUP SESSION

Opening Time (¼ session time)

1. Welcome the members back to group. Inquire what concerns they might have about the issue of confidentiality. Ask whether the ground rules need any adjustment.

2. Ask what changes in their behavior they were able to make because of the editorials they wrote during the last session. What new ideas do they have for dealing with conflicts about use of technology/electronics?

Working Time (½ session time)

1. Invite the group members to discuss some of their frustrations with balancing all of the things they do and want to do in the following areas:

    School: Homework, long-term projects, keeping lockers in order, managing books and other materials, getting help when needed

Home: Household jobs, baby-sitting younger siblings, yard work, keeping bedrooms in order, doing laundry, helping parents do extra things, going to and helping with family get-togethers, buying and caring for clothes

Friends: Where to go, when to go, what friends to go with, and how to get there; money to spend with and on friends; managing problems with friends and ex-friends; doing things you want to do and dealing with pressure to do things you don't want to do

Work: Finding a job, working more or less, problems at work with bosses or other workers. (If your group is underage for work, discuss baby-sitting, lawn mowing, dog walking, and so on.)

Sports or hobbies: Horseback riding, golf, football, tennis, cross-country, baseball, hockey, music lessons and performances, art lessons and shows, and so forth (finding time to do enjoyable things and still meet your responsibilities, becoming swamped by adding more and more sports/activities to an overloaded schedule)

Discuss the fact that our bodies, minds, and spirits can take only so much, and if we push ourselves beyond what we can deal with we can become ill in many different ways: exhaustion, depression, physical ailments, psychological problems, burnout.

2. Pass out the balancing rods and pieces of cardboard or posterboard, scissors, and marking pens. Instruct group members to cut out several different geometric shapes (circles, squares, triangles, rectangles, polygons, and so forth). You can have some models to show them. Each person should cut out a total of about 10. On each shape have them write one major area: school, home, friends, work, sports, or other (whatever other categories you come up with) and a couple words describing the exact issue relating to that area. They then write one number representing where they are on a scale of 1 to 10, with 1 being the lowest and 10 being the highest, to indicate how important the topic is in terms of time, energy, and personal resources. For example:

Home: Chores for allowance—6

Sports: Working my horses—9

School: Math classes—10

Work: Baby-sitting—4

Friends: Hanging out at the mall—7

Home: Doing stuff with family—6

Sports: Basketball practice and games—10

School: Working on school newspaper—7

Friends: Bringing cards or hobby items to school to look at and trade—8

Have group members punch a hole at the top of each of their shapes, then thread a piece of string or yarn about 8 inches long through each hole. (They will tie each shape to the balancing rod so the shape hangs down 3 or 4 inches.)

3. After they get their shapes cut out, written on, punched, and tied, instruct them to form pairs. One at a time, each person in the pair attaches a clothespin to the bottom of any cardboard shapes numbered 9 or 10. Then the person must decide how he or she is going to tie all of the shapes on either end of the rod so the rod stays evenly balanced when the person balances it on a single finger. When added, the numbers on each side must be nearly equal—for example, there can't be a total of 98 points on one side and 37 on the other. If the rod tips to one side or the other, the person must figure out how to subtract or add points to the shapes to make the rod balance.

4. When both members of the pair have attempted this procedure, stop and discuss the idea that the rod represents the physical and mental self. If a person's self is out of balance, physical or psychological distress will result. What this tells the person is to review and

adjust his or her investment of energy and resources to keep from getting frustrated and burned out. Ask the following questions:

What did you like least about having to get your life "in balance"?

What did you like most about working out your balance?

What does "working it out" mean to you?

What changes do you think you might need to make?

How about your partner—what changes did you notice that he or she didn't notice or mention that you think that person needs to work on?

What is the first step you need to take to get going on making things balance better in your life?

How frustrating is it for you to think about giving up things you like to do because you can't handle everything?

Processing Time (¼ session time)

1. Ask at least one question from each of the four levels of processing:

   INTRAPERSONAL

   What were you thinking and feeling today as you worked on getting in touch with the important issues in your life and getting them "in balance"?

   INTERPERSONAL

   What did you notice about other group members as they were trying to get the idea of balance going for them?

   NEW LEARNING

   What new ideas might you have from being involved in this activity?

   APPLICATION

   What would you be willing to do between now and the next session to reduce a little stress in your life and give yourself the gift of more balance?

2. Thank group members for coming and remind them that the next session is the last "working session" of the group. The last session will be a review of learning and goal setting for the future. Give them hope statement, remind them of the day and time for the next session, and share the snacks.

The Gifts I Bring

GOALS

Affective

To experience altruism and generosity toward family and friends

Behavioral

To learn how to be of service to others for the sake of service, not for what one receives in return

Cognitive

To recognize other people's needs, dilemmas, and problems, and be able to empathize and offer help

To learn what the concept of "giving support" means

MATERIALS

Empathy Leads and Situations (Handout 12)

Healthy snacks

GROUP SESSION

Opening Time (¼ session time)

1. Welcome the members back to group. Inquire what concerns they might have about the issue of confidentiality. Do any of the ground rules need work?

2. Ask:

    What did you notice about balancing your schedule and what might need to be changed for better balance?

    How have the changes helped or hurt your stress level?

    Have you noticed things that might need to be added, instead of taken away, for you to have better balance?

Working Time (½ session time)

1. Discuss the idea that as the group draws to a close, you would like to invite members to use some of their new ideas and skills to help other people as well as themselves. In order to get along at home, giving and taking is the important balance. Today they are invited to analyze situations that they could choose to become involved in to help someone else. (In other words, "What goes around, comes around.")

2. Pass out the Empathy Leads and Situations (Handout 12). Share the idea that empathy statements are a way to show someone else that you are 100 percent paying attention to what the person is saying or doing and that you want to give the gift of letting the person know you have listened, understand, and care.

3. Explain that empathy statements have two parts, a content part and a feeling part. Read the examples from the Empathy Leads and Situations handout. Have them use the empathy leads to create statements for the first four situations. The last item suggests that the group relate some situations that have actually occurred or are likely to occur. For each situation, they use an empathy statement and tell how else they could help the person.

4. Ask the following questions:

How could using empathy statements and offering to help your family members make a difference in the feelings among family members?

Even if you just use the empathy statements by themselves in situations where another person may or may not need help, what changes do you think might occur in your relationship with that person?

What would it feel like to you to have others make empathy statements to you?

5. Have the group members each share a brief situation that is going on with them now, at school or home. After each member shares his or her situation, the other group members make one or more empathy statements to that group member. After all have shared, ask, "Now, how does it feel to have others recognize your feelings about a situation and share that with you?"

Processing Time (¼ session time)

1. Ask at least one question from each of the four processing levels:

INTRAPERSONAL

What feelings did you experience today as you gave and received empathy statements?

What did you think about using this kind of technique to give a gift of help to others?

INTERPERSONAL

What have you noticed about the group lately? Anything surprising?

NEW LEARNING

What new ideas do you have today to fuel your search for better communication and relationships in your family?

APPLICATION

What would you be willing to make a commitment to doing with empathy statements between now and the next session?

2. Give group members a hope statement and explain that during the last part of the next session, it's party time! Ask what group members would like to do to celebrate. Thank them for coming, remind them of the next session's day and time, and share the snacks.

Empathy Leads and Situations

1. It looks like you feel _____ because _____ .

2. You must feel _____ because _____ .

3. I imagine you're feeling _____ because _____ .

4. It sounds like you feel _____ because _____ .

5. I wonder if you're feeling _____ because _____ .

6. Could it be that you're feeling _____ because _____ ?

SITUATION 1

You get home from school, and your mom has just arrived from the grocery and has many bags of groceries and other household supplies in the car. You feel like running into the house and turning on your favorite after-school TV program, but you recognize that she could use some help. You decide it would be the kind thing to do to use an empathy statement and then offer to help her, so you say _____ .

SITUATION 2

Your little brother, Shawn, age 18 months, has just messed his diaper something awful. You and your dad are taking care of him and watching the ball game together while your mom goes to night school at the university. Your dad has worked really hard that day cleaning out the whole garage and getting things in the yard ready for winter. He falls asleep watching the ball game. You'd like to wake him up and tell him Shawn needs his diaper changed because you definitely don't like the job. But you make a silent empathy statement to your snoring papa and take Shawn to the bathroom for a scrubdown. What empathy statement do you make to your dad?

SITUATION 3

Your older sister, not your favorite family member to begin with, is going to a BIG dance with a guy she is crazy about and has wanted to date for a long time. She has a lot to do to get ready for the dance and is running late. She hasn't eaten all day and says she is starved and her stomach is really getting upset. Your mom is ironing your sister's dress and doing other things for her. So you use an empathy statement and then offer to get your sister a sandwich or some soup so she won't go to the dance with an upset stomach from not eating all day. What empathy statement do you make to your sister?

SITUATION 4

It's your brother's turn to clean up after dinner. He has a bad cut on his hand and doesn't want to put his hand in the dishwater because the cut will hurt. You use an empathy statement and offer to help him. What exactly do you say?

OPEN SITUATION

Come up with your own situations, then develop your own empathy statements in response. If there are other ways you could help the person in the situation, explain.

That's a Wrap

GOALS

Affective

To experience the loss of the group as it has been

To feel satisfaction for progress made toward personal goals

Behavioral

To celebrate the group's hard work and changes group members have made

To say good-bye

Cognitive

To review what has been learned and practiced throughout the life of the group

To think about continuing to work toward personal goals and supporting other group members in the future

To recognize when to ask for help dealing with a major family issue

MATERIALS

A "magic wand," homemade or purchased at a costume or toy store

Whatever treats group members decided on during the last session for their celebration

GROUP SESSION

Opening Time (¼ session time)

1. Welcome the members back to group. Inquire what concerns they might have about the issue of confidentiality or the ground rules at this last session. Remind them that confidentiality extends even after the group is over.

2. Ask:

    How did it go for you this week, using empathy statements and helping out family members?

    What did you feel like when you used this new skill?

    How did family members react?

    How have the attitudes or feelings of family members changed toward you at this time?

Working Time (½ session time)

1. Discuss the idea that as the group draws to a close, you would like to invite members to think through the sessions one by one and share a "magic moment" or two with the rest of the group. Your magic moment would be a special time when:

    You realized something very special about yourself or others that has made a difference, a change in your life, in the way you do things

    You experienced very special, new, or different feelings toward yourself or someone else

    You practiced some new behavior you learned in the group with a family member or friend, and it made a difference

    You have a new attitude about something as a result of being a member of this group

2. Review the topics of each session, starting at the beginning. Mention any special event that might have occurred during a given session to help jog their memories. After describing each session, ask if anyone had his or her magic moment because of or during that session. That person may hold the magic wand and share with the group.

> Session 1—Getting Started
>
> Using the gears model to think about how thinking, feeling, and behaving are different and having each member describe a situation at home that he or she could work to improve
>
> Session 2—Power Struggles
>
> Using "family sculpts" to help each member clarify and show other members a situation that happens at home
>
> Session 3—My Freedoms and Responsibilities
>
> Reading the "Home Rules" and thinking about getting a family's-eye-view of tasks that need to be accomplished to keep things running smoothly
>
> Session 4—I'm Not the Only One Living Here
>
> Drawing a current family conflict to help us give one another feedback on how to get past "stuck points"
>
> Session 5—Cutting Edge: Technology at Home
>
> Writing editorials to focus in a grown-up way on a situation that bugged us
>
> Session 6—Teeter-Totter: Balancing Family, Friends, School, and Other Responsibilities
>
> Making a weighted scale to show which responsibilities and activities need to be rearranged, limited, or eliminated
>
> Session 7—The Gifts I Bring
>
> Learning to be empathic and sensitive to other people's difficulties and thinking of ways to help them out—a mature, responsible way to be

Processing Time (¼ session time)

1. Ask the following questions:

> If you were starting the group all over again, what would you make sure that you talked about and got help with?
>
> If you could make a difference in the work of one group member, who would that be? Tell him or her.
>
> How could you be a support to other group members in the future?
>
> How can you tell if you have a major issue going on with family members that you need help with? Where can you go to get help dealing with these situations?

2. Thank the group as a whole for participating, then thank and share an encouragement statement with each member. For example:

> Krissi, I appreciate your efforts to put into practice many of the new skills and ideas you learned. My hope for you is that you continue to use and practice them.
>
> Matt, you have grown a lot in being more aware of others' needs and less insistent on your own way. My hope for you is that you continue to make good choices in this area.

3. Explain any plans you have for follow-up—maybe set a time in a month to have members bring a brown-bag or cafeteria lunch to your office to give support and see how everyone is doing on using their new skills.

4. Share the party treats and celebrate!

The Brain Laundromat: Cognitive Coping Skills _____

Children have very little understanding of the "whys" of their behavior and feelings, yet early adolescence brings dramatic changes in the intensity and expression of both. With limited understanding and control over their own cognitive and affective functioning, life is often very confusing. It is therefore easy to understand why young adolescents often feel battered about emotionally, experiencing intense feelings because of their rapid physical changes and perplexing roller-coaster emotions, as well as in response to complicated social messages from peers and parents.

Although young adolescents have experienced life for only a few years (relative to the adult lifespan), their patterns of behavior, attitudes, and habitual emotions are often already present. I do not subscribe to the deficit model of adolescent development—that maladjustment and significant emotional and psychological trauma occur universally—but believe like many others (e.g., Newcomb, 1966) that adolescence is a time of excitement, joy, hope, uncertainty, and positive expectations. There are, however, large numbers of adolescents from families where the adults are unable to provide stable emotional, social, financial, and moral support. With some, antisocial behavior is becoming established, and negative reactions to adult attempts to teach self-control, positive motivation, and prosocial skills result in a pattern of predelinquent and delinquent behavior (DeLange, Lanham, & Barton, 1981; Dupper & Krishef, 1993; Guerra & Slaby, 1990).

This group experience deals broadly with established negative thinking and behaving patterns in young adolescents. It is a group that has the potential for greatly improving youths' thinking and behavior, but it also calls for a leader experienced in group counseling who can deal with the variety of issues presented. For the experience to be successful, the leader must be well-grounded in group counseling skills and possess an in-depth understanding of and ability to apply activities based on cognitive-behavioral theory.

The research literature at this point is replete with positive outcome studies of cognitive-behavioral therapy with children and adolescents experiencing a wide range of maladaptive behaviors. The approach has been successful in addressing anger (Deffenbacher, Lynch, & Oetting, 1996; Feindler, Mariott, & Iwata, 1984), isolation (Edelson & Rose, 1981), impulsivity (Kendall & Braswell, 1985), aggression (Lochman, Nelson, & Sims, 1981), depression (Reynolds & Coats, 1986; Wilkes, Belsher, Rush, & Frank, 1994), test anxiety (D'Alelio & Murray, 1981), and adolescent pregnancy (Schinke, Blythe, & Gilchrist, 1981).

Both individual and group counseling approaches appear to be successful in modifying negative attitudes and behaviors via cognitive-behavioral techniques. As well, significant individual change has been measured through the use of small-group therapy (Sarri & Galinsky, 1985; Schopler & Galinsky, 1985). The sessions here employ researched cognitive-behavioral techniques and focus on helping young adolescents learn cognitive coping skills, practice those behavioral skills, and participate in an affective experience with peers as they work toward group and individual goals.

The sessions in this group are as follows:

Session 1—Getting Started

Session 2—ABC's of Feelings

Session 3—Garbage In/Garbage Out: My Responsibility for My Feelings

Session 4—How to Get Your Brain to Work Right

Session 5—No Neggies

Session 6—Self-as-Model: I Can Do This!

Session 7—Healing Painful Words

Session 8—That's a Wrap

GROUP GOALS

1. To facilitate development of a trusting, supportive environment in which members feel secure to risk and share

2. To promote the group norms of becoming a supportive, encouraging person

3. To raise awareness of the power of thinking to determine feelings and behaviors

4. To learn the ABC's of where and how we control feelings and behaviors

5. To recognize personal responsibility for thoughts and feelings, and for making changes based on this recognition

6. To understand different types of self-talk

7. To become aware of how self-talk begins, is maintained, and can be changed

8. To learn cognitive coping skills as a technique to change negative self-talk

9. To identify a target behavior to change

10. To learn and practice how to role-play as a method to enhance learning that can be transferred to experiences outside the group

11. To learn, practice, and apply training in coping skills to replace negative habits and behaviors

12. To review the group experience and set goals for future personal work

SELECTION AND OTHER ISSUES

Choose youth with a variety of established problems that appear to be directly influenced by negative attitudes and behaviors. These problems may relate to academic work, family issues, interpersonal problems, and intrapersonal conflicts. Make certain that every candidate for the group has a problem situation that is influenced by negative cognitions; you will be using cognitive counseling techniques to help group members make changes that will affect these problems.

Keep in mind that the youth selected must bring some positive aspects to the group so members have the opportunity to learn from one another. Do not load the group with generally low-functioning youth, aggressive youth, or youth currently in major conflicts at home or school. Because the group involves cognitive therapy, it does not lend itself to youth whose cognitive development is not sufficiently mature to deal with the abstract thinking required.

An individual selection interview is absolutely essential to determine the motivation level, clarity of goals, willingness to self-disclose, and ability of students to use this intervention at this time. This type of counseling cannot be successful unless the clients are at a "reachable moment." At this individual interview, explain (in language the students can understand) that the purpose of the group is to work on problems maintained by irrational thinking and negative self-talk. Help each potential group member identify a behavior to work on in the group. With your approval, group members may change the target situation from the one chosen during pregroup selection, but it must be a behavior maintained by irrational thinking and negative self-talk.

Choose six to eight group members. The mix might include the following:

A youth who is doing well academically but who describes his or her abilities to meet opposite-sex friends negatively (negative self-talk) and who has a high desire to be more socially involved

A youth with moderate academic success but who has high anxiety about tests and is concerned this will prevent future academic success

A youth who has difficulty making decisions and sticking with them

A youth who has many friends but who cannot sustain friendships because he or she is unaware of having an abrasive communication style or is unwilling to deal with it

A youth who did well academically in elementary school but can't seem to deal with the transition to and added responsibilities of middle school

A youth who appears to be going through several losses, which seem to compound a sense of frustration (not a clinically depressed youth, however)

A youth who has a "temper" and is not accepting responsibility for his or her own negative responses to anger situations

REFERENCES AND SELECTED RESOURCES FOR PROFESSIONALS

D'Alelio, W. A., & Murray, E. J. (1981). Cognitive therapy for test anxiety. *Cognitive Therapy and Research, 5,* 299–307.

Deffenbacher, J. L., Lynch, R. S., & Oetting, E. R. (1996). Anger reduction in early adolescents. *Journal of Counseling Psychology, 43,* 149–157.

DeLange, J. M., Lanham, S. L., & Barton, J. A. (1981). Social skills training for juvenile delinquents: Behavioral skill training and cognitive techniques. In D. Upper & S. M. Ross (Eds.), *Behavioral group therapy.* Champaign, IL: Research Press.

Dupper, D. R., & Krishef, C. H. (1993). School-based social-cognitive skills training for middle school students with school behavior problems. *Children and Youth Services Review, 15*(2), 131–143.

Edelson, J. L., & Rose, S. D. (1981). Investigation into the efficacy of short term group social skill training for socially isolated children. *Child Behavior Therapy, 3*(2), 1–16.

Feindler, E. L., Marriott, S. A., & Iwata, M. (1984). Group anger-control training for junior high school delinquents. *Cognitive Therapy and Research, 8,* 299–311.

Forman, S. G. (1993). *Coping skills interventions for children and adolescents.* San Francisco: Jossey-Bass.

Guerra, N. G., & Slaby, R. G. (1990). Cognitive mediators of aggression in adolescent offenders. *Developmental Psychology, 26,* 269–277.

Kendall, P. C., & Braswell, L. (1985). *Cognitive-based therapy for impulsive children.* New York: Guilford.

Lochman, J. E. (1985). Effects of different treatment lengths in cognitive behavioral interventions with aggressive boys. *Child Psychiatry and Human Development, 16,* 45–56.

Lochman, J. E., Nelson, W. M., & Sims, J. P. (1981). A cognitive-behavioral program for use with aggressive children. *Journal of Clinical Child Psychology, 10,* 146–148.

Nelson, W. M., & Birkimer, J. (1978). Role of self-instruction and self-reinforcement in the modification of impulsivity. *Journal of Consulting and Clinical Psychology, 46,* 183.

Newcomb, M. D. (1996). Adolescence: Pathologizing a normal process. *The Counseling Psychologist, 24*(3), 482–490.

Reynolds, W. M., & Coats, K. I. (1986). A comparison of cognitive-behavioral therapy and relaxation training for the treatment of depression in adolescents. *Journal of Consulting and Clinical Psychology, 54,* 653–660.

Sarri, R. L., & Galinsky, M. J. (1985). A conceptual framework for group development. In M. Sundel, P. Glasser, R. L. Sarri, & M. Vinter (Eds.), *Individual change through small groups* (2nd ed.). New York: Macmillan.

Schinke, S. T., Blythe, B. J., & Gilchrist, L. D. (1981). Cognitive-behavioral prevention of adolescent pregnancy. *Journal of Counseling Psychology, 28,* 451–454.

Schopler, J. J., & Galinsky, M. J. (1985). The open-ended group. In M. Sundel, P. Glasser, R. L. Sarri, & R. Vinter (Eds.), *Individual change through small groups* (2nd ed.). New York: Macmillan.

Wilkes, T. C. R., Belsher, G., Rush, A. J., & Frank, E. (Eds.). (1994). *Cognitive therapy for depressed adolescents.* New York: Guilford.

Getting Started

GOALS

Affective

To begin to feel comfortable with the group format

Behavioral

To work with other group members to develop ground rules

To have a fun experience getting to know one another

Cognitive

To understand the purpose and goals of the group

To learn what confidentiality is and understand its importance

To learn to discriminate thinking, feeling, and behaving

To set some initial target goals to work toward during the group

MATERIALS

Limits of Confidentiality sign (see Appendix A, page 270)

Easel pad or posterboard and marker

Thinking-Feeling-Behaving Gears (see Appendix A, page 271)

Colored markers

A large sheet of newsprint

Healthy snacks (such as fruit, crackers, juice, raisins)

GROUP SESSION

Opening Time

For sessions after this first one, Opening Time will take up about one-fourth of the typical 40- to 50-minute session time, or about 10 minutes. For this session, however, you will need to plan on more time to discuss confidentiality, develop ground rules, and conduct a getting-acquainted activity. See the book's introduction for some ideas on how to schedule this extra time.

---

1. Welcome the boys and girls, and go over the name, purpose, and general goals of the group. Stress that the focus of this group is on identifying a "target behavior" that is causing a problem and on learning a new way to think, feel, and behave regarding that situation. Emphasize that each member is expected to identify and work toward a personal goal during the group experience.

2. Thoroughly discuss confidentiality (the "no-blab" rule): What is said and done in the group stays in the group. Give examples of things adults or peers outside the group might say to pressure group members to share what happens in group. For example:

I'm your dad, and I want to know what you are telling those other kids in that group.

What do you guys say about your friends that you aren't supposed to tell?

What do you mean, it's confidential? That's not true—you can tell if you want to.

After members are clear on the meaning of confidentiality, share the Limits of Confidentiality sign (either as a handout or poster) and discuss: Let group members know you are bound by the confidentiality rule but that as the leader you are required to tell about what goes on in the group if you think someone will do harm to self or others, if someone says anything about child abuse or criminal activity going on, or if a judge orders you to turn over information.

3. Discuss the basic ground rules you have decided on for your group and request the group's input in developing a few more that would enhance their comfort in sharing with one another. For example:

Take turns.

Everyone has the right to "pass" (not share unless that's comfortable).

Agree to disagree (no put-downs).

Come on time.

Don't move on until the group agrees on the ground rules. Write or have the group write the rules on an easel pad or piece of posterboard and have each member sign the document to show agreement. You can then post these rules every session.

---

4. To get acquainted, have members form dyads and share the following information; remind them they have the right to "pass" if they don't want to respond. Each person will share with the group whatever information about the partner he or she remembers or chooses to share.

My name, and what I like or don't like about it

The season of the year I like best

My favorite pizza topping

The best movie I have ever seen

The most important person in my life, other than a family member

What I like best about being in this group

What I worry most about being in this group

What I hope to accomplish by being in the group

Working Time

Working Time will take half of a typical session, or about 20 to 25 minutes.

---

1. Discuss the idea that this group experience is designed to help group members gain control over some life situation that is causing them distress. The way this will happen is that each group member will share a target behavior that is causing problems. DO NOT ASK THEM TO SHARE THEIR SITUATIONS YET. Since you have already discussed the target behavior and the purpose of the group with each member during the selection process, you don't need to repeat your explanation at this point.

2. Discuss the idea that we have many "parts" to us, but that the functions of thinking, feeling, and behaving are important ones we must focus on to keep our lives in balance. Show the group the Thinking-Feeling-Behaving Gears and explain that these parts are like gears that

must work together to keep a clock or machine working right. In your own words, convey the following ideas:

Thinking, feeling, and behaving all work together to keep us mentally healthy. If one "gear"—our thoughts, our feelings, or our actions—is not working right, is out of alignment with the other gears, nothing works right. So, if you are thinking negative thoughts, your thinking isn't working right, and your behavior and feelings won't work right either. If your behavior is not right, then your feelings and thinking will not be right or helpful to you. If your feelings are negative and hurtful, then your thinking and behaving won't be right.

3. Share with the members that the first step to making changes is to be sure everyone can tell how thinking, feeling, and behaving are different. Give some examples of what you mean and ask group members to add their own ideas:

    Thinking: Scheming, imagining, calculating, dreaming, organizing

    Feeling: Angry, afraid, joyful, guilty, worried, irritated, hurt, loving

    Behaving: Screaming, erasing, lifting, cussing out, dating, studying, shopping, driving

4. Pass out the colored markers and sheet of newsprint. Invite group members to think of and illustrate their own way of expressing the thinking-feeling-behaving relationship. They could use something like a train, with the engine representing the thinking part (write thinking words on it); the cars, the behaviors (write behavior words on them), and the wheels, emotions (write feeling words on them). They could choose a butterfly, computer, car, tree, whatever—as long as it has related parts. They must work together, making it a group project, and they can move around the room, sit on the floor, or use a table while making their picture. Allow at least half of the working time for this activity.

5. Then, in the group circle, have members talk about what they drew. Ask them to explain how they chose the metaphor they chose and how they made decisions about what they drew. Praise them for their work and ideas, and hang the drawing up if possible. If they depicted the brain, they might want to name the group after their picture—for example, "The Geniuses" or "The Brain Drainers."

6. Discuss the idea that now they have the "right handles" to put on goals for their behavior self-change projects. Invite them to share the target behaviors they want to work on, one by one. As members speak, help them clarify exactly what they are going to aim for by reframing their statements as cognitive-behavioral goals. For example:

    Randall: I want to stop being so afraid of tests so I can do better on tests 'cause I'm not so scared.

    Leader: So let me check to see if I understand you clearly. You want to stop saying negative things to yourself about tests and your test-taking skills and replace those negative thoughts with coping skills that will help you pass tests with less anxiety and more confidence—is that right?

    Judy: I hate junior high because it is so confusing—there are so many changes, and nobody cares if you understand or not. I hate changing classes all the time, and I never know where I'm supposed to be.

    Leader: Help me understand your goal here. It sounds like you want to stop feeling confused and frustrated about the many and changing responsibilities, such as classes in different parts of a large building and many teachers with different personalities and requirements, and you want to get a better handle on how things work around here so you can get organized and feel more a part of it. Is that correct?

Terry:	I have a temper because my dad is Irish and they all have tempers, so it's not my fault, but it gets me in trouble. I don't like being in trouble all the time—I can't help it, but I want to stop it.
Leader:	It sounds to me like you are really bugged by your way of expressing anger and that you end up in trouble, losing privileges and such. You are wanting to get control of your temper and stop blaming other people and situations for your loss of control over your behavior and emotions—am I correct?
Rashad:	I feel so crummy all the time because my best friend died last year in that car wreck that the three ninth and tenth graders died in, and then my best gramma died this summer, and now I don't have anyone who really listens to me. All I think about is that I don't have any friends now, and I can't do anything to get new ones. So I don't want to feel crummy all the time.
Leader:	Since you've lost two very special people in your life, you are feeling alone and like there is no one who really hears you. Perhaps your feelings include being down in the dumps, helplessness, anger at others and at yourself, and maybe some grief that is still there, and you want to put some names on your feelings and get some of them processed. True?

7. Explain:

Now we have identified what you want to work on and have made a commitment to the group to make the effort, you can all get started learning some new ways of dealing with the problems that are making your life unpleasant and a hassle at this point. Thank you for being so up-front and mature to put your issues right out there and take responsibility for your part in maintaining them.

Processing Time

Processing Time will take one-quarter of a typical session, or about 10 minutes.

1. Ask at least one question from each of the four processing levels:

INTRAPERSONAL

Our first session together brought a lot of new ideas and sharing on goals. While you were learning about thinking-feeling-behaving and hearing the goals group members want to work on, what were you thinking, or what were you feeling inside yourself?

INTERPERSONAL

Group is different than a classroom. You have more opportunity to be part of the group and listened to and given positive support by other group members and me as the leader. What was it like for you today to come and be a part of this group?

NEW LEARNING

What new ideas, thoughts, surprises, frustrations, or other feelings do you have about being a group member today?

APPLICATION

Between now and the next session, you may have some different kinds of thoughts, feelings, and behaviors. Who might be willing to come back next time and share their new ideas or attitudes about their situations?

2. Thank group members for coming and give them a hope statement like the following example:

> You have shared some very personal ideas and feelings today, and set some goals to work toward. I have a great deal of hope and belief that each of you can reach your goals and can support and encourage other group members along the way.

Remind them of the next session's day and time, then enjoy the snacks.

ABC's of Feelings

GOALS

Affective

To experience how it is to take personal responsibility for choosing one's own feelings

Behavioral

To share situations with peers while learning to discriminate events, beliefs/attitudes about events, and resulting feelings

Cognitive

To learn the "ABC approach" to understanding where feelings come from

To begin to recognize personal responsibility for feelings and behaviors

MATERIALS

ABC's of Where Feelings Come From (Handout 13)

Proof That People and Events Don't Cause Feelings (Handout 14)

Healthy snacks

GROUP SESSION

Opening Time (¼ session time)

1. Welcome the group members to the second session and invite them to share any concerns or questions about confidentiality. Ask if they have any additions or changes they would like to make to the ground rules.

2. Briefly review the first session, regarding thinking-feeling-behaving discrimination, and ask if they have ideas or comments to share about anything that might have changed with regard to their target behaviors.

Working Time (½ session time)

1. Share the ABC's of Where Feelings Come From (Handout 13). Ask these questions:

   Your friend takes a CD of yours and breaks it. This makes you feel absolutely furious. True or false?

   Your mom won't let you stay up until 1:00 on Saturday night watching TV with your friend, who is sleeping over. This makes you angry and embarrassed in front of your friend. True or false?

   Your teacher gives a surprise test. You forgot to study the chapter the night before, so your grade goes from a B to a C, and this makes you guilty and outraged. True or false?

   Your girlfriend/boyfriend accepts a date with someone else. This makes you feel like breaking rocks. True or false?

2. Let the members give true or false guesses, then tell them that all of these statements are false because in each case the situation or other person doesn't cause the feeling—what the person THINKS about the situation causes the feelings. Discuss Part 1 of Handout 13, going through the ABC's of each situation. Next discuss Part 2, having group members substitute changed beliefs or attitudes.

3. Share Handout 14, Proof That People and Events Don't Cause Feelings. Discuss Part 1, the situation of moving and how different people perceive the situation in different ways.

4. Go through Part 2, the question-and-answer examples, asking what group members think about each. Let members give other situations that appear to be caused by someone or something else, and invite others to refute this.

5. Next ask group members to volunteer to read the statements under Part 3 aloud. After they have done so, invite them to describe their own situations and feelings by saying, "I feel _____ , and I choose to feel _____ ." Discuss how it feels to take responsibility for your own feelings instead of blaming them on someone or something else.

It is important for you to go first and model this step. Reinforce the group members highly during this exercise! If some remain "nonbelievers" at this point, allow them to do so.

Processing Time (¼ session time)

1. Ask at least one question from each of the four processing levels:

INTRAPERSONAL

This was a new idea today: that we are the ones responsible for our feelings. Pretty heavy duty stuff, because we can't blame others for making us miserable if we make ourselves miserable! What were you thinking and feeling today during our session?

INTERPERSONAL

What did you notice about the group today? Did anything surprise you about our group?

NEW LEARNING

What new ideas or feelings did you have today because of what we talked about and shared?

APPLICATION

What do you think you could do with this new way of thinking about things during the time until our next session? Don't go changing everything in your life around until we learn more about this! (Your suggestion that group members not proceed actually may encourage them to do so.)

2. Thank group members warmly, praise them for participating in an important session, and give them a hope statement. Remind them of the day and time for the next session, then share the snacks.

ABC's of Where Feelings Come From

PART 1

A = EVENT

1. A friend breaks your CD.

2. Your mom won't let you stay up late.

3. Your boyfriend/girlfriend goes out with someone else.

4. A teacher gives an unannounced test; this affects your grade.

B = YOUR BELIEF OR ATTITUDE ABOUT THE EVENT

1. My friend is really mean, and I should never lend him/her my stuff.

2. My mom is just trying to control me.

3. My boyfriend/girlfriend is a jerk for going out with someone else.

4. Mrs. Johnson is unfair and mean for giving a pop quiz.

C = FEELINGS AS A RESULT OF BELIEFS

1. I am furious, and I'd like to smash his/her CD's, too!

2. I resent my mom, and I can't stand it that she won't let me stay up late.

3. I hate my boyfriend/girlfriend for not being truthful when he/she promised not to go out with anyone else.

4. I feel miserable and defeated because Mrs. Johnson gave us a pop quiz.

PART 2

What if you change your beliefs or attitudes about these events?
Your feelings and behaviors will probably change, too!

1. Change "My friend is mean" to "My friend is clumsy."

   Then I would feel: Not furious, just irritated

2. Change "My mom is controlling" to "My mom wants me to rest."

   Then I would feel: Not resentful, just bugged

3. Change "My boyfriend/girlfriend is a jerk" to "My boyfriend/girlfriend isn't really committed."

   Then I would feel: Not hateful or crushed, just hurt

4. Change "My teacher is mean" to "She could have warned us."

   Then I would feel: Not miserable, just guilty and blue

Proof That People and Events Don't Cause Feelings

PART 1

Suppose 100 eighth graders go home tonight and their parents say the family is going to move 1,000 miles away to another state. Does this situation CAUSE these kids' feelings? If it caused their feelings, all 100 would feel the same, wouldn't they? BUT . . .

20 of the 100 eighth graders feel devastated, horrible, and like their world is crashing in.

20 more feel like it is a real bummer, but not crushed or horrible.

20 more feel like it might be OK—they could adjust to it.

20 more think it would be fun to move and get new friends, a fresh start in school, a cool house.

10 more think it would be exciting to live in XYZ City and be able to go to school by the ocean and have lots of interesting things to do and see.

10 more are absolutely ecstatic! It's the best thing that ever happened, moving to XYZ City! It's the greatest adventure of their lives! Wow!

PART 2

Q: Do red lights CAUSE a driver to stop a car?

A: No, what drivers believe about red lights does.

Q: Do tests CAUSE you to get panicky?

A: No, what you think about them causes panic.

Q: Do doctors' offices CAUSE you to get anxious?

A: No, what you think about doctors and possible pain does.

Q: Do bullies CAUSE you to get scared?

A: No, what you think about what they do causes it.

Q: Do computer games CAUSE you to feel excited?

A: No, what you think about them causes it.

Q: Do dogs CAUSE you to be afraid?

A: No, what you think about dogs causes you to be afraid or not.

PART 3

IT IS INACCURATE TO SAY . . .	SAY . . .
1. Josh made me mad!	I choose to be mad.
2. Mom makes me furious!	I choose to be upset.
3. My sister makes me miserable.	I choose to be miserable.
4. Homework makes me sick!	I choose to dislike homework.
5. The coach makes me feel defeated.	I choose to feel defeated.
6. Tyler made me feel humiliated.	I choose to be humiliated.
7. My boyfriend/girlfriend makes me frustrated.	I choose to be frustrated.
8. School makes me feel confused.	I choose to feel confused.
9. My dad makes me feel guilty.	I choose to feel guilty.
10. Rainy days make me feel depressed.	I choose to feel depressed.

Garbage In/Garbage Out: My Responsibility for My Feelings

GOALS

Affective
To have a fun experience learning about self-talk

Behavioral
To practice replacing negative self-talk with positive self-talk

Cognitive
To learn to discriminate between positive and negative self-talk

MATERIALS

Two small, clean trash cans, one with a sign that says *GARBAGE IN*, the other with a sign that says *GOOD STUFF IN*

Small wrapped candy, approximately five pieces for each member

Scraps of paper with *BRAIN GARBAGE* and/or *NEGATIVE SELF-TALK* written in large marker letters on each, about five per member

Positive and Negative Self-Talk Examples (Handout 15)

Healthy snacks

GROUP SESSION

Opening Time (¼ session time)

1. Welcome group members to the third session and invite them to share any concerns or questions about confidentiality. How are the ground rules working for them at this point? Discuss any concerns.

2. Invite the group to share any observations, questions, ideas, or personal experiences related to situations in which they noticed their own beliefs or attitudes about events. How did they feel about having these insights? Did they notice the ABC sequence occurring with anyone besides themselves? Reinforce group members for even thinking about the previous topic and learning experience.

Working Time (½ session time)

1. Review the idea from the last session that it is your beliefs or attitudes about a situation that cause your feelings, not the situation or person. Let group members ask questions or disagree. Discuss the idea of how people get their beliefs or attitudes about situations:

   They come from programming, which means past experience. Just like a computer, if your programming—what you and other people have put into your brain—is BRAIN TRASH or BRAIN GARBAGE, then you aren't going to get good things or ideas (positive, helpful to you) back out. As they say about computers, "Garbage in, garbage out."

2. Point out that we are constantly having conversations with ourselves about what is going on around us:

Even when someone else is talking, we are talking to ourselves as well as listening. Sometimes we aren't even listening to the other person—for example, when we are very angry. We are just going on inside our heads saying whatever we'd like to say aloud. This talking to ourselves is called SELF-TALK. We self-talk about 5,000 times every day! If we use negative, hurtful self-talk, like "I can't do anything right—I'm dumb," then we think negative, hurtful thoughts, and we have negative feelings and do negative things. That is how the brain works. What you put into it is what comes out of it, in your behaviors, feelings, and actions: "Garbage in, garbage out."

3. Explain that the opposite of negative self-talk is positive self-talk:

   If you say positive things to yourself, like "I am lovable and capable, and I can do this," then you will have positive feelings and be able to do positive things. It isn't as simple as saying this once because you sometimes have to overcome years and thousands and thousands of negative messages you have put into your brain/computer. Once your brain learns negative ways of self-talk, it is difficult to change, BUT IT CAN BE DONE BECAUSE YOU ARE IN CHARGE OF CHANGING IT!

4. Share the Positive and Negative Self-Talk Examples (Handout 15) and invite group members to take turns reading the items. When they are finished, ask them what they think.

5. Place the two small trash cans in the center of the group circle, and the wrapped candy and slips of paper on a plate or container beside the trash cans. Invite group members to come to the center of the circle one at a time and make one brain-garbage, negative self-talk statement and one positive self-talk statement. As each one does so, he or she picks up a piece of candy and a slip of paper and tosses them into the appropriately labeled cans—the candy in the *GOOD STUFF IN* can and the slips of paper in the *GARBAGE IN* can. Let every member have several turns coming up with positive and negative self-talk statements. (At this point, you could share the candy, or you could wait until the end of the session.)

6. Ask, "What have you been noticing about how easy or difficult it is to come up with negative and positive self-talk statements?" Let group members respond, then convey the following ideas:

   It's much easier to come up with negatives because, if we grow up in a fairly average positive home, we might hear what we can NOT do more than 148,000 times by age 18. In a very positive home, we might hear NO only about 50,000 times. Most people hear YES only a couple hundred times by age 19: Yes, you can accomplish this, believe that, and so on. Some people only have positive statements made to them a few times in their lives—no wonder they are negative!

Processing Time (¼ session time)

1. Ask at least one question from each of the four processing levels:

   INTRAPERSONAL

   While we were talking about self-talk today and explaining that if you put negative statements into your brain you are going to get negative feelings and behaviors back, what were you thinking and feeling?

   INTERPERSONAL

   How is it going for you in the group?

   What kinds of feelings are you having about being a group member at this point?

   What are you noticing about our group?

NEW LEARNING

What new ideas or feelings do you have as a result of learning this new stuff about self-talk and how important it is to take responsibility for our own feelings and behaviors?

APPLICATION

Say, "This week I'd like to invite you to get in touch with your negative self-talk—just notice that you are doing it and how you feel after you have beat yourself up with negatives. Don't try to change yet; just notice what you're doing and let us know at the next session how it went."

2. Thank the group for coming and give them a hope statement. Remind them of the day and time for the next session, then share the candies (if you haven't already) and snacks.

Positive and Negative Self-Talk Examples

NEGATIVE SELF-TALK (GARBAGE IN)

1. I can't do this math!
2. I should do my homework, but I won't.
3. I never do things right.
4. I can't get a girlfriend/boyfriend.
5. I ought to keep my room clean.
6. Today's just not my day.
7. I just know I can't do _____ .
8. I need to stop eating junk food.
9. I just want to get by, that's all.
10. I could never (go to college, get a job).

NEGATIVE FEELINGS AND BEHAVIORS (GARBAGE OUT)

1. Incompetent, stupid/drop geometry
2. Guilty, hate science class/cut class tomorrow
3. Dumb, resentful, embarrassed/don't try
4. Lonely, out of it, ashamed/don't try
5. Worried, messy, unorganized/hope I don't get caught again with old food under the bed
6. Frustrated, defeated/give up on doing right
7. Miserable, jealous, irritated/don't try
8. Fat, unappreciated, lonely/eat more to "relax"
9. Lazy, exhausted, no motivation/don't try
10. Discouraged, confused, afraid/don't try

POSITIVE SELF-TALK (GOOD STUFF IN)

1. I can learn this—I'll get help.
2. Science is OK. I'll do it.
3. I can do a lot of things if I try.
4. I'm going to watch X and Y talk to girls/boys and learn how they do it.
5. I'll clean up for 5 minutes—I can do that.
6. Today I will do several things right.
7. I know I can do it a little at a time.
8. I will eat junk food only on weekends.
9. I will get at least a B in three subjects.
10. I can do it if I try and get help.

POSITIVE FEELINGS AND BEHAVIORS (GOOD STUFF OUT)

1. Competent, in charge/successful at math
2. Proud, happy/OK about going to class
3. Successful, competent/take risks, try new things
4. Happy I tried, playful/keep trying
5. Proud, relaxed/happy about helping Mom
6. Surprised, in charge/take the time to do things right
7. In charge, coping, surviving/trying my best
8. In control, handling diet/eat healthy during the week
9. Proud, in charge, happy/doing homework every night, getting help from teachers
10. Capable, competent, assertive/having successes

How to Get Your Brain to Work Right

GOALS

Affective

To feel more comfortable thinking about and using improved self-talk skills

Behavioral

To review and share individual goals stated at the beginning of the group

Cognitive

To identify personal negative self-statements to be eliminated

To identify personal positive self-statements to enhance coping

MATERIALS

Large index cards, enough for each group member to have four or five

Paper and pencils

Healthy snacks

GROUP SESSION

Opening Time (¼ session time)

1. Welcome the members back to the fourth session and ask what questions or concerns they might have about confidentiality. Encourage discussion of the ground rules.

2. Ask if there are any observations, comments, or successes they might want to report on about their between-session behavior and feelings concerning self-talk.

Working Time (½ session time)

1. Explain that today the session will help each group member get a clearer idea of what his or her issue is. Do not mention that you will also be discussing what negative things group members are saying about their situations (negative self-talk) and what positive thoughts could replace the negative thoughts. Instead, say that each person will be given an opportunity to share and clarify his or her target behavior and that everyone in the group is invited to be a special support person for every other member.

2. Ask for a volunteer who will permit you to talk about his or her target behavior. Suppose Jonathan volunteers: You would begin by summarizing your understanding of his target behavior (you'll have a good idea from his previous self-disclosures):

   Correct me on this as I go along, OK, Jonathan? "My issue is that I hate science, and I avoid doing science assignments or homework, and I daydream in science class."

My NEGATIVE self-talk goes like this:

- "I hate science."
- "I hate Mr. Thompson because he loves science and is always telling us to like it."
- "I can't do science experiments."
- "Science is too hard and boring anyway."
- "No one I know likes science either."
- "I don't care if I get a D in science."

My new POSITIVE coping self-talk is going to go like this:

- "Science isn't so bad. There are some interesting parts to it, like space and telescopes."
- "I'm going to make my own decisions about what subjects I like and dislike."
- "Science takes patience and practice to learn. I am going to be more patient."
- "I know a couple of kids who get A's in science, and they are really cool."
- "I am going to get at least a C in science because I'm going to try harder this time."

3. Confer with the volunteer all along, building the model for the rest of the kids, then have each group member go through the process. Invite group members to help develop positive coping statements for one another. (You might want to do this first one as a model from your own self-disclosures. Kids love to hear that adults are not perfect and are trying to improve themselves, too.)

4. As you are helping clarify each group member's target behavior, have that person write down, on a piece of paper, all the positive statements he or she thinks will "work." Instruct members to write down only clear, short statements, and only those with which they agree.

5. After everyone has gone through the process, tell group members not to try to make any changes from negative to positive self-statements. Say that at this point you are only identifying what you will work on in the future. (Paradoxically, group members will begin working on their changes because it is not supposed to happen!)

6. Ask if group members feel clear about what they are going to be working on in a week or so, then have them copy their positive self-talk statements, each one on a separate index card. Collect the cards and make photocopies of them so they don't get lost and so there is a record for comparison at the end of the group. (For now, group members may keep their original lists.)

Processing Time (¼ session time)

1. Ask at least one question from each of the four processing levels:

   INTRAPERSONAL

   As you and other group members were sharing and supporting one another in your change projects, what were you thinking? What were you feeling?

   INTERPERSONAL

   What have you noticed about us as a group?

   NEW LEARNING

   What new feelings or thoughts have you had today about making some positive changes in your life and not falling back into old, negative patterns?

   How hard or easy do you think these changes are going to be?

   APPLICATION

   During the time between now and our next session, who feels ready to make a serious effort to try pay attention to the times before, during, or right after a negative self-statement—just notice when negative thinking occurs and what would need to happen to change it to positive? (Remind group members not to make any actual changes from negative self-talk to positive self-talk.)

2. Thank group members for participating and give them a hope statement. Remind them of the day and time for the next session, then share the snacks.

No Neggies

GOALS

Affective

To increase group cohesion by working together on a self-talk activity

Behavioral

To reinforce the use of positive self-talk and coping statements

To self-disclose by completing sentence stems

To receive positive feedback from peers on use of coping self-talk

Cognitive

To reinforce understanding of how damaging negative self-statements can be

MATERIALS

Self-Talk Sentence Stems (Handout 16)

Index cards

Transparent tape

Healthy snacks

GROUP SESSION

Opening Time (¼ session time)

1. Welcome the members to the fifth session and ask what they are thinking about confidentiality. Do they feel any changes need to be made to the ground rules at this point?

2. Ask if there are any comments about last week's session, about clarifying target behaviors. What was it like for group members to catch themselves in a "neggie"? If despite your instructions any group members actually tried substituting a positive coping statement, act surprised in a humorous way and give praise.

Working Time (½ session time)

1. Explain that today you invite group members to play a card game to practice changing negative self-talk to positive self-talk. They will team up with a partner. One person will practice while the other helps out, then the partners will switch roles. When you call time, the pairs will choose other partners and practice with someone else.

2. Give each pair three or four cards from the deck of Self-Talk Sentence Stems (Handout 16). The first team member shows a card at a time to the second team member, who completes the negative self-statement and then responds with a positive self-talk alternative. If the first team member needs help or encouragement, the partner provides it. After the first team member has responded to all the cards, he or she passes them to the second team member, who now has a chance to respond with different negative and positive self-statements.

3. Monitor the teams, and when both team members have had a chance to respond to the cards, call time and have the pairs switch partners (and sets of cards). Continue until there have been about three different teams and all the cards have been responded to by all the groups.

4. Reconvene in the group circle and discuss:

> What did you like best about doing this activity?
>
> What didn't you like about responding to the sentence stems?
>
> What was it like for you to have to think of a positive statement and say it aloud?
>
> How did your partners help you?

5. Encourage group members to use the linking and connecting skill with one or more of their partners and tell those partners in what way they helped. Thank them for participating!

Processing Time (¼ session time)

1. Ask at least one question from each of the four processing levels:

INTRAPERSONAL

In today's activity you really had to think on your feet to respond to the sentence stems. What were you thinking and feeling when you were either responding to or holding the cards?

INTERPERSONAL

What was it like to be a group member today?

What did you notice about our group from today's activity?

NEW LEARNING

What new ideas or feelings do you have as a result of doing this activity?

APPLICATION

You're getting pretty good at positive self-talk now. Who would be willing to begin really practicing identifying and changing negative self-talk, then come back and tell the group about it?

2. Thank group members for coming regularly and sharing with others in the group, then give them a hope statement. Remind them of the day and time for the next session, then share the snacks.

Self-Talk Sentence Stems

Photocopy this page, then cut out the statements and tape them to the index cards.

I just don't . . . I can . . .	I must _____ , but I'm not. I am _____ now.
I wish I could . . . I certainly can . . .	I can't be . . . I am becoming . . .
I just can't seem to . . . I absolutely can . . .	I despise . . . I am learning to like/tolerate . . .
I just don't know . . . I know I . . .	I am always scared to . . . I am learning to deal with . . .
If only I could . . . I surely can . . .	I've always wanted to but don't . . . I have started to . . .
I could never . . . I can now do . . .	I am never going to . . . I have started to . . .
I don't have the motivation to . . . I am determined to . . .	My greatest fear is . . . I am overcoming my fear by . . .
Today is not my . . . Today is my . . .	My worst subject is . . . But I am beginning to do better in . . .
I should _____ , but I won't. I will . . .	I hate disagreeing with people when . . . But I'm learning to be assertive when . . .
I ought to start . . . I have started to . . .	I never have been able to . . . Yet now I can _____ somewhat.
I'd really like to _____ , but I won't. I am going to . . .	I'm afraid of _____ when I grow up. But I'm trying to get over . . .
I need to get going on . . . I am working on . . .	I used to be afraid to . . . But now I am no longer afraid to . . .
It would be fun to _____ , but I can't. I am having fun . . .	I always feel like a goofball when . . . I feel good about myself when . . .
I really should try to _____ , but I won't. I am trying very hard to . . .	I am out of control when I . . . I feel in charge now that I . . .
I feel disgusted about myself when . . . I feel in control of myself when . . .	Most of my friends think I'm nuts when . . . My friends respect me because I'm . . .

Self-as-Model: I Can Do This!

GOALS

Affective

To increase sense of belonging to the group by being of assistance to others

To increase self-esteem by practicing to a higher level of competence

To enjoy receiving positive feedback from other group members

Behavioral

To practice assertive, positive statements to others by using audiotape-recorded modeling

To increase comfort level and response fluidity in making positive self-statements

Cognitive

To understand that through practice positive responses can become more comfortable

To learn that others must also work to achieve mastery

MATERIALS

Tape recorder and one blank audiotape for each member of the group

Healthy snacks

GROUP SESSION

Opening Time (¼ session time)

1. Welcome the members to the sixth session. Discuss any concerns about confidentiality. Are the ground rules working at this point?

2. Ask if there are any comments about last session's "card game" to change negative self-talk to positive self-talk and whether anyone would be willing to share observations or events outside of group since the last session.

Working Time (½ session time)

1. Describe the activity for today as a technique to help group members deal with other people around the issue of the behaviors they have targeted for change. Not only must members stop negative self-talk in their heads, they must also stop saying it aloud to other people and responding negatively to people in their target situations. In your own words, summarize:

   > The technique today is called SELF-AS-MODEL. This means instead of having someone else show you how to do or say something, you will be using yourself as your own model. Each group member will have a chance to share a situation where he or she usually says negative things to someone else, such as whining and complaining about a certain teacher, all teachers, a school subject, boyfriends or girlfriends, parents, or some other situation. Instead of whining about the situation, you will have the opportunity to practice saying positive things about the situation. I will play the part of the other person in your situation, so you will need to tell me a little bit about what you usually talk about so I can play that role.

2. Ask one member to volunteer to go first. Have that person describe right there in the group the situation in which he or she usually ends up talking negatively. Practice a couple of negative lines first, checking out with the group member to be sure what you are saying

sounds realistic. Then audiotape yourself repeating these negative statements. Stop the tape recorder. Instruct the member to add his or her own negative thoughts about the issue. For example:

Group Leader: (As Jenny's friend) Jenny, I heard that Jill and Sarah are mean, nasty, gritches who tell on everyone, and I'd just like to smack them silly, wouldn't you?

Jenny: Yeah, I heard that, too, and I also heard they're weird and do weirdo things like maybe they're witches or something. I can't stand it when they make faces and shoot the bird at me and my friends, and I'm gonna tell them to get sick.

3. Record a second conversation on the same topic, instructing the group member to counter your negative introductory statements with positive responses.

Group Leader: Jenny, I heard that Jill and Sarah are mean, nasty gritches who tell on everyone, and I'd just like to smack them silly, wouldn't you?

Jenny: Yeah, they say mean things to a lot of people, but I am not going to let it get to me because I don't need that negative stuff in my life.

Ask the group member if the positive approach sounds like something he or she could actually say and do. If necessary, allow the member to record the positive response two or three times, practicing until the statements are smooth, with no stumbling in delivery.

4. Let all the group members practice a few statements geared toward a target behavior they want to change. (Use a separate tape for each person.) The following types of situations work well with the self-as-model technique:

> Asking a teacher for an extension on a project he or she has told the class there will be no extensions on
>
> Asking a parent for a special privilege
>
> Confronting a boyfriend or girlfriend about a negative incident
>
> Asking for donations for a class trip

5. When everyone has had a chance to participate, give them the tape recordings of themselves using positive statements to deal with their target situations. Ask them to listen to their tapes several times at home (or in the school library, if they don't have audiotape equipment at home), until they feel comfortable using those positive statements in real life.

Processing Time (¼ session time)

1. Ask at least one question from each of the four processing levels:

> INTRAPERSONAL
>
> What kinds of things were you thinking and feeling while we were recording our positive statements today?
>
> INTERPERSONAL
>
> What did you notice about other group members when they were doing their role-play recordings, using themselves as models?
>
> NEW LEARNING
>
> What new ideas do you have from watching and participating in this activity today?
>
> APPLICATION
>
> How do you think you could use this information, this self-as-model technique, to improve your target behavior?
>
> What new challenges are you ready to take on with this skill?

2. Explain that the next session will be the last "working" session and that the final session will be a review/evaluation of where the group has been and a celebration. Remind the group of the day and time for the next session; ask them to think about how they want to celebrate.

3. Thank the group for coming and give them a hope statement, then share the snacks.

Healing Painful Words

Due to the nature of the self-disclosures involved, this group experience requires members to have a moderately strong sense of cohesion and trust. Group members are likely to share painful situations in front of others only if they trust that confidentiality will be honored.

GOALS

Affective

To get in touch with painful experiences caused by negative, hurtful words from peers

To experience positive energy and support from peers while learning to deal with past hurts and negative experiences

Behavioral

To process painful verbal exchanges by naming and talking about them

To practice new verbal skills to deal with such exchanges as they happen

Cognitive

To understand what drives peers to respond in hurtful ways

To learn coping skills to deal with these situations as they occur

MATERIALS

Pencils and enough strips of paper so each member can have two (a regular piece of paper cut into four or five horizontal strips is about the right size)

Healthy snacks

GROUP SESSION

Opening Time (¼ session time)

1. Welcome members to the seventh session and remind them that this is the last working session. Explain that you will save some time at the end of this session to discuss how members would like to celebrate during the last session.

2. Ask what comments the group might have about confidentiality. Stress that the confidentiality rule is especially important for this session: What is said and done in the group stays in the group. Also ask, "What comments do you have about the ground rules?" and let members discuss any issues.

3. Ask, "How did it go with your recordings of self-as-model of positive assertive statements? Who would like to share?" Give lots of encouragement for trying.

Working Time (½ session time)

1. Describe the activity for today as a technique to help each person deal with the hurtful words, statements, and behaviors of others. Explain that the purpose of the activity is to apply new skills in changing negative self-talk (which becomes negative statements and behaviors toward others) to coping statements and to begin to heal sore, tender feelings.

2. Give each group member one or two strips of paper and a pencil, and explain that because this activity is for the purpose of getting in touch with hurtful feelings, it could get them in

touch with something hurtful from the past that they might not want to remember or deal with. If so, they have the right to "pass," or they could choose less emotionally hurtful or disturbing situations.

3. Instruct group members to write down on each slip of paper about two sentences per situation: "What they said, what you said—NOT THE WHOLE STORY." For example:

> Sharissa and Carya told me my boyfriend is a liar and a thief, and called me a stupid bitch for hanging around with him. I hated them for that.

> My dad told me a lot of times and still does that I am the dumbest kid in the world. It makes me sick when he does that.

> Elena and Jiri come from the Czech Republic, and they are really nice. I was walking with them, and some guys came by and shouted, "Hey, you queer foreigners." We were really mad and hurt.

> My older sister, Tara, is always putting me down. She is jealous of everything I do and think, and I get furious when she calls me her dorky-ditsy sister in front of her friends.

> I get off the bus by a store where some guys hang out, and they always yell at me and shoot me the bird and call me the biggest wuss at Jarvey School. I feel like strangling all of them.

4. Follow these steps for each group member:

Step 1: Have the group member share what he or she has written.

Step 2: Give an empathy statement to the group member (for example, "It sounds like you felt crushed and resentful when the girls called you wounding names for sticking with your boyfriend").

Step 3: Ask all group members to share ideas about what could be said or done in the IMMEDIATE situation.

Step 4: Ask all group members to give examples of what positive self-talk could replace negative self-talk AFTER the immediate situation.

Don't hurry through this part of the activity. It is better to do only one situation and do it thoroughly than to rush through two or three. Group members are sharing very painful experiences and need time to process and get support from one another.

---

5. After each group member has had a chance to go through the process, thank him or her for being willing to share these situations. Ask the group what they have learned from one another, reminding them to talk directly to the person they learned something from or who gave them special support. Encourage linking and connecting.

Processing Time (¼ session time)

1. In your own words, explain:

> Today's experience raked up a lot of feelings you may have wanted to forget and push to the back of your mind. But these feelings are still there because they haven't been processed yet— they need to be experienced and healed through exactly what we are doing now: Getting them out, getting a new perspective on them, and learning new skills to deal with these situations and feelings in the future.

2. Ask at least one question from each of the four processing levels:

INTRAPERSONAL

What were you thinking and feeling as we did this activity?

INTERPERSONAL

What did you learn from the other group members?

What feelings do you have about being a group member now?

NEW LEARNING

What new ideas do you have now about having had other people be hurtful to you?

APPLICATION

What would you be willing to try outside the group to help you cope better with these kinds of tough situations?

3. Ask, "What would you like to do during the last session to celebrate all of the hard work we have been doing on changing negative self-talk and replacing it with positive self-talk and coping statements?" Let everyone discuss.

4. Give the group a hope statement, remind them of the last session's day and time, then share the snacks.

That's a Wrap

GOALS

Affective

To enjoy positive feedback from other group members for one's efforts and changes

To increase self-esteem by sending and receiving "warm fuzzy" notes

To have an opportunity to deal with feelings about the group's ending

Behavioral

To write out positive statements to other group members so they have a concrete way to review and remember the learning experience in the future

To celebrate and say good-bye

Cognitive

To get in touch with ideas and experiences that had an impact during the life of the group

To plan goals to work toward in the future

MATERIALS

Thin-tipped marking pens or pencils

Enough strips of paper for each group member (and yourself) to have one strip for every other member of the group. (I usually use colored copy paper, cut sheets in eight strips across, and paper clip together for each member.)

Brown lunch bags, one for each member and yourself

Whatever party or celebration food the group has chosen

GROUP SESSION

Opening Time (¼ session time)

1. Welcome the members to the last session and ask what comments they might have about the ground rules. Remind them that the confidentiality rule extends even after the group is over and discuss any concerns.

2. Ask what progress they might have made using their new positive self-talk skills outside of group. Spend some time here allowing each person to describe how he or she has used the skills and what impact they have had outside the group.

Working Time (½ session time)

1. Spend a few minutes reminiscing about how the group experience has been for you as the group leader, from your own perspective

2. Briefly review the topic of each session, getting members' feedback and reactions:

    Session 1—Getting Started

    Understanding how our thoughts, feelings, and behaviors are connected and pinpointing the target problem we wanted to work on in the group

    Session 2—ABC's of Feelings

    Learning a new approach to personal responsibility for our feelings and behaviors, helpful in motivating us to make changes in our target problem behavior

Session 3—Garbage In/Garbage Out: My Responsibility for My Feelings

Beginning to grapple with the idea that if we hear a constant stream of negative self-talk that we are going to get back negative feelings and behaviors

Session 4—How to Get Your Brain to Work Right

Really making progress learning to identify personal negative self-statements and some alternative positive coping statements

Session 5—No Neggies

Giving one another help and support for using positive self-statements instead of negative ones

Session 6—Self-as-Model: I Can Do This!

Gaining confidence by recording, reviewing, editing, and rerecording better ways of getting our messages across

Session 7—Healing Painful Words

Sharing painful exchanges with peers and encouraging one another as we practiced new verbal skills to deal with others' insensitive comments

3. Following the review, pass out the lunch bags, markers, and strips of paper. Instruct group members to take a bag (folded flat), place a hand on it, then trace around the hand. Explain that the hand is a symbol, a "helping hand," showing willingness to be of assistance to others. Have each group member write his or her name in the middle of the hand.

4. Invite group members to write a "warm fuzzy" message—something positive, supportive, encouraging, or appreciative—to each other group member. Members place their bags in front of them. On the separate slips of paper, they then write one positive statement for each other member, fold the slip, and place it in that person's helping-hand bag. After the group is over, especially if members are feeling down about something, they can take out their "warm fuzzies" and read them! For example:

Sandy, thank you for telling me I had a bad attitude. Now I see why I didn't have friends, and I am doing much better.

Shawn, I really like how you tell it like it is, and I learned not to be so shy and speak up for myself.

Joshua, you helped me a lot because I want to talk like you and be more positive and less mean.

Mañuel, I want you to know I support you, and you can come and talk to me about your stuff anytime.

Yellow Feather, I like how you think. You are very patient, and I really need to be more like you. Please keep helping me, and I'll help you, OK?

5. This activity will take the rest of the Working Time. (You might play some music in the background and let them talk and laugh while they are writing their warm fuzzy statements.)

Processing Time (¼ session time)

1. Ask the following questions:

What were you thinking and feeling as we went back over all the sessions and came up with special times and feelings and ideas we experienced together?

What were you thinking about yourself as a group member? What were you thinking about the other group members?

What is one new thing you learned that you will definitely keep in mind and keep practicing in the future?

2. Explain your plans for follow-up. For example:

Today we end our group as we know it. We will be meeting two more times, one in one month, and then another month later. We can meet as a brown-bag lunch group to review how you are doing with your new positive self-talk skills and gain encouragement and reinforcement from everyone else. We can also problem solve to see how we can help one another move forward if we are stuck.

3. Thank group members for participating and give them a hope statement like the following:

I feel joyful and confident about the steps you've taken during the group to learn and practice several new coping skills. I know it was difficult and painful at times to "hang in there" and try when you felt like giving up or that the techniques wouldn't work for you. I have hope and faith in you that you will keep on growing and stronger and more in charge of your own lives.

4. Have your celebration!

Agree to Disagree: Learning to Manage Anger ___

Managing emotions that go up and down like a roller-coaster is a major task for young adolescents. Even youth with the most supportive family environments have difficulty negotiating major emotional events such as family moves, adjusting to new school environments, breakups between boyfriends/girlfriends, and pressure from peers to be accepted. The rest of the picture, youth without many family resources, includes the 15.7 million children that by 1993 lived in poverty and the one in four children under age 6 who now live below the poverty line (Annie E. Casey Foundation, 1994, 1995; Children's Defense Fund, 1994, 1995). Minority youth take the hardest hit. In 1993, 33 percent of Asian American children, 41 percent of Hispanic American children, and more than 46 percent of African American children lived in poverty, compared with 14 percent of European American children.

According to research cited by McWhirter, McWhirter, McWhirter, and McWhirter (1998), two-thirds of all high school seniors have used illegal drugs, and 90 percent of high school seniors have used alcohol; 77 percent of eighth graders report having used alcohol. Furthermore, nearly 3 million students and teachers are crime victims in U. S. secondary schools every month. For African American teenagers, murder is the major cause of death.

This is a depressing catalog of information! However, such research results are a reality check and an opportunity to confirm what we sense is going on in our culture. We know that at-risk, dysfunctional families are affecting youth through inconsistent, negative parenting. Children from such families are subject to stresses that can lead to antisocial and delinquent behavior, and these children then perpetuate the cycle of abuse, violence, and psychopathology. In the school system, youth act out their anger, hatred, deep losses and sorrow, and abuses in physical, verbal, emotional, and sexual ways. The school milieu is often the stage where these frustrations are played out, and teachers, peers, and community are impacted by this wide range of distressing behaviors. In the last few decades, research about the effects of different types of parenting on children's behavior has increased dramatically. Three fundamental, bipolar dimensions are consistently described in the literature as having a major impact on children's behavior: permissiveness–restrictiveness, hostility–warmth, and anxious/emotional involvement–calm/detachment. Parents who fall at the extremes of or whose parenting is continually inconsistent along these dimensions appear to place their children at high risk for school problems, interpersonal problems, and antisocial, maladaptive behaviors (McWhirter et al., 1998).

Anger is a secondary emotion, a result of other emotions and ideation. The expression of anger in negative ways affects children, teachers, and parents of young adolescents nearly every day. Anger erupts in violence against peers, teachers, administrators, community members, and, unfortunately, parents. Group counseling is a special vehicle that allows small numbers of youth who lack skills to express anger in appropriate ways to learn or relearn more adaptive ways to understand their feelings and behave more appropriately. In addition to instruction and encouragement by the group leader, members can receive help from peers who have some of these skills and from other youth who have been through counseling. The literature shows group counseling can have a significant effect on adolescents' anger control, especially when cognitive-behavioral techniques and skills are taught (Arbuthnot & Gordon, 1986; DiGiuseppe, Tafrate, & Eckhardt, 1994; Feindler, Ecton, Kingsley, & Dubey, 1986).

The session sequence for this group is as follows:

Session 1—Getting Started
Session 2—Peace in Any Language
Session 3—Agree to Disagree: Compromising and Negotiating
Session 4—Moody Blues
Session 5—Get a Life

GROUP GOALS

1. To develop an environment where youth can feel safe to disclose ideas, feelings, behaviors, and hopes for a better future

2. To promote the group norms of becoming a supportive, encouraging person

3. To ensure that members can discriminate thinking, feeling, and behaving

4. To experience an adult role model for new skills and attitudes, as well as different ways to respond to angering situations

5. To learn what anger is—how it is experienced and expressed

6. To develop a sense of being able to control and dissipate anger

7. To recognize that situations that provoke anger can be negotiated

8. To develop an understanding of how moods affect self and others

9. To recognize how we deny and hide negative feelings

10. To explore fears about expressing anger and other emotions

11. To increase self-esteem and confidence in dealing with negative emotions

12. To review the group experience and set goals for future personal work

SELECTION AND OTHER GUIDELINES

The purpose of this group is to assist youth who have various kinds of difficulties dealing with anger:

> Those who "act out" in antisocial ways

> Those who "act in" their anger in personally hurtful ways, such as depression or psychosomatic illnesses (asthma, stomachaches, headaches)

> Those who channel their anger about an external event (such as a divorce) in indirect ways (for example, excellence in sports, music, a hobby, or academics) but who do not yet have anger management skills

It is important not to select youth who are so angry that they cannot work together with others or any members who are so emotionally needy as to require substantially more attention and counseling than other members. Role-balancing is the key to getting this topical group to the working stage.

A good mix would be two or three youths with moderate acting-out behaviors, two who act in their anger, and two who have positive skills and abilities to deal with anger but perhaps have difficulty dealing with academics or school attendance. Be sure to have one male and one female who are socially desirable role models for the group—they can have anger issues but must possess qualities that the rest of the group admires, such as popularity or athletic ability. For inexperienced leaders, six members might be more workable than eight.

REFERENCES AND SUGGESTED RESOURCES FOR PROFESSIONALS

Annie E. Casey Foundation. (1994). *Kids count data book: State profiles of child well-being.* Washington, DC: Author.

Annie E. Casey Foundation. (1995). *Kids count data book: State profiles of child well-being.* Washington, DC: Author.

Arbuthnot, J., & Gordon, D. A. (1986). Behavioral and cognitive effects of a moral reasoning development intervention for high-risk behavior-disordered adolescents. *Journal of Consulting and Clinical Psychology, 54,* 208–216.

Burns, D. (1980). *Feeling good: The new mood therapy.* New York: Avon.

Children's Defense Fund. (1994). *The state of America's children yearbook.* Washington, DC: Author.

Children's Defense Fund. (1995). *The state of America's children yearbook.* Washington, DC: Author.

DiGiuseppe, R., Tafrate, R., & Eckardt, C. (1994). Critical issues in the treatment of anger. *Cognitive and Behavioral Practice, 1,* 111–132.

Feindler, E. L., Ecton, R. B., Kingsley, D., & Dubey, D. R. (1986). Group anger-control training for institutionalized male adolescents. *Behavior Therapy, 17,* 109–123.

Goldstein, A. P., Palumbo, J., & Striepling, S. (1995). *Break it up: A teacher's guide to managing student aggression* [Book and Video]. Champaign, IL: Research Press.

Guerra, N. G., Moore, A., & Slaby, R. G. (1995). *Viewpoints: A guide to conflict resolution and decision making for adolescents.* Champaign, IL: Research Press.

Hammond, W. R., & Gipson, V. (1991). *Dealing with anger: A violence prevention program for African American youth* [Video]. Champaign, IL: Research Press.

Institute for Mental Health Initiatives. (1991). *Anger management for parents: The RETHINK method* [Video and Program Guide]. Champaign, IL: Research Press.

Katz, N. H., & Lawyer, J. W. (1994). Resolving conflict successfully: Needed knowledge and skills. In J. J. Herman & J. L. Herman (Eds.), *The practicing administrator's leadership series.* Portsmouth, NH: Heinemann.

McWhirter, J. J., McWhirter, B. T., McWhirter, A. M., & McWhirter, E. H. (1998). *At-risk youth: A comprehensive response.* Pacific Grove, CA: Brooks/Cole.

Peace in 100 languages: A one-word multilingual dictionary. Rolling Hills Estates, CA: Jalmar.

Steinberg, P. (1998). *Theatre for conflict resolution: In the classroom and beyond.* Portsmouth, NH: Heinemann.

Getting Started

GOALS

Affective
To begin to relax and get to know other group members

To develop self-confidence to share in the group

Behavioral
To work with other group members to develop ground rules for the group

To participate in a fun getting-acquainted activity

Cognitive
To understand the purpose and goals of the group

To learn what confidentiality is and understand its importance

To learn how the thinking, feeling, and behaving processes are different

To begin to understand that self-talk, not external events, causes anger

To begin to distinguish between productive and unproductive anger

MATERIALS

Limits of Confidentiality sign (see Appendix A, page 270)

Easel pad or posterboard and marker

Three large sheets of newsprint, with a drawing of a head, heart, and hand or the words *THINKING, FEELING,* and *BEHAVING* (one item on each sheet)

Pens or pencils

Autographs of Famous People (Handout 17)

Scented colored markers (nonscented will do)

Small candy bars or other individually wrapped treats, enough for all members

Healthy snacks (such as fruit, crackers, juice, raisins)

GROUP SESSION

Opening Time

> For sessions after this first one, Opening Time will take up about one-fourth of the typical 40- to 50-minute session time, or about 10 minutes. For this session, however, you will need to plan on more time to discuss confidentiality, develop ground rules, and conduct a getting-acquainted activity. See the book's introduction for some ideas on how to schedule this extra time.

1. Welcome members to group and go over the general goals for the group. Explain why the group is called "Agree to Disagree"—to agree that it is OK for each person to have a different point of view instead of fighting, condemning, hurting, or hating.

The two rules for understanding anger mentioned in this session are from *Feeling Good: The New Mood Therapy,* by David Burns (New York: Avon, 1980).

2. Thoroughly discuss confidentiality (the "no-blab" rule): What is said and done in the group stays in the group. Give examples of things adults or peers outside the group might say to pressure group members to share what happens in group. For example:

> I heard that group is for kids who fight and get in trouble. Why are you in there?

> Confidentiality just means Mr. Lewis is going to tell on you but you can't tell on him.

> You can tell me—we're tight.

After members are clear on the meaning of confidentiality, share the Limits of Confidentiality sign (either as a handout or poster) and discuss: Let group members know you are bound by the confidentiality rule but that as the leader you are required to tell about what goes on in the group if you think someone will do harm to self or others, if someone says anything about child abuse or criminal activity going on, or if a judge orders you to turn over information.

3. Discuss the basic ground rules you have decided on for your group and request the group's input in developing a few more that would enhance their comfort in sharing with one another. For example:

> Take turns.

> Everyone has the right to "pass" (not share unless that's comfortable).

> Agree to disagree (no put-downs).

> Come on time.

Don't move on until the group agrees on the ground rules. Write or have the group write the rules on an easel pad or piece of posterboard and have each member sign the document to show agreement. You can then post these rules every session.

---

4. Invite group members to do a get-acquainted activity called "Autographs of Famous People." Distribute copies of Handout 17 and have them read through the categories. There are more categories than they can possibly get autographs for, but the object of the game is to get as many autographs as possible within a time limit. Mention that there will be prizes for all winners. (There is no definition of *winner*—all are winners who make the effort.) Ask each group member to give a "hint" before the game begins by having a share-around: "Whoever wants to may go first. Say your name and favorite pizza topping, and give one hint about what you are like."

5. Give group members about 5 minutes to get as many autographs as they can. Reassemble the group when the time is up and have them share their autographs—a quick way of getting to know lots of fun things about other group members. Give treats to all for being winners.

Working Time

Working Time will take half of a typical session, or about 20 to 25 minutes.

---

1. Begin by saying there are two goals for today: First, to learn how thoughts, feelings, and behaviors are different, and, second, to learn a new way of thinking about what anger is and what we think causes anger. Explain the following idea:

> *During the eight sessions of this group, we will be talking about how you are feeling, what you are thinking, and what you are doing. So it makes sense for everyone to know what we are talking about when we ask, "How did you feel about that?" Sometimes we don't say how*

we feel—we say what we did or what we think, but in group we are going to focus quite a bit on feelings.

2. Divide the group into three smaller groups, and show them the three sheets of newsprint with the thinking, feeling, and behaving symbols or words. Give each group one sheet and some markers and encourage them to write words that fit within their category. For example:

   Thinking: Wondering, daydreaming, calculating, forgetting, worrying

   Feeling: Silly, wild, curious, badgered, apprehensive, whipped

   Behaving: Dating, driving, watching TV, hugging, walking

   Explain that someone in their minigroup can be the "scribe," who will write down the words when the group thinks of them, or they can all write words down.

3. Have the groups take the posters to different parts of the room and work for 5 or 6 minutes. Then call them back to the group circle and ask them to share their words. Ask if there were any disagreements about any words. If so, how did they settle the disagreements?

4. Repeat the idea that the second goal for today's session is to hear a new way of thinking about where anger comes from, then summarize, in your own words:

   You are in this group because you have shared that at this point in your life you do not have enough or the right kind of coping skills to deal with anger. You might think that you experience anger because something outside of yourself happens, some external event—for example, a friend tells you a lie, your teacher gets on you really hard for not doing your homework, someone scratches your new CD, or your girlfriend or boyfriend tells you he or she is going to date your best friend. But these external events DO NOT CAUSE YOUR ANGER. What causes your anger is YOU: your beliefs, thoughts, and attitudes about external events. Events do not have the power to cause you any feelings; only YOU have the power to decide what feelings you will have. This means that YOU ARE IN CONTROL OF YOUR FEELINGS. If you feel negative feelings, you are probably using negative self-talk, saying things to yourself like "Boy, is he mean—he deserves to have his butt kicked" or "I'm gonna get him back for telling ME a lie—I can't stand liars." So if you are feeling angry, it is because YOU are telling yourself to feel angry thoughts and do angry things.

   You probably don't accept this idea because we find it much easier to blame the other person in a situation than to take responsibility for our anger. This is exactly why anger gets us in trouble. Let's look at a few examples, then YOU think of some situations, and we will play detective and find out how you can take control of your anger. Remember, we don't "lose" our temper—we give it away.

5. Explain that there are two rules to help us understand if our anger is productive or unproductive. *Productive* means that you can learn something from the situation and deal with it in a way that does not hurt you or other people. *Unproductive* means that you respond in ways that are hurtful to yourself and other people.

   Rule 1: Is my anger directed toward someone who has knowingly, intentionally, and unnecessarily acted in a hurtful manner?

   Rule 2: Is my anger useful? Does it help me achieve a desired goal, or does it simply defeat me?

6. Discuss the following situations.

Situation 1

You are doing math homework in study hall and someone walking by knocks your book off your desk, knowingly and intentionally to irritate you. You are really mad but decide to channel your anger into working even harder to get all your math finished so you don't have to take it home. So far, you are using your anger for a productive, or adaptive, purpose. But after study hall you see the person who knocked your book off your desk by the lockers, and you feel like going over and slamming the locker door right on the person. Now your anger could be channeled into unproductive, or maladaptive, behavior, which would serve no useful purpose but just get you in trouble.

Situation 2

Your little sister comes into your bedroom and goes through all your drawers looking for where you keep your money. She takes 2 dollars out of the money you have been saving. When you come home and realize your privacy has been violated and your money taken, you are furious and want to get back at her. You realize that the violation isn't what is making you mad, what you are telling yourself is making you mad . . . that she had no right to go through your things, she is hateful for stealing your money and should be punished, and you have a right to do the same thing or something as bad to her. What if she took your money to buy a gift for your mom that would be from both of you and couldn't tell you because you weren't there and she wanted to be able to have the birthday gift that night for your mom? Would you feel the same intensity of anger?

7. Ask members to describe one or two situations from their experience, then ask, "What were you telling yourself that resulted in your feeling angry?"

8. Discuss the following questions:

Before this session, where did you think anger comes from?

Who do you think is to blame for your feelings?

Do we need to blame anyone, or can we just accept the fact that we cause our own feelings?

Say, "If we accept responsibility for our own feelings, then we definitely don't need to get in trouble for our actions because we can stop needing to respond that way. Think about all of this, then let's process what we've done."

Processing Time

Processing Time will take one-quarter of a typical session, or about 10 minutes.

1. Discuss at least one question from each of the four processing levels:

INTRAPERSONAL

This was a different kind of experience today. What thoughts and feelings did you have during the session?

INTERPERSONAL

How was it for you to be a member of the group today? What do you think about being a member of this special kind of team?

NEW LEARNING

What new ideas or feelings have you had as a result of talking or listening to others talk about how thinking, feeling, and behaving are different?

APPLICATION

Who might be willing to take time between now and the next session to think about what happens in situations where you get really steamed about something? (Think about choices of feelings that you could have and what it would be like if you chose to feel a different way, such as irritated instead of furious.)

2. Thank group members for coming and give them a hope statement like the following example:

> *You have shared some very personal ideas and feelings today, and set some goals to work toward. I have a great deal of hope and belief that each of you can reach your goals and can support and encourage other group members along the way. I hope you will keep coming for the fun, togetherness, and new things you will learn to make life better. You are here to help one another, and this is a joint venture—like a family buying a new house with many rooms they will begin decorating, one at a time.*

3. Remind group members of the next session's day and time, then share the snacks.

Autographs of Famous People

A person who . . .

1. Has a birthday in April _____

2. Loves computers _____

3. Has a pet parakeet _____

4. Went to the beach for vacation _____

5. Loves spinach _____

6. Plays the guitar _____

7. Knows how to dive off the high dive _____

8. Wants a career in television broadcasting _____

9. Believes in equal rights for men and women _____

10. Has an aunt named "Auntie" _____

11. Favorite color is purple _____

12. Might be afraid of the dark _____

13. Knows how to make people laugh _____

14. Is new in this school _____

15. Has a dad who travels for his job _____

16. Loves anchovies _____

17. Has been to caves exploring _____

18. Thinks school is very important _____

19. Reads a lot of library books _____

20. Considers herself/himself adventurous _____

Peace in Any Language

The focus of this session is on discussion and sharing. You can develop the discussion into a very interesting and powerful activity at a second session, if that is appropriate for your group. Have the group members pick out their favorite word or words for peace. Then have each one draw a picture of what peace might look like at home, what they might be doing to promote peace, and so on. Group members then share their word(s) and pictures.

GOALS

Affective

To explore and develop a positive attitude and feeling toward peacemaking

To develop further self-confidence as a group member

Behavioral

To discuss the many meanings of the word *peace*

Cognitive

To understand what peace and peacemaking mean

To realize that it is worth making an effort to begin at home to create peace

MATERIALS

A copy of *Peace in 100 Languages: A One-Word Multilingual Dictionary.* Available from Jalmar Press, World Peace Project, 45 Hitching Post Drive, Building 2, Rolling Hills Estates, CA 90274–4297 (Telephone: 1–800–662–9662).

Healthy snacks

GROUP SESSION

Opening Time (¼ session time)

1. Welcome members to group and ask them what concerns they have at this point about confidentiality. What questions and issues might have come up since the last session? Ask them if they are still in agreement with the ground rules, or if anything needs to be changed at this time.

2. Connect back to the previous session's new ideas about anger and other feelings—that we are responsible for choosing how we feel and that other people or situations don't cause our feelings. Ask what group members have been thinking or feeling about this idea: "How does it change things when you stop to think that you and no one else is in charge of your feelings?"

Working Time (½ session time)

1. Ask how the group would define the word *peace*. Do they think peace is important? Why or why not?

2. Pass around the book *Peace in 100 Languages* and tell members that it is the first attempt by a group of people to find the word *peace* in as many languages as possible. The book also includes some very special sayings about peace and is a candidate for the *Guinness Book of World Records* as largest AND smallest dictionary ever published.

3. Read the group a few of the observations on peace. For example:

    Peace is more difficult than war. (Aristotle)

    Peace cannot be kept by force. It can only be achieved by understanding. (Albert Einstein)

    True peace is not merely the absence of tension but is the presence of Justice and Brotherhood. (Martin Luther King, Jr.)

    Give peace a chance. (John Lennon)

    If you want peace, work for justice. (Pope Paul VI)

4. Share a few of the words for peace from the book—for example, Bengali (*ashanti*); Russian (*mir*); Hebrew (*shalom*); the phonetic alphabet (P-apa E-cho A-lpha C-harlie E-cho); Swahili (*amani*).

5. Ask the following questions:

    What is it about peace that so many millions of people throughout the world and for all the past centuries have valued so much?

    What is it about peace that is so difficult to keep?

    Why do you think people start wars and do terrible things to one another?

    What wars do you know about, and what caused them?

    What would happen if we didn't air our feelings and kept everything inside to "keep the peace" at all costs? (It would come out later as passive aggression.)

    What does the saying "Peace begins at home" mean?

    What would your life be like if there were more peace in your family?

    How can you contribute directly to peace in your own family? In our city? State? Country? The world?

    How can taking responsibility to control and reduce your anger contribute to a more peaceful world?

Processing Time (¼ session time)

1. Summarize, then ask at least one question from each of the four processing levels:

    This was a different kind of session today . . . exploring the concept of peace. Perhaps at first when I started talking about peace, you might have thought that it was only a word you hear on the news, or maybe in church, but not actually something that applies to you every day. Now after your responses and discussion it seems as though you are making contact with peace and rethinking it.

    INTRAPERSONAL

    What thoughts and feelings have you had as we discussed how peace relates to us?

    INTERPERSONAL

    How does the concept or idea of peace apply to us as a group?

    NEW LEARNING

    What new ideas or feelings about peace do you have now that you didn't have before the session started?

    APPLICATION

    What might you notice and think about between now and the next session concerning being a person who values peace?

2. Thank group members for coming and give them a hope statement. Remind them of the day and time for the next session, then share the snacks.

Agree to Disagree: Compromising and Negotiating

GOALS

Affective

To feel more confident and less angry when dealing with unpleasant situations

Behavioral

To use a step-by-step process to practice negotiating a difference

To increase assertive skills through group practice

Cognitive

To understand that negotiation is an alternative to passive or aggressive behavior

To recognize one's personal rights to use assertive skills to rectify perceived injustices

MATERIALS

Negotiation Steps (Handout 18)

Pens or pencils

Small index cards

Healthy snacks

GROUP SESSION

Opening Time (¼ session time)

1. Welcome the members back to group. Ask what comments, concerns, or problems they might want to discuss about confidentiality. How are the ground rules working for them at this point—any additions or changes needed?

2. Revisit last session's discussion about peace. Ask:

   What did you notice since the last session about peace in your life?

   What were you able to do toward adding just a little bit more peace to the world?

   How did it feel to be a peacekeeper?

Working Time (½ session time)

1. Introduce the session's topic by discussing the meaning of compromise:

   The focus today is on learning some steps to follow to COMPROMISE when you get your-self in a situation where you have a disagreement or want fair treatment from someone. In a compromise, both people give a little and perhaps do not get all of what they want in order for each one to get something. In other words, nobody gets all of what he or she wants, but both win some.

   If you feel you must win and the other person must lose whenever you have a conflict, then you have a "win-lose" situation. NEGOTIATION is the name of the skill where each person gives a little in order for both to get something out of it. If you are able to negotiate a com-

promise, it is a "win-win" situation, rather than a win-lose situation, because each person wins by getting something.

2. Invite group members to come up with some situations that can be negotiated. For example:

   Your mom wants you to do your chores NOW, but you want to watch the rest of a favorite TV show. You negotiate to do the chores immediately after the show.

   Your teacher gives you the opportunity to do an extra project to bring up your science grade, but you hate that kind of project. You negotiate with her to help her organize all the science stuff after school instead doing of the project.

   Your neighbor wants you to mow and edge her yard all summer. You negotiate fair pay for your work.

   Your friend wants to borrow 4 dollars. He says he will pay you back 4 dollars and 50 cents. You only have 5 dollars to get by for the rest of the week. You want to help him out, so you negotiate.

3. Ask group members to pair up. Give each pair a copy of the Negotiation Steps (Handout 18). Encourage them to come up with a situation where there could be a negotiation, then work it out between themselves, using the Negotiation Steps as a guide. (If necessary, do one negotiation with the whole group before breaking into dyads.)

4. After a few minutes, call members back to the group circle and ask them to present their situations and negotiations to the group. Work through as many situations as time permits.

5. Ask the following questions:

   What have you learned from using the negotiation skill?

   How could the skill help you get what you want without getting into an argument or fight?

   How difficult do you think this skill is to use?

   In what area of your life would this skill work the best?

6. Encourage group members to write down the negotiation steps on an index card to keep in their wallets or purses so the steps will be handy when members need to work something out.

Processing Time (¼ session time)

1. Ask at least one question from each of the four processing levels:

   INTRAPERSONAL

   What ideas or feelings were you having today as we talked about this negotiation, compromise skill?

   Were you attracted to the idea, or was it negative for you?

   INTERPERSONAL

   Which group members are you linking with at this time in the group?

   Which group members do you need to get to know better?

   NEW LEARNING

   What new ideas or feelings do you have as a result of today's discussion?

   APPLICATION

   Before the next session, in what area of your life do you think you would be willing to try negotiating?

2. Thank group members for coming and give them a hope statement. Remind them of the day and time for the next session, then share the snacks.

215

Negotiation Steps

STEP 1

Ask yourself: What is the problem?

STEP 2

Tell the other person you have a disagreement and want to talk about it when you both have time and privacy.

STEP 3

Ask the other person's ideas on the problem while you listen closely.

STEP 4

Tell the other person you would like to suggest a compromise.

STEP 5

Suggest your compromise. Listen to the other person's comments.

STEP 6

Keep on working back and forth until you both agree.

Moody Blues

GOALS

Affective
To have fun exploring feelings and mood states

Behavioral
To relate to a prop to help focus on being "crabby" and experiencing other moods

Cognitive
To develop awareness of how moods affect one's own and others' behavior and perceptions

MATERIALS

An assortment of crabs, any kind. You can use crab shells, pictures of crabs, whatever is available, but kids love the multicolor Beanie Baby crabs!

Healthy snacks

GROUP SESSION

Opening Time (¼ session time)

1. Welcome the members back to group. Say that this is the half-way point in the group and ask what concerns they might have about confidentiality. How are the ground rules working?

2. Revisit the last session's topic of negotiating. Ask, "How did that go for you since the last session? Would anyone like to share how the practice went?"

Working Time (½ session time)

1. Show the group members the crabs—perhaps toss the Beanie Baby crabs out if you have more than one. Ask them what it means to be "crabby." Let members give examples from their own experience; tell them they must have possession of a crab before they speak.

2. Next ask what a *mood* is—work toward a definition of the term as an extended emotional state with a specific or nonspecific cause. Ask, "What kinds of situations seem to spark your crabby moods? Is it something in particular, or do lots of things stimulate you to give a crabby response?" Let everyone respond to this and the following questions:

    When you find yourself in a crabby mood, how exactly do you feel? What are some descriptors you would use about yourself as a crabby person that day?

    How does being crabby affect what you have to get done that day?

    How would your family describe you when you are crabby?

    How about your friends? How would they know you are in a crabby mood?

    How does being crabby affect your relationships with family members and friends?

    How do you think it would affect you on the job if you were working at a store or restaurant?

    How does being crabby affect your schoolwork?

    How long do you usually stay crabby? A couple of hours, a day, days, weeks?

    What do you usually do to get yourself out of a crabby mood? Does it work?

What is the worst thing about being crabby? The best thing?

Is there any way you can prevent yourself from getting crabby or get out of a crabby mood more quickly?

What can you do to help a family member or friend or teacher if you sense that he or she is in a crabby mood?

3. Say, "Enough about crabs! Let's enjoy the happy side of ourselves for the rest of the day!"

Processing Time (¼ session time)

1. Ask at least one question from each of the four processing levels:

    INTRAPERSONAL

    Today we talked about the mood called being crabby. We really got into being crabby from every direction! What kind of thoughts and feelings did you have as we explored this mood from every angle?

    INTERPERSONAL

    We've had four sessions together. What have you noticed about the members of this group?

    How are we relating to one another?

    What kind of trust issues do you think we have at this point?

    How safe are you feeling about being a group member?

    NEW LEARNING

    What new ideas, thoughts, or feelings do you have about being in moods, crabby or otherwise, after we have explored how you think, feel, and behave when crabby?

    APPLICATION

    What are you willing to do between this session and the next to work on being crabby and some of your other moods?

2. Thank group members for coming and give them a hope statement. Remind them of the day and time for the next session, then share the snacks.

Get a Life

GOALS

Affective

To experience feelings related to a deeper level of self-disclosure

To identify feelings related to immature behaviors

Behavioral

To relate to a pacifier as a prop to discuss immature behaviors that need to be eliminated in order to earn adult respect and freedoms

Cognitive

To increase awareness of leaving certain aspects of childhood behind

To facilitate a process of identifying and planning to change immature behaviors that are interfering with growing up

MATERIALS

One or more pacifiers

Healthy snacks

GROUP SESSION

Opening Time (¼ session time)

1. Welcome the members back to group. Ask, "What would you like to discuss about confidentiality?" and "How are the ground rules working for you?"

2. Review the last session's topic of dealing with moods and ask what group members have noticed about their moods since the last session. Were they able to make changes in them or see them any differently?

Working Time (½ session time)

1. Pass out the pacifiers to the group members. Ask what pacifiers are used for (to keep babies quiet and help them manage the stress of wanting or needing something).

2. Discuss the idea that pacifiers work wonders for babies. They are very effective in helping babies and small children deal with stress, anxiety, fearfulness, and lots of other negative things.

3. Recreate the following dialogue, in general outline:

   Leader: What would happen if a first or second grader brought a pacifier to school and sucked on it during the day?

   Group: The other kids would laugh and tease and call him or her a baby.

   Leader: Why would they tease a second grader?

   Group: Pacifiers are for babies; a second grader is too old.

   Leader: What do you think would happen if you took a pacifier to school when you were 10 years old?

   Group: Lots of laughs, snickers, name-calling, and so on.

Leader: Why would they tease you so much if you brought a pacifier and used it when you were 10?

Group: It's way past the time when it is OK.

Leader: What if the pacifier helped you manage your stress and feel better?

Group: The other kids wouldn't understand and would tease you terribly.

Leader: OK, now you are (whatever age your group members are). What would happen if you brought a pacifier NOW?

Group: You would get laughed out of school by other kids, and the teachers would think you were weird!

Leader: Why?

Group: Because pacifiers are for babies.

Summarize: "OK, pacifiers work well for babies and little children, helping them manage their stress and feel calm because they are a certain age."

4. Invite the group members to share an immature behavior they are still doing that worked for them when they were younger but that isn't working as well now and that they are beginning to see has to go if they are going to have their parents' and other adults' trust and respect and be able to have more adult privileges and opportunities, like driving, having a job, and going out with other kids in cars on dates. For example:

Sassing back your mom when she wants you to do something and you don't want to do it

Stomping your foot and sulking off when you don't get your way

Ignoring a request to do something

Throwing a temper tantrum like a 2-year-old

Crying and whining to get your way

Arguing/accusing back instead of accepting responsibility

5. Ask the following questions:

How do you think these behaviors will work when you turn 16 and get that really cool job you have been wanting? What if you throw a temper tantrum because your boss or supervisor tells you to do something you don't want to do? How would that work? (Not very well—you'd be walkin' !)

How about some of the other behaviors you mentioned? What would happen if you keep using them to get your way and manage your stress?

6. Have a share-around and invite everyone to tell about his or her plan to replace an immature behavior with a more mature behavior. They can say it like this:

I need to change my behavior _____ (for example, tantrums)

and replace it with the more mature behavior _____ .

7. Thank each one and use an empathy statement to let them know you recognize how difficult it is for them to be so up-front with this issue. Ask:

What was the hardest thing about sharing your immature behavior that needs to be changed?

What have you learned about yourself today by sharing this?

Processing Time (¼ session time)

1. Summarize, then ask at least one question from each of the four processing levels:

    Today we talked about some really personal feelings and behaviors. I want to thank you again for taking the risk to share and making an effort to help everyone in the group get in touch with behaviors that aren't working anymore and need to be changed.

    INTRAPERSONAL

    As we were talking and sharing today, what kind of things were you thinking about and feeling?

    INTERPERSONAL

    What did you notice about the other group members as we shared?

    NEW LEARNING

    What new ideas do you have for making your life more fun and less hassle by giving up some of the behaviors of babyhood and childhood for more adult ways of thinking and acting?

    APPLICATION

    What would you be willing to do before the next session to get started on making the change, "giving up the pacifier," so to speak, and behaving in the more mature way you described?

2. Give group members a hope statement, remind them of the day and time for the next session, and share the snacks.

I-Messages

GOALS

Affective

To increase feelings of competence with regard to expressing anger

To experience a feeling of altruism by helping others

Behavioral

To use the I-message format to express anger appropriately

To practice dealing with anger and angering situations

To give and receive help and support

Cognitive

To recognize the need for expressing negative feelings such as anger, frustration, and irritation in healthy ways that respect one's own and others' rights

MATERIALS

I-Message Skill Sheet (Handout 19)

Healthy snacks

GROUP SESSION

Opening Time (¼ session time)

1. Welcome the members back to group. Ask what concerns or comments they have about confidentiality at this point. Inquire how the ground rules are working out for them. Do any changes or additions need to be made?

2. Talk briefly about the last session, in which the group used pacifiers to help get in touch with behaviors left over from childhood that are keeping them from becoming more mature and responsible, and therefore earning the right to have more grown-up responsibilities and privileges. Ask, "What have you noticed since the last session about your behavior, and what have you started working on to make changes possible?"

Working Time (½ session time)

1. Explain, in your own words:

> We all have the right to express our positive feelings, such as liking, loving, and happiness, as well our negative feelings, such as anger, irritation, guilt, fear, hurt, and sadness. Many times when we express negative feelings we do so using "You-messages." "You spilled Coke on the rug again!" "You took my CD and scratched it!" "You never help me, and I always do all the work!" When we use You-messages, the other person feels blamed, hostile, and certainly not like wanting to help you or change the behavior! The person closes down the communication, and you end up feeling angry and resentful.
>
> There is another way to get over anger and negative feelings toward someone, a way that helps build a bridge to and won't alienate the other person. It is called using "I-messages." I-messages help us take responsibility for our own feelings, not placing the blame for our feelings on the other person, and give us the opportunity to ask the other person to change or

treat us in a different way. There is a formula for I-messages, which means that we must include certain things for the message to work best.

2. Give each group member a copy of the I-Message Skill Sheet (Handout 19) and go over the formula:

    I feel . . . (Here you state your feelings.)

    When . . . (Here you say what the other person is doing that stimulates your negative feelings.)

    Because . . . (Here you say why you feel that way.)

    And I want/need . . . (Here you say what you would like the person to start doing, stop doing, increase, decrease, or otherwise change.)

3. Discuss with group members some of the possible negative effects of using I-messages:

    You must be aware that when you use I-messages you can expect the other person to respond to you differently because you are behaving differently. The person may be very surprised that you are so assertive, not passive or aggressive, and respond in a positive way. The person also might respond in a negative way, such as teasing you or making cruel statements. The point is that YOU HAVE A RIGHT TO EXPRESS YOUR NEGATIVE FEELINGS AND ASK SOMEONE FOR A BEHAVIOR CHANGE IN A WAY THAT DOES NOT VIOLATE THE PERSON'S RIGHTS. If the person does not like your new way of communicating, he or she might feel threatened because you are now in control, in charge of yourself. Maybe the person wants you to lose your cool and get angry and blow up, perhaps as you have done in the past. But, if you continue to use I-messages with people, most will begin to respect you a great deal because you are not putting them down or expressing yourself in a way that is hurtful or threatening to them. You must continue using I-messages if you want them to work.

    It is important for group members not to use I-messages if doing so will provoke someone else to react in a truly hurtful way (for example, a parent might react with harsh punishment). Stress that anyone who feels he or she will be at risk because of being more assertive should speak with you or another counselor before using I-messages in that situation.

    ---

4. Have group members form dyads and share situations in which they were angry and upset with someone, and wanted to tell that person in a respectful way and ask for a change in behavior. Encourage members to work out several possible I-message responses on the I-Message Skill Sheet. Give them a time limit so both may share equally. Let them know you will get back together as a group to share so you can learn from one another.

5. When the time is up, reassemble the group and invite them to share what they did as a dyad, giving praise and reinforcement to both members of the dyad for helping each other, not just themselves. After everyone has shared, ask:

    What have you learned from developing these I-messages for your target situation?

    What are some of the worries you have about going ahead and using this technique when a situation arises?

    What help do you need in order to use I-messages?

    What if you use an I-message and it doesn't work—in other words, the other person teases you or says something hurtful? What could you do?

    What if the other person just doesn't change? (Keep trying, have patience—it takes time.)

Processing Time (¼ session time)

1. Ask at least one question from each of the four processing levels:

    INTRAPERSONAL

    While we were talking about and practicing I-messages today, what kind of feelings were you experiencing? What ideas ran through your head?

    INTERPERSONAL

    What was it like helping someone else come up with I-messages?

    NEW LEARNING

    What new ideas, feelings, or possibilities do you have from today's activity?

    APPLICATION

    Who might be willing to try I-messages and come back next session and tell the group how it went? Who needs more work on this and wants more instruction and practice?

2. Thank group members for coming and give them a hope statement. Let group members know that the next session will be the last "working" session and that the last session will be a review of what has been learned and a celebration, so they should be thinking of what they might like to do to celebrate. Remind them of the day and time for the next session, then share the snacks.

I-Message Skill Sheet

SITUATION 1

_____

_____

_____

_____

_____

I feel _____

When _____

Because _____

And I want/need _____

SITUATION 2

_____

_____

_____

_____

_____

I feel _____

When _____

Because _____

And I want/need _____

SITUATION 3

_____

_____

_____

_____

_____

I feel _____

When _____

Because _____

And I want/need _____

Big Spiders and Little Spiders

GOALS

Affective

To get in touch with feelings of fear, worry, and anxiety

Behavioral

To increase self-control by disclosing fears and worries

To practice using the technique of thought stopping to replace negative fears and worries with positive coping statements

Cognitive

To learn to discriminate between fears we can do something about and those we need to let go

To recognize that some problems are solvable if we make and follow a plan to do so

To raise awareness that others also have major worries with which they must deal

MATERIALS

Toy spiders—Beanie Baby spiders are great, or use plastic or rubber ones.

Thick rubber bands, enough for each group member to have at least one

Healthy snacks

GROUP SESSION

Opening Time (¼ session time)

1. Welcome members back to group. Ask what concerns they have regarding confidentiality. Are the ground rules working?

2. Refer back to the previous session, on the topic of I-messages. Ask group members who had the opportunity to practice since the last session how the I-messages worked for them. What difficulties did they encounter? What successes did they have?

Working Time (½ session time)

1. Explain, in your own words:

   Fear is one of our major emotions. Sometimes we don't even recognize it because fear wears many faces. For example, sometimes when we are scared, we show it as anger, striking out at the person(s) we fear and trying to get control of the situation by being aggressive.

2. Discuss the following examples, showing the negative effects of too much stress, then summarize:

   Because you are afraid of what a parent might do or say, you keep your feelings bottled up inside and eventually develop headaches, depression, or asthma attacks. (This is called "somatizing" negative feelings, turning them into physical or psychological ailments.)

   Because you are afraid of a bully, you become very aggressive yourself, shouting and name-calling, bullying back. Sometimes we hear people say, "The best defense is a strong offense," which means if you want to defend yourself, come on strong, use an attack mode, and the other person will usually back off.

Perhaps you are afraid of not making a team, passing a class, or being selected for the cheerleading squad. The worry, anxiety, and concern cause you to be awake at night and maybe have nightmares, disturb your eating habits, affect your ability to study and concentrate, and you become easily angered and irritated.

As you can tell by the examples, sometimes we don't even recognize that the feeling we are experiencing is fear because it looks like something else: anger, sadness, physical problems, sleep disturbances—anything but fear!

3. Toss out the spiders to the group members, telling them that there are some fears we can learn to recognize and do something about and some fears we can't do anything about. Say, "Let's brainstorm some of your fears and try to decide if they are the type that can be worked on and changed or the type it would be better to 'cut loose' and worry about less because you don't have any control over them and they can't be changed."

4. Encourage group members to share fears, worries, and anxieties. Examples of uncontrollable concerns/worries:

> Wanting my parents to get back together and/or remarry
>
> Becoming a major league sports player
>
> Not growing any taller
>
> Hoping my girlfriend/boyfriend won't ever leave me for someone else
>
> Hoping my teachers will give me straight A's so I can be valedictorian
>
> Hoping my foster parents won't decide to get rid of me

Examples of things worth planning for and working on to change:

> Going from a D to a C in math this term
>
> Improving communication with my stepmom
>
> Negotiating for more space and privacy
>
> Changing an "attitude" that gets me in trouble
>
> Finding another way to have fun between classes rather than horsing around, which gets me in trouble
>
> Getting a job I like that pays pretty well

5. Communicate the following:

"Letting go" means stopping yourself from thinking about something over and over. Sometimes when we worry or are afraid of a situation we keep thinking about it hundreds of times a day. We can actually stop ourselves from thinking about it, if we choose to do so, because we have control over our thoughts. We can tell our brains to stop thinking about something, but we have to put something else, something positive, in its place. One way to learn to stop thinking about something we can't do anything about is called THOUGHT STOPPING. You can place a thick rubber band around your wrist, and when you notice you are thinking your unproductive thought, just pull back the rubber band and zap your wrist once. Since it hurts a little, your brain will immediately stop thinking about the negative or unproductive thought and be open, like a clean sheet of paper, for you to put something positive into your thoughts.

6. Pass out the rubber bands. Invite group members to participate in an activity to demonstrate this. You will be asking them to close their eyes and visualize something they do not want to keep thinking about because they cannot control the situation. Then you will ask them to zap themselves with the rubber band and at the same time say "STOP!" silently to themselves. The thought will disappear. Then they are to replace the negative thought with a

coping statement about something they can make a plan to change. Remind members that they have the right to pass if they are uncomfortable about doing this. Examples:

Negative thought: I can't stand it if my mom and dad don't get back together! ZAP!

Coping statement: I am going to work on communicating my feelings better to both my mom and dad.

Negative thought: If I don't get picked for JV Cheerleading Squad I'm never going to any games, and I'll lose my friends. ZAP!

Coping statement: I'm going to try my best and work on flips and dance steps for next year's tryouts.

7. Invite group members to close their eyes and visualize a situation and negative self-statement they make to themselves. When you say "ZAP," they snap their rubber bands. They will open their eyes and remark about how it hurts! Have them close their eyes again and concentrate on a positive coping statement for that situation. If they need help figuring out a coping statement, assist them individually before you begin. Continue until they all have had the opportunity to replace a negative statement with a positive one.

8. Ask, then summarize:

What have you learned about changing and controlling fearful thoughts and ideas?

What do you think about replacing them with coping statements that are more positive and have a better chance of working?

You must make a plan to work on these situations—change doesn't just happen like magic. It takes a lot of work, but the idea is, you don't have to be controlled by awful thoughts that just keep coming back over and over.

Processing Time (¼ session time)

1. Ask at least one question from each of the four processing levels:

INTRAPERSONAL

What thoughts and feelings are you experiencing because of getting in touch with fears, worries, and concerns?

INTERPERSONAL

What was it like for you to be a member of the group today, and what have you noticed about the other group members?

NEW LEARNING

What new ideas do you have to take away from this experience to help you during the coming week?

APPLICATION

What are you willing to try between now and the next session to take control of negative feelings such as fear, worry, and anxiety?

2. Remind group members that the next session is the group's last and that you won't have a special topic. Instead, you will be processing what happened during the whole group experience and afterward the group will have some extra time to celebrate in some special way. Say, "All of you have tried very hard and worked on your problems during the group. We have learned from one another, through sharing and modeling. So it's time to celebrate! How would you like to do this?"

3. Thank group members for participating and give them a hope statement. Remind them of the day and time for the next group, then share the snacks.

That's a Wrap

GOALS

Affective

To have an opportunity to deal with feelings about the group's ending

To increase self-esteem by recalling special times and learning moments during the group experience

To experience a sense of altruism by helping others

Behavioral

To participate in writing a group poem as a way to review the group experience

To demonstrate appreciation for peers' helping one another to grow

Cognitive

To recognize progress in making life changes

To think about ways to continue to work toward goals and to self-reward for patience, practice, and persistence

MATERIALS

A sheet of construction paper (a seasonal color if possible) for each member and yourself

Pens, pencils, or narrow-tipped marking pens

Party food

GROUP SESSION

Opening Time (¼ session time)

1. Welcome members to the last group session. Ask what comments they have about the ground rules. Invite discussion of any concerns over confidentiality; remind them that confidentiality extends even after the group is over.

2. Review the previous session's topic of fears and the use of thought stopping to interrupt fearful thoughts about situations that are not changeable. Ask, "How did the thought-stopping process go? What was it like to replace negative thoughts with something you had more control over?"

Working Time (½ session time)

1. Spend some time praising, thanking, and encouraging group members for their work on learning new ways to deal with anger and for expressing themselves during the group. Explain that today is a review of the learning experiences:

   Session 1—Getting Started

   Getting acquainted, learning about thinking-feeling-behaving, and identifying anger strength and growth areas

   Session 2—Peace in Any Language

   Talking about the meaning of peace and peacekeeping

Session 3—Agree to Disagree: Compromising and Negotiating

Learning the steps in negotiating a win-win agreement

Session 4—Moody Blues

Understanding being "crabby" and having other moods

Session 5—Get a Life

Letting go of immature behaviors (remember the pacifiers?)

Session 6—I-Messages

Learning an assertive way to say what you want and need, and to ask others to change

Session 7—Big and Little Spiders

Understanding fears—ones we can't do anything about and others we can

2. Next explain that you will be writing a group poem to help remember your experiences together. Pass out the construction paper and markers. Give directions slowly and clearly:

Hold the paper vertically in front of you; write your initials in the TOP RIGHT-HAND CORNER.

This is YOUR poem: It belongs to you—your initials are on it—so you are going to write the first line to your poem. Then every other group member is going to write one line on your poem.

The poem must be about the group experience, not other stuff. It can be serious, funny, silly, or all of these.

After you write the first line to your poem, fold the top over about 1 to 2 inches and PASS IT TO THE PERSON ON YOUR RIGHT.

The person who gets your poem then looks at your line and writes a line of his or her own. It can rhyme with your line or not have anything to do with it. Then that person folds over the top so only his or her line shows and passes it on to the next person on the RIGHT.

Each person is allowed to read only the line written by the person before: You can't unfold the page and read the previous ones.

Write one line and pass it on! Examples of first lines:

- We worked, we cried, we laughed, we shared . . .
- What a group! Eight guys and gals got together . . .
- Group is like the flowers in spring . . .
- Group is like the leaves turning colors . . .
- All of us tried, all of us cried, all of us felt good inside . . .

Continue until you have written a line on every other member's poem as well as your own. You should have your own poem back at this time. Unfold and read to yourself. Then let's read them all aloud to the other group members.

The group poem experience is magical. It always works, producing delightful poems for group members to keep as a reminder of the group experience. If the members wish, poems can also be duplicated and put them together in a booklet so everyone can have a copy of everyone else's poem.

230

Processing Time (¼ session time)

1. Ask the following questions:

    What memory will you take away from the group experience that will help you the most to deal with anger and related feelings?

    What would you like to say to any other group member to show appreciation for what you learned from that person?

2. Explain any follow-up arrangements and convey your own appreciation for group members' efforts and your hopes for the future. For example:

    Sometimes it is very hard to say good-bye. But this isn't good-bye forever! It is good-bye for the time being. We can get together in (4 or 5 weeks—whatever is appropriate) to find out how we are doing on working toward our goals and to keep our connections going. You might feel that you have just gotten started on your personal growth and have lots more wonderful things to discover and improve about yourself. Maybe you can work on them by yourself, and maybe you need more help. Please come see me if you think you do because maybe I can refer you to another counselor or place where you can get more help.

    I want to tell you how much progress you have made, and how important and wonderful it is that you are taking risks and making big changes in your life. This itself is the sign of growing up, and you are all taking giant steps forward.

Guys' Club: Issues from a Male Perspective _____

Preadolescent boys live in a world of frustrations. Many of them do not receive the nurturing and support needed both physically and psychologically from infancy and therefore grow up lacking in confidence and skills to deal with the stresses of adolescent years in healthy ways. With their basic needs not met, many youth are targets for physical and sexual abuse, and their frustrations grow. These frustrations play out in society in myriad ways: antisocial behaviors, predelinquent and delinquent behaviors, school problems, school violence, juvenile crime, self-inflicted crime, gang membership and violence, and family violence (Donmoyer & Kos, 1993; Dryfoos, 1990; Mishel & Bernstein, 1995).

Teachers and counselors are constantly confronted with boys and young men who are victims and perpetrators of violence on others as expressions of their own anger and frustrations. Sadly, many of these youth learn their behaviors from parents and older siblings, who are themselves victims and perpetrators of violence. Whole families are caught up an intergenerational cycle of violence. Although boys are not the only ones involved in these maladaptive behaviors, they tend to engage in clusters of violent behavior more often than girls and are considered more at risk for continuing in intergenerational social devastation (Jessor, 1993; Jessor, Donovan, & Costa, 1991).

For all of the screaming headlines on the news, there are thousands of less noteworthy tales of troubled, battered, depressed, scared, bored, angry, and bewildered youth we never hear about. But their teachers and school counselors come in contact with them every day and confirm the voiceless thousands virtually abandoned emotionally by their parents and the system. How do we help give voice to the voiceless, who attempt to gain attention by being "bad," by doing negative, hurtful things to one another and adults? Youth who engage in early delinquent behaviors often do so after a childhood bereft of emotional and social support. They ache to get back at those who are the cause of their feelings of loneliness, abandonment, depression, and anger.

Although the prevailing models for many youth are aggressive, negative, and often violent adults and other youth, significant research demonstrates that even one prosocial model can make a difference. Werner and Smith (1982, 1992) document a longitudinal study of aggressive and nonaggressive youth, confirming that enduring contact with even one prosocial model (coach, teacher, parent, peer) can result in a troubled adolescent's developing into a prosocially functioning adult.

Because they have few skills or behavioral referents for responding in more positive, effective ways, young adolescents are especially prone to responding negatively to provocative stimuli by peers. It is essential that some type of intervention take place early on so that maladaptive behavior patterns from childhood are not entrenched as adult behaviors, more resistant to change. Group counseling is a forum for learning and relearning social behaviors that are more appropriate ways to deal with social and coping skill deficits, interpersonal problems, and negative and corrosive thinking. This group experience focuses on a variety of issues that contribute to help boys develop insights into new ways of thinking and behaving in stressful situations, as well as become more comfortable sharing and inquiring about personal feelings and behaviors. It includes several high-interest activities to keep them involved and motivated.

The session sequence is as follows:

Session 1—Getting Started

Session 2—The Secret World of Body Language

Session 3—Friends

Session 4—I Am the President

Session 5—On Camera: Video Modeling I

Session 6—On Camera: Video Modeling II

Session 7—The Big Wuss Club

Session 8—That's a Wrap

GROUP GOALS

1. To facilitate development of a trusting, supportive environment in which members feel secure to risk and share

2. To ensure members can discriminate thinking, feeling, and behaving

3. To promote the group norm of becoming a supportive, encouraging person

4. To promote members' understanding of nonverbal body language and how it affects interpersonal communication

5. To help members develop awareness that understanding others is a very difficult task requiring good communication skills

6. To offer a humorous way of dealing with name-callers, bullies, and teasers

7. To review the group experience and learn how to set goals for future personal work

SELECTION AND OTHER GUIDELINES

Appropriate candidates for this group would be youth who exhibit poor interpersonal skills, cognitive coping skills, problem-solving skills, and self-management skills. Youth with these issues frequently have low self-esteem and exhibit this through passive, passive-aggressive, or aggressive behaviors toward family and friends. The homogeneous factor for selection in this group is actually broad-based social and cognitive skill deficits, rather than a particular problem such as loss or divorce. The youth may have difficulty relating to one another because of different manifestations of these deficits and not because of any identifiable issue. Such difficulty can be overcome if you establish the purpose of the group as being an accepting place to learn new skills and ideas for developing successful friendships with other guys. You will want to include at least two boys who are of high social status and who possess positive prosocial skills. In addition to these high-functioning youths, who are desirable and attractive to other group members by virtue of their status, each other member must have something positive to model for the group, such as a positive attitude or values, an effective coping skill, patience, or survivorship of life difficulties. Do not overload the group with negative or depressed members, or it will not work! Role-balance instead.

REFERENCES AND SELECTED RESOURCES FOR PROFESSIONALS

DeVito, J. A. (1989). *The nonverbal communication workbook.* Prospect Heights, IL: Waveland.

Donmoyer, R., & Kos, R. (1993). *At-risk students: Portraits, policies, programs, and practices.* Albany, NY: State University of New York Press.

Dryfoos, J. G. (1990). *Adolescents at risk: Prevalence and prevention.* New York: Oxford University Press.

Jessor, R. (1993). Successful adolescent development among youth in high-risk settings. *American Psychologist, 48,* 117–126.

Jessor, R., Donovan, J. E., & Costa, F. M. (1991). *Beyond adolescence: Problem behavior and young adult development.* New York: Cambridge University Press.

Kahn, J. S., Kehle, T. J., Jensen, W. R., & Clarke, E. (1990). Comparison of cognitive-behavioral, relaxation, and self-modeling intervention for depression among middle-school students. *School Psychology Review, 19,* 195–210.

Karns, M. (1994). *How to create positive relationships with students: A handbook of group activities and teaching strategies.* Champaign, IL: Research Press.

Kaufman, G., & Raphael, L. (1991). *Stick up for yourself.* St. Petersburg, FL: Trend.

Lal, S. R., Lal, D., & Achilles, C. M. (1993). *Handbook on gangs in schools: Strategies to reduce gang-related activities.* Thousand Oaks, CA: Corwin Press.

Meggert, S. S. (1996). Who cares what I think? Problems of low self-esteem. In D. Capuzzi & D. R. Gross (Eds.), *Youth at risk: A preventive resource for counselors, teachers, and parents* (2nd ed.). Alexandria, VA: American Association for Counseling and Development.

Mishel, L., & Bernstein, J. (1995). *State of working America, 1994–95* (Economic Policy Institute Series). Armonk, NY: M. E. Sharpe.

Shure, M. B. (1992). *I Can Problem Solve (ICPS): An interpersonal problem-solving program for children* (Intermediate Elementary Grades). Champaign, IL: Research Press.

Vernon, A. (1989). *Thinking, feeling, behaving: An emotional education curriculum for adolescents*. Champaign, IL: Research Press.

Werner, E. E., & Smith, R. S. (1982). *Vulnerable but invincible*. New York: McGraw-Hill.

Werner, E. E., & Smith, R. S. (1992). *Overcoming the odds: High-risk children from birth to adulthood*. Ithaca, NY: Cornell University Press.

Willis-Brandon, C. (1990). *Learning to say no: Establishing healthy boundaries*. Deerfield Beach, FL: Health Communication.

Getting Started

GOALS

Affective

To begin to relax and feel connected to the group

Behavioral

To thoroughly discuss confidentiality and its limits

To work with other members to select ground rules for the group

To participate in an activity to get acquainted with other group members

Cognitive

To understand the purpose and goals of the group

To discriminate thinking, feeling, and behaving

To identify thoughts, feelings, and behaviors related to problem situations

MATERIALS

Limits of Confidentiality sign (see Appendix A, page 270)

Easel pad or posterboard and marker

Get Acquainted in a Hurry (Handout 20)

Bean-bags, enough for each member to have 8 to 10

Three large containers, such as wastebaskets or popcorn cans, labeled separately as follows: *THINKING, FEELING,* and *BEHAVING/DOING*

Rewards for get-acquainted activity. (Tootsie Pops work great.)

Healthy snacks (such as fruit, crackers, juice, raisins)

GROUP SESSION

Opening Time

> For sessions after this first one, Opening Time will take up about one-fourth of the typical 40- to 50-minute session time, or about 10 minutes. For this first session, however, you will need to plan on more time to discuss confidentiality, develop ground rules, and conduct a getting-acquainted activity. See the book's introduction for some ideas on how to schedule this extra time.

1. Welcome the boys to group, going over the name, purpose, and general goals of the group. Stress that the purpose of the group is to get to know one another and help one another learn new skills and get ideas for developing successful friendships with other guys. Discuss that the group is a cooperative venture, meaning that they will pull together as a team, like other teams they are on, to make some positive steps toward their behavior-change goals. Everyone in the group has been selected because he has something positive to contribute.

2. Discuss confidentiality (the "no-blab" rule): What is said and done in the group stays in the group. Give several examples of what other kids or adults might say to pressure group members to share what happens in group. For instance:

What do you talk about in group, anyway?

Do you tell whether you do drugs in that group?

What does Alex say about me?

After members are clear on the meaning of confidentiality, share the Limits of Confidentiality sign (either as a handout or poster) and discuss: Let group members know you are bound by the confidentiality rule but that as the leader you are required to tell about what goes on in the group if you think someone will harm self or others, if someone says anything about child abuse or criminal activity going on, or if a judge orders you to turn over information. Summarize:

> *The reason I am asking you, and you are asking one another, to keep what we say in group confidential is that each person must feel safe and trusting in order to share personal business. Sharing is based on trust. We must be able to trust and take the risk to share for the wonderful learning and growing to happen.*

3. Explain that in addition to confidentiality, the group needs a few other basic rules so members can feel safe. Present the ground rules you have decided on for your group. For example:

Take turns.

Everyone has the right to "pass" (not share unless that's comfortable).

Agree to disagree (no put-downs).

Come on time.

Encourage members to add to these basic ground rules. Tell them that they can add or change ground rules as the group goes along according to what they need to feel comfortable in the group.

Don't move on until the group agrees on the ground rules. Write or have the group write the rules on an easel pad or piece of posterboard and have each member sign the document to show agreement. You can then post these rules every session.

---

4. Give each member a copy of the Get Acquainted in a Hurry page (Handout 20) and invite the group to participate in an activity to get to know one another better. (If you can copy this handout on both sides, members will have a total of eight sets of fill-in-the-blanks.) They will need to get up and walk around to find out the information on the list from each other group member. Let them know there will be a reward for writing down their responses in under 8 minutes. Read through the questions aloud once, then begin.

5. Invite members to sit down in the group circle after time is up and give rewards to all for "giving it their best shot." Let them talk for a minute or two about what connections they made.

Working Time

Working Time will take half of a typical session, or about 20 to 25 minutes.

---

1. Discuss the idea that during the eight sessions the group has together members will often be asking themselves and one another, "How do I feel?" "What am I thinking?" and "What am I (or others) doing?" In order to make sure everyone in the group understands clearly what these thinking-feeling-doing/behaving questions mean, you would like to invite them to play a game.

2. Place the three containers in the center of the group. Write the three categories (thinking, feeling, behaving/doing) at the top of the easel pad or another piece of posterboard, then ask the group to suggest words for those categories. Write the words as group members come up with them. The following examples may help get them started:

> Thinking: Imagining, deciding, examining, learning, remembering, wondering

> Feeling: Annoyed, confused, joyful, furious, humiliated, thankful, weary

> Doing/behaving: Arguing, jumping, digesting, imitating, laughing, throwing

3. After group members get the idea, give them the bean-bags and tell them how to play the game. First, any group member says a word (thinking, feeling, or doing/behaving) and tosses his bean-bag into the correctly labeled container. The first group member to say another word in the same category and toss his bean-bag accurately becomes the new leader. The new leader changes categories, says his new word, and tosses another bean-bag into the matching container. For example:

> Jesse starts as leader, says "daydreaming," and tosses a bean-bag into the *THINKING* container.

> Josh says "ideas" and tosses a bag into the *THINKING* container, then assumes leadership and changes the category. Josh says "playing ball" and tosses another bag into the *DOING/BEHAVING* container.

> Marshall says "swimming," tosses a bean-bag into the *DOING/BEHAVING* container, then assumes leadership, changing categories again.

Continue playing for several rounds until everyone has had a couple of turns and you are sure the group is making the discriminations.

4. Thank them for their work bringing everyone up to speed on this important issue. Invite them now to share something they would like to learn in the group experience, something that would help them get along better at school and at home (keep it broad based). Tell them that whatever they choose to work on they are expected to continue with throughout the group, so it isn't something they can change around each session—it is something important they really need to improve on now. Help each group member articulate what he wants to be thinking, feeling, and doing by the end of the group. For example:

> Ramon: "I would like to stop exaggerating all the time. My friends hate it, and I have lost some friends because of it. I would like to feel like I didn't need to exaggerate to have friends. I want to think I am OK and not have to do stupid stuff to be liked."

> LeShan: "I would like to know how to meet a girlfriend and have her like me. I want to have a girlfriend to go places with me like the games and feel like she likes me the same as I like her. I want to stop saying I can't meet anybody that likes me because it makes me feel bad about myself."

This is a big step for them! Give lots of encouragement.

Processing Time

Processing Time will take one-quarter of a typical session, or about 10 minutes.

---

1. Say, "Today we met for the first time, got acquainted, and learned about thinking, feeling, and behaving, three main areas we will be working on during this group," then ask at least one question from each of the processing levels:

INTRAPERSONAL

While we were doing these activities today, from the get-acquainted activity all the way through, what kinds of things were you thinking or feeling about being here and being a group member?

INTERPERSONAL

How does it feel now to be a member of this group, after we have shared some things, as compared to when you first came in the door and didn't know what group was going to be like?

NEW LEARNING

What new ideas or feelings do you have now about being a part of this experience?

APPLICATION

What tiny step do you think you could take between now and the next session to move toward your goal?

2. Thank group members for coming and give them a hope statement like the following example:

You have shared some very personal ideas and feelings today, and set some goals to work toward. I have a great deal of hope and belief that each of you can reach your goals and can support and encourage other group members along the way.

Remind them of the next session's day and time, and share the snacks.

Get Acquainted in a Hurry

Member's name _____

1. Birthday: month _____ day _____ year _____

2. Favorite pizza topping _____

3. Best movie of all time _____

4. Favorite food _____

5. Best game _____

6. Likes to do in free time _____

Member's name _____

1. Birthday: month _____ day _____ year _____

2. Favorite pizza topping _____

3. Best movie of all time _____

4. Favorite food _____

5. Best game _____

6. Likes to do in free time _____

Member's name _____

1. Birthday: month _____ day _____ year _____

2. Favorite pizza topping _____

3. Best movie of all time _____

4. Favorite food _____

5. Best game _____

6. Likes to do in free time _____

Member's name _____

1. Birthday: month _____ day _____ year _____

2. Favorite pizza topping _____

3. Best movie of all time _____

4. Favorite food _____

5. Best game _____

6. Likes to do in free time _____

The Secret World of Body Language

GOALS

Affective

To develop a sense of cohesion as a group through a shared activity

Behavioral

To participate in an activity to help become aware of the meaning of one's own and others' body language

To practice using appropriate body language to get a message across

Cognitive

To understand how body language affects people's perceptions of others

To recognize the messages body language sends in order to avoid potentially risky situations and/or deal with them

MATERIALS

Shadow Shapes (Handout 21)

Healthy snacks

GROUP SESSION

Opening Time (¼ session time)

1. Welcome the boys back to the group and ask what concerns they might be having regarding confidentiality. What do they need to discuss about it at this time? How are the ground rules working for them? Does the group need any changes or additions?

2. Briefly review the last session's content: discriminating thinking, feeling, and behaving, and identifying some goals to work toward during the group. Ask: "What have you noticed about your behavior since the last session? Have there been some changes in your behavior or thinking in relation to the goals you stated last time?"

Working Time (½ session time)

1. Discuss the idea that *body language* is a silent way of communicating with other people. Body language sends messages all the time, whether we realize it or not:

   Body language means our facial expressions or the way we stand, sit, walk, or move certain parts of our bodies. If we understand what our own and other people's body language means, it can help us get along with them better, avoid problem situations, and have more control of our own lives. Some people are really good at "reading" body language, and they have an advantage because they are not only getting verbal messages but are also understanding what someone is not saying. Some communication experts say we communicate about 60 percent through body language and only 40 percent by verbal language, so that gives the body language reader a head start on knowing what's going on.

   Suppose you are walking down the hall toward your locker and another guy starts making obscene gestures and silently mouthing, "You big wuss." Technically, he isn't saying any-thing, yet you are getting a very negative message. On a scale of 1 to 10, 1 meaning a little and 10 meaning very, very mad, how angry would you be in this situation? (Group members will probably say they would be very angry.) *If this person can poke your anger buttons, and you pop up to a 10, can you see how powerful body language messages can be? Without a word, you could be in a situation where you get in serious trouble because of your response to nonverbal language!*

2. Demonstrate the following and ask group members to tell you what they think your body language means:

> Rolling eyes around, looking up (aggravated, irritated)
>
> Crossed legs, crossed arms, slouched back in chair (bored, don't want to participate)
>
> Leaning forward, looking left and right, left and right (anticipation)
>
> Jumping up and down, waving arms back and forth (I did it!)
>
> Snarling face, making "tsk" noise (mad)
>
> Arms crossed, looking away from other person (mad, put out, hurt)
>
> Shoulders down, looking down, won't make eye contact (sad, guilty)
>
> Looking down, big, deep sigh (lonely)

3. Give group members copies of the Shadow Shapes (Handout 21) and ask them to guess what the people in the pictures are doing. (For example, a figure or figures may look angry, worried, or excited about something.)

4. Next ask group members to pair up and decide on a short, wordless scene they will act out for the rest of the group. Explain that the scene must have one main, identifiable emotion and message. Give them 5 minutes to go to corners of the room and decide what they are going to do. Instruct them to use arms, legs, whole body, and facial expressions to get their point across.

5. Reassemble and give each pair the center of the group to act out their scene. For example:

> I'm mad because I hurt my knee and can't do cross country.
>
> I'm red-faced (embarrassed) because I lost my ticket money.
>
> My book is damaged, and I'm gonna be in trouble!

6. Ask and discuss:

> What have you learned about watching other people to get in touch with how they may be feeling and what their attitudes are, as shown by their body language?
>
> What can you do when you notice someone is upset in some way?
>
> - Ask the person if he or she needs help.
> - Stay away, avoid the situation.
> - Acknowledge the person's feelings.
> - Discuss it.
> - Listen to the person's opinion.
> - Change your tone of voice.
> - Relax, take a deep breath, and try to compromise.
> - Analyze what you should say to the person, then say it.
> - Go get help.

Processing Time (¼ session time)

1. Ask at least one question from each of the processing levels:

    INTRAPERSONAL

    What have you been thinking and feeling today as we talked and acted out scenes about how people communicate with body language?

    INTERPERSONAL

    This was our second session together. How are you feeling about being a group member at this time? What is it like for you to be here in group?

    NEW LEARNING

    What have you learned today about body language that you might have found surprising? What is helpful? What is scary?

    What new ideas or feelings do you have now because of learning how body language affects you?

    APPLICATION

    How could you use this information before the next session to get a little closer to your goals for coming to the group?

2. Thank group members for coming and participating. Reinforce them for sharing their ideas, thoughts, and feelings—you know it is new and scary at first. Give them a hope statement, remind them of the day and time for the next session, then share the snacks.

Shadow Shapes

Friends

GOALS

Affective

To get in touch with feelings associated with having a loyal, trusting friend

Behavioral

To identify personal friendship values by creating a "chair sculpt"

Cognitive

To recognize the value of having a trustworthy friend

To explore the concept of loyalty

MATERIALS

Approximately four chairs per group member. (Folding chairs or children's chairs will work fine.)

Healthy snacks

GROUP SESSION

Opening Time (¼ session time)

1. Welcome the members back to group. Ask what concerns, questions, or issues they might have regarding confidentiality. How are the ground rules working for them at this point? Any additions or changes required for them to feel safe?

2. Ask: "What were you able to recognize about your own and other people's body language after the last session? What changes or responses have you made as a result of what someone's body language was telling you?"

Working Time (½ session time)

1. Explain that the focus of this session is becoming more aware of what friendship really means. Invite group members to talk about what they think are absolutely the most important parts of friendship, so important that the friendship does not work right or last if these parts are not there. (Group members will most likely name some or all of the qualities listed next.)

    Trust: What is trust? Why should you be able to trust a friend and that friend trust you?

    Respect: What is respect? Why should you respect a friend and that friend respect you?

    Loyalty: What is loyalty? Why should friends be loyal to each other?

    Concern/caring: What does *caring* mean? Why should friends care and be concerned about each other?

    Honesty: Why is honesty important in a friendship? What happens to a friendship when one or both are not honest?

2. Next invite the group to participate in creating a "chair sculpt." Have each member take a number of chairs and place them in a row, one in front of the other, with each chair representing a friend or another person who has the special qualities of friendship he values. Group members are to put the chairs in order of importance—the first chair represents the most important friendship value, the second chair represents the second most important value, and so forth.

3. Let group members arrange their chairs, then have everyone sit down except the person explaining his chair sculpt. That person walks over to the chairs and describes who is sitting in them. This is what Jeremiah's chair sculpt looks like and what he says about it, for example:

> Chair 1: "Coach Cramer, 'cause he always talks about being respectful. I respect him a lot. He pushes me to do my best and gets after me when I need it."
>
> Chair 2: "John Yellow Feather, who is the best friend I ever had because he is ALWAYS loyal and helps me, and he is the person I tell my deepest, darkest secrets to."
>
> Chair 3: "My big brother, Tommy, who is at college but he is also my best friend. I respect him a lot because he is smart and cool, and I know he likes me whatever I do."
>
> Chair 4: "Mr. Bastin, my biology teacher, has a lot of good values, too, like he helps you when you need it and stuff."

4. After each group member has had a turn, return to the group circle and ask:

> What did you learn from arranging the chairs to show what is important about your friends?
>
> What have you learned about why certain other people are not your friends?
>
> Why would you not choose a person for your friend? What kind of behaviors would he be doing?
>
> What kind of things would cause you to end a friendship with someone?
>
> What kind of friend would you want as a friend for life?

Processing Time (¼ session time)

1. Summarize, then ask at least one question from each of the four processing levels.

> *Today we did an activity to help get in touch with important parts of being a friend. You were able to identify people in your life you value as friends, how they affect you, and what kind of attitudes and behaviors you value in a friend.*

> INTRAPERSONAL
>
> What kind of thoughts and feelings did you have as we talked about all of this and did the chair sculpt activity?

> INTERPERSONAL
>
> What was it like for you to be a member of the group today?
>
> How is your trust level at this time?
>
> What have you noticed about the other group members?

> NEW LEARNING
>
> What new ideas or feelings do you have after thinking about friendships in this way?

> APPLICATION
>
> What could you say to a friend of yours before the next session to let him or her know how much you value your friendship? Would you be willing to try this if you feel ready?

2. Thank group members for coming. Give them a hope statement, remind them of the day and time for the next session, and share the snacks.

I Am the President

This energizing and discovery-filled activity requires an hour if each group member is to get a turn. You could also arrange for an extra session so all members will have a chance to participate.

GOALS

Affective

To get in touch with feelings associated with having and not having control

Behavioral

To participate in a spontaneous, imaginative, and fun activity

Cognitive

To recognize and disclose personal views on a variety of issues

To raise awareness of power and personal effectiveness in oneself and others

MATERIALS

One "special" chair. (You can make it a special chair by draping a red cloth over it.)

A penny or nickel, taped to the bottom of one group member's chair. Whoever sits in that chair is the first "president."

Healthy snacks

GROUP SESSION

Opening Time (¼ session time)

1. Welcome the members back to group. Ask what comments, questions, or concerns they might have about confidentiality at this time and how the ground rules are working for them.

2. Revisit the last session's topic of friendship values: "At the end of the I session asked if you would be willing to let a friend know how much you value that person's friendship. How did that go for you?"

Working Time (½ session time)

1. Discuss the idea that the president of the United States has the ability to make changes and do things his or her own way for 4 years while holding office. Sometimes the Congress does not go along with the president, so the president doesn't ALWAYS get what he (or she) wants, but often that is the case.

2. Invite group members to play a game where, one at a time, they will each get to be president for 3 minutes. Explain that the purpose is to recognize how they feel about control and to discover and disclose their personal views about a variety of issues. During the 3 minutes members are president they can make five changes, wishes, or events come true. The rest of the members of the group are the Congress; they will have 2 minutes to give their opinions about or rebut any of the president's changes or wishes, but they don't have the power to make the changes—only the president has that.

3. Tell members to look under their chairs: Whoever has the penny or nickel taped underneath is "elected" the first president. That group member then comes and sits in the special chair. Say "go" and begin the 3-minute timing. The president shares his changes, wishes, or events, then the Congress has 2 minutes for comments and rebuttals.

4. Congress then elects a new president, who takes over the special chair and begins 3 minutes of control. Continue until all group members have been president.

5. Reassemble everyone in the group circle and ask:

   What was it like for you to be president? What were you feeling?

   What was it like to have control over your whole life and make changes as if it could really happen?

   What was it like to hear other people disagree with you and not want your changes to occur?

   How did you feel when your time as president was ending and you had to give up the power?

   What would you be willing to give up or do to be president longer?

   What was the worst thing about being president? What was the best thing?

Processing Time (¼ session time)

1. Ask at least one question from the four processing levels:

   INTRAPERSONAL

   While you were president, what were you thinking and feeling that no one else knew about?

   INTERPERSONAL

   What did you notice about all of the group members as we did this activity today?

   What was happening?

   What was surprising?

   NEW LEARNING

   What new ideas or feelings do you have as a result of doing this activity today?

   APPLICATION

   What would it be like to observe how your peers, friends, teachers, school administrators, and family members behave in authority situations and consider what they might be feeling? Who feels ready to try that?

2. Thank the group for participating and give them a hope statement. Remind them of the day and time for the next session, then share the snacks.

On Camera: Video Modeling I

This is a two-session activity, the first one using prewritten situations and the second using situations, either real or imagined, that group members contribute.

GOALS

Affective

To increase feelings of self-confidence and competence in dealing with anger

Behavioral

To practice a problem-solving procedure to use in high-stress situations

To experience participant modeling as a way of learning a prosocial skill

Cognitive

To analyze angering situations

To understand that there is a behavioral alternative to losing control in angering situations

MATERIALS

Video camera, VCR and monitor, and blank videotape

Anger Role-Play Situations (Handout 22)

Easel pad or posterboard chart with the words *STOP, THINK, CHOOSE,* and *ACT* written on it in large letters, placed in full view

Healthy snacks

GROUP SESSION

Opening Time (¼ session time)

1. Welcome the members to group. Ask how they are feeling about the "no-blab" (confidentiality) rule at this point. What would they like to discuss about it? How are the ground rules working for them at this time?

2. Ask what ideas they have had since the last session's activity, about being president:

   What have you noticed about how power and authority influence people's behavior?

   What did you notice about yourself when you felt in control of a situation?

   How did you treat others that you had power or control over (like a younger brother or sister)?

   How did you feel when friends or adults exerted control over you? How would you like to have been treated?

Working Time (½ session time)

1. Discuss the idea that it has been found that videotaping and then watching yourself saying and doing new and more helpful things can help you overcome some difficult behavioral and emotional problems. Explain that today the focus is working through some role-plays of situations that are like ones group members face every day.

2. Pass out copies of the Anger Role-Play Situations (Handout 22). Explain that some group members will play the part of the antagonists, the people in the situation who start the problem, pick the fight, or in some way aggravate the other person. These members are called the "A's." Other group members will be the "B's" and will try using the STOP-THINK-CHOOSE-ACT way of dealing with the situation. (Tell the group that during the next session the B's will be A's and the A's will be B's, so everyone will get a chance to be in both roles.)

For this first session, select the two or three group members who have the best social and coping skills to play the B, or modeling, roles. Tell them that next time they will be the A's.

---

3. Read Situation 1 aloud. Explain that the process will go like this:

   A's: Act out your role in your own words. You may keep the situation description in hand and stop to read it whenever you want. Your performance doesn't have to be perfect.

   B's: Try using the STOP-THINK-CHOOSE-ACT way of dealing with the situation: You may take as much time as you want and ask for help and coaching from those watching. After the A player(s) perform the aggravating behavior, you will turn your body away. You will say STOP! THINK: If I do this, then this will happen; if I do that, then this is likely to happen. Say as many alternatives as you can think of. Then say, I CHOOSE _____ (behavior) and ACT (do it). This first trial may be rough, but it is just a practice.

   Specific instructions for the first situation might sound something like this:

   Joe, you play Pedro, the B role, and Thomas and Lenny, you are Matt and Paul, the A roles. Joe, get as mad as you want when you see your locker, but then look away from Matt and Paul toward the STOP-THINK-CHOOSE-ACT chart. Say STOP! THINK: What are some better ways to deal with this? Name a few things you could do instead of going after them and starting a fight. CHOOSE one and ACT (do it).

4. Videotape the role-play as group members perform it. Afterwards, rewind the video and have everyone watch. Use open-ended questions to help the group explore the role-playing:

   What did the B player do well in the role-play? Tell him directly what he did well.

   What needs to be improved on—what could B have done better? Tell him directly what he could do.

5. Have A's and B replay Situation 1, making corrections according to the group's feedback.

6. Rewind and replay the second trial. Reward and reinforce.

7. Follow the same procedure for Situation 2 with different actors: Role-play and videotape the situation, rewind and have the group view the tape and give feedback, role-play and videotape the situation again (with the group's corrections), then have the group view the second attempt. Give lots of encouragement for positive changes.

Processing Time (¼ session time)

1. Ask at least one question from each of the four processing levels:

   INTRAPERSONAL

   What were you thinking or feeling as you watched or participated in the role-plays?

   What have you learned from watching the video about dealing with angering situations in ways that require thinking and making better choices?

INTERPERSONAL

What did you notice while watching the other group members participate and give feedback during the group experience?

NEW LEARNING

What new ideas or feelings have you had today about using this technique to help you deal with angering situations?

APPLICATION

During the time between now and the next session, who would be willing to try to use the STOP-THINK-CHOOSE-ACT way of dealing with things instead of giving in to angering situations?

2. Thank group members for trying the new video technique to deal with situations. Tell them that the next session they are invited to act out their own situations, so be thinking of ideas. Give them a hope statement, remind them of the day and time for the next session, then share the snacks.

Anger Role-Play Situations

Photocopy, then cut out and give group members only the situations. Retain the lists of alternatives so the role-players can generate their own "better ways of dealing with it."

SITUATION 1: DEALING WITH PREJUDICE

Pedro is putting his books in his locker and getting his basketball out to go shoot some hoops in the gym after school. He notices that someone has written on the locker with lipstick, and it says, "Spics can't kiss." He hears someone laughing, looks over, and sees Matt and Paul across the hall. These two guys have been mean toward him all week. Pedro is furious and ready to take Matt and Paul on in a fight.

SITUATION 2: LYING AND STEALING

Jason doesn't have time to put his wallet in his locker, which is all the way at the other end of the building. He has 35 dollars in 5-dollar bills he has saved to pay for a new soccer jersey. He makes a decision to hide the money on a shelf in the science lab and come back to get the wallet after math, which is right across the hall. There are a lot of science papers and projects left all over and stuck on the shelf, so he thinks his wallet is well hidden. Just as he walks into the math room, he looks back and sees Jerome headed toward the shelf. Jerome rarely has enough money even for lunch, let alone extra to show off. Jerome comes into math class late, from the science lab, with a bunch of 5-dollar bills. Jason whispers to Jerome, "Hey, where'd you get those fives?" and Jerome says, "None of your damn business." Jason is so mad he can't concentrate on math, and Mr. Washington, the math teacher, calls him to get to work and finish the problems assigned.

Situation 1

Examples of "better ways of dealing with it" are . . .

1. Get a basketball and go straight to the gym and shoot until your anger wears down.
2. Go out and jog around the quarter-mile track a few times.
3. Take a few deep breaths and go about your business.
4. Find your best friend and ask for support.
5. Go outside and scream and yell.
6. Look for your girlfriend and kiss her a couple of times really great and ask her to tell you how well you kiss.
7. When you see Matt and Paul say, "It's obvious you're jealous of my sexy lips."

Situation 2

Examples of "better ways of dealing with it" are . . .

1. Don't leave the money anywhere but your locked locker in the first place.
2. Go to the teacher immediately after class and explain the situation; take witnesses to Jerome's having the fives.
3. Go to the school counselor immediately after class, explain the situation, and ask for help.
4. Confront Jerome, saying, "I expect you to repay every cent immediately, or I will report it as theft."

On Camera: Video Modeling II

GOALS

Affective

To increase feelings of self-confidence and competence in dealing with anger

Behavioral

To practice a problem-solving procedure to use in high-stress situations

To experience participant modeling as a way of learning a prosocial skill

Cognitive

To analyze angering situations

To understand that there is a behavioral alternative to losing control in angering situations

MATERIALS

Video camera, VCR and monitor, and blank videotape

Easel pad or posterboard chart with the words *STOP, THINK, CHOOSE,* and *ACT* written on it in large letters, placed in full view

Healthy snacks

GROUP SESSION

Opening Time (¼ session time)

1. Welcome the members back to group. Ask what concerns they might have about confidentiality. Are there any comments about the ground rules at this point?

2. Ask: "What did you notice about angering situations last week after we did the STOP-THINK-CHOOSE-ACT videos? Who would like to share how it was to use this technique in a situation outside the group?"

Working Time (½ session time)

1. Ask what kinds of situations group members thought of to use for the videotaping today. Help them clarify exactly what went on in these situations and reduce the scene to a manageable interchange. (They usually want to go on and on about a long, involved problem.) The focus here is more on doing short scenes using the STOP-THINK-CHOOSE-ACT technique than on dealing with complicated relationship issues.

2. Ask the group members who were A's during the last session if, after watching the B's model last time, they would be willing to switch roles (do the modeling) this time.

3. Repeat the role-play process:

   A's: Act out the aggravating behavior (your role) in your own words.

   B's: Try using the STOP-THINK-CHOOSE-ACT way of dealing with the situation. Take as much time as you want, asking for help from other group members as needed. Say STOP! THINK: If I do this, then this will happen; if I do that, this is likely to happen. Say as many alternatives as you can think of. Then say, I CHOOSE _____ (behavior) and ACT (do it).

4. After videotaping, rewind the video; everyone watches and critiques the role-play. Use open-ended questions to help explore the situation:

What did the B player do well in the role-play? Tell him directly what he did well.

What needs to be improved on—what could B have done better? Tell him directly what he could do.

5. Have the actors replay the scene, making corrections according to the group's feedback, while you videotape.

6. Rewind and replay the second trial. Reward and reinforce.

7. Do as many more scenes as you can, leaving time to process.

Processing Time (¼ session time)

1. Ask at least one question from each of the four processing levels:

INTRAPERSONAL

Today we worked on your tough situations using the STOP-THINK-CHOOSE-ACT approach. While you were doing the role-plays, or observing and giving feedback, what were you thinking and feeling?

INTERPERSONAL

What was it like to observe the other group members learning this technique?

NEW LEARNING

As you observed and participated, what new thoughts or feelings did you have that you would like to describe?

APPLICATION

Who is at a point to make a commitment to practice the STOP-THINK-CHOOSE-ACT technique some time before the next session? If you don't feel comfortable saying you will, you don't have to—this is only for those who feel ready for it.

2. Remind the group members that there is only one more working session in the group, the next session. The last session will be a review of experiences, goal setting for the future, and a celebration. Tell them to be thinking of what kind of celebration they would like to have at the end of the last session.

3. Thank them for coming and give them a hope statement. Remind them of the day and time for the next session, and share the snacks.

The Big Wuss Club

GOALS

Affective

To enhance a sense of self-control and efficacy in dealing with peer pressure

Behavioral

To learn a technique to deal with peer pressure cues

To practice a skill with group members that will transfer to experiences outside the group

Cognitive

To understand why peers use teasing, threatening, and name-calling to control situations

To learn how to replace passive and aggressive behavior with an assertive, humorous response

MATERIALS

Easel pad or posterboard chart with the following written in large letters:

> **NOT JUST A WUSS, A DOUBLE DIG-DOG WUSS**
>
> And too smart to fall for that.
>
> And too wuss-y for cool guy(s) like you.
>
> And I'm in control of me, not you.

Big Wuss Situations (Handout 23)

Healthy snacks

GROUP SESSION

Opening Time (¼ session time)

1. Welcome the members back to group. Inquire what concerns they might have about confidentiality. Are any changes needed in the ground rules at this point?

2. Ask how it went for those who made a commitment to practicing the STOP-THINK-CHOOSE-ACT technique. Encourage and reward even small approximations of success.

Working Time (½ session time)

1. Ask group members the following questions:

> Why do you think other kids do and say things that make you mad, poke your buttons so you will respond in some way that gets you in trouble?
>
> Are those tactics successful in getting you to be really mad?
>
> How good are you at saying aggravating things that result in someone else's getting mad?
>
> If you respond by fighting or saying something back to a person for making an aggravating statement, why do you do this? (To get back at the person)
>
> Who is in control here? Are you in control, or is the person making the aggravating statement in control? (The other person)
>
> The other person poked your anger button, and you responded just the way that person expected, so YOU are the loser here, not the other person. How does it feel to be the loser when you give in to someone else's stimulus?
>
> What would it be like to turn this situation around so you get control for a change?

2. Summarize, then ask the following questions:

   Today we are going to learn a way to respond to name-calling that might sound like it wouldn't work. It does work, though, because it puts YOU back in control so you don't respond in ways that do damage to yourself. One name-calling situation that happens every day and is very angering because it jabs at your self-esteem in a very powerful way is when other kids call you a "wuss" for doing something, or being something, or not doing something, or whatever.

   What is a wuss anyway? (A weakling, crybaby, jerk, someone who is scared of doing something, gutless, won't take a risk)

   Why is it so bad to be called a wuss?

3. Make the connection between name-calling and the other person's need for control:

   The reason you call someone a wuss is a power thing—it is to control the other person, to be a "winner" by calling the other person a loser, a wuss. But calling you a wuss or anything else is not what makes you lose in a situation. It is your behavior in response to the name-calling that can put you in a situation where you might make poor choices, where you WOULD end up losing your self-respect or maybe getting in trouble in school or at home. If you take hold of the situation and don't pay attention to the names, then YOU TAKE BACK CONTROL of the situation. The other person no longer has control if you are not negatively affected by the names, whatever they are.

4. Invite group members to try the new way of responding:

   Since name-callers want you to have a negative response, to get mad, start a fight, whatever, which is not in your best interest, we'll use a different approach to the name-calling. The reason you react negatively is that you have told yourself that being called a wuss is something awful that you can't stand. Instead of reacting with hurtful responses, change the idea that it is awful and terrible to be called a wuss to the idea that it doesn't mean a thing if someone calls you a wuss because . . .

   You aren't a wuss. (No one has ever seen one!)

   It doesn't matter what someone calls you—you are still a worthwhile, competent person.

   People who call you names don't deserve having you as their friend anyway.

5. Show the chart and explain that one way of defusing a volatile situation is to say something that is surprising to the other person, something unexpected, instead of getting mad:

   If name-calling doesn't work, you have called the other person's bluff. What you can say back is that not only ARE you a wuss, you are a big, huge, extraordinary wuss, a DOUBLE DIG-DOG WUSS. This is so unexpected that it takes the wind out of the other person's sails, and you can then leave the situation and go debrief with someone else and reward yourself for not falling into the trap. You are using "reverse psychology": The name-caller won't understand it, so it changes a potentially harmful situation into one where you are in control. NOW IT TAKES A BIG WHOPPING HELPING OF COURAGE FOR YOU TO TRY THIS BECAUSE IT IS SO DIFFERENT. BUT IT WORKS IF YOU STICK WITH IT.

6. Pass out the Big Wuss Situations (Handout 23) and ask for one volunteer to be the sender and another to be the receiver. The sender sends a negative message, and the receiver responds with one of the "reverse psychology" statements on the chart.

7. Encourage group members to come up with their own responses and add these to the chart as you go. Have as many senders and receivers practice as time permits.

Processing Time (¼ session time)

1. Ask at least one question from each of the four processing levels:

   INTRAPERSONAL

   Goofy as this idea sounded at first, what were you thinking and feeling as we were trying it out?

   INTERPERSONAL

   What did you notice about how group members acted in this situation today?

   NEW LEARNING

   What new ideas or feelings do you have now about dealing with situations where you are called a wuss or any other names?

   APPLICATION

   How can getting control of yourself and your responses to provoking situations help you get along better at home and school?

   What would it be like to try out this technique? Does anyone feel ready to do that?

2. Explain that the next session will be the last one and ask how group members would like to celebrate the end of the group. Decide what special party food they would like and who will bring what.

3. Thank group members for coming and give them a hope statement. Remind them of the day and time for the next session, and share the snacks.

Big Wuss Situations

SITUATION 1

You are sitting in math class minding your own business when Mike whispers to you, "Hey, buddy, give me your homework—I need it now." You say, "Heck, no, I worked an hour on it." Mike says back, "You didn't either, you big brown-noser wuss." You say . . .

SITUATION 2

You and your best friend, Charlie, are at the football game on Friday night. There are a zillion girls running around, and all the guys are talking to them or talking about talking to them and having fun. You and Charlie don't have girlfriends but would like to. Some high school guys see you watching the girls and making comments, and one of them, Nathan, says to you and Charlie, "You two wusses couldn't get a look, much less a phone call, from those girls—keep your eyes to yourself." Charlie is really steamed. You tell Charlie to be cool and let you say something, and then you'll both go and get hot dogs. You say to Nathan . . .

SITUATION 3

Your grade has the early lunch time, and you are in line in the cafeteria. You're not as hungry as usual because your mom was home from work today and made bacon and eggs for breakfast, and you ate them and a big pile of toaster waffles, too. So you just take one chocolate milk and some mashed potatoes, your favorite. All the rest of the guys are taking the biggest portions they can get and piling up the food. Your tray looks a little empty. Leon and Juan look at your tray and start laughing out loud. You give them a nasty look. They love it, laugh more, and turn around to some other guys in line and say, "Hey, look at that kid's stuff—no wonder he's so skinny and ugly. Hey, kid, don't ya wanna eat some more, ya big wuss?" You say . . .

SITUATION 4

You and some other guys go to K-Mart to look at some stuff they have for fishing and camping. You are looking at the fishing lures and trying to decide whether to get some or not, when one of the guys says, "Why don't you just stick that lure in your pocket and get it on outta here?" You say, "You think I want to get caught stealing? No way." The other guys start snickering, and one of them says, "You always were a big wuss. We'd do it." You say . . .

That's a Wrap

GOALS

Affective

To deal with feelings associated with the ending of the group

To feel satisfaction for making progress toward a personal goal

Behavioral

To express appreciation to other group members in writing

To celebrate the group's work together and say good-bye

Cognitive

To review and reinforce what has been learned in the group

To realize progress and set goals for the future

To recognize that other group members have contributed to one's changes in attitudes and behaviors

MATERIALS

Brown paper lunch bags, enough for each group member to have one

Thin-tipped colored markers

Plain paper, cut into four or five strips horizontally, enough for each member to have eight strips

Party food

GROUP SESSION

Opening Time (¼ session time)

1. Welcome members to the final group. Ask how the confidentiality rule has helped them feel safe during the group experience and how the ground rules have worked for them. Remind them that the "no-blab" rule continues even after the group is over.

2. Review the previous session, on rethinking name-calling and using "reverse psychology" on the person sending the message. Has anyone tried the technique? How did it work?

Working Time (½ session time)

1. Briefly review the topics of the previous group sessions and invite comments:

> Session 1—Getting Started
>
> Getting acquainted, learning about thinking-feeling-behaving, and setting and sharing goals for ourselves
>
> Session 2—The Secret World of Body Language
>
> Becoming aware of body language as an important part of communication
>
> Session 3—Friends
>
> Identifying important values and behaviors involved in friendship

Session 4—I Am the President

Recognizing power and control in ourselves and others

Session 5—On Camera: Video Modeling I

Practicing the STOP-THINK-CHOOSE-ACT way of dealing with angering situations

Session 6—On Camera: Video Modeling II

Practicing this new way of dealing with anger in situations from real life

Session 7—The Big Wuss Club

Learning a humorous way of responding to teasing and peer pressure

2. Convey your appreciation and respect for group members' participation in the whole group experience. Explain that each of them contributed in his own way and that each person learns from every other group member, sometimes more as time goes on rather than immediately.

It is important to keep track of the time during the following thank-you activity. Be sure to save enough time to have a share-around in which members identify goals for the future.

---

3. Explain that in order to thank and give appreciation statements to one another, you have provided a bag and some strips of paper for them to do so in a private way. Pass out the bags, strips, and marking pens. Invite members to write out a short statement of thanks, appreciation, or respect for each other group member, one per strip of paper. Each group member writes his name on the paper bag, opens it, and sets it in front of him. As members write their appreciation notes, they drop them in one another's bags. Some examples of things they could say include the following:

Joe, I respect you, man. You really worked hard and did some tough stuff.

Paolo, thanks for telling me to get on with it and stop being so mean. I'm doing better.

Bohdan, you really changed, and I like you a lot more now.

Skip, I appreciate your ideas—you have neat ideas, and I like that.

Processing Time (¼ session time)

1. Ask the following questions:

What did you like best about coming to this group experience? What did you like least?

What was the most important/useful thing you learned by coming to the group?

What happened to us as a group that was a special learning experience?

Would you recommend a group experience to your friends? Why or why not?

What would you like to continue working on in the future? Would each of you be willing to state a goal you would like to work toward in the next month? (Conduct a share-around.)

2. Explain any follow-up plans and give the group a hope statement for the future. You might say, for example:

Sometimes it is very hard to say good-bye. But this isn't good-bye forever! It is good-bye for the time being. We will be getting together in 4 or 5 weeks for a follow-up session to find out how we are doing on working toward our goals and to keep our connections going. You might feel that you have just gotten started identifying things about guys' issues and your own personal challenges to discover and improve yourself. Maybe you can work on them by yourself, and maybe you need more help. Please come see me if you think you do because maybe I can refer you to another counselor or place where you can get more help, or even another group experience. Don't forget, you have other guys in the group for your support system now.

You have taken some big steps toward improving your lives, and I believe in each one of you. You have shown me you have the ability to make changes for the better in your life. I have a great deal of hope and confidence that each of you will continue to take the risks to grow as a beautiful, kind, and loving person.

3. Share the party snacks and celebrate!

SAMPLE FORMS

Faculty Group Counseling Needs Assessment

Dear Faculty Member:

The counseling staff will be conducting small-group counseling experiences during the academic year. We are seeking your support and input so that we can better meet your needs and the needs of the youth in our school. Please help us provide the best and most appropriate services possible. Each of the following topics represents a major issue to be covered in an eight- or nine-session group counseling experience. A counselor or counselor team will lead the group. Please place a check mark beside the topics you think are most valuable at this time. Thank you very much!

_____ 1. Anger management skills

_____ 2. Dealing with a divorce in the family

_____ 3. Meeting, making, and keeping friends

_____ 4. Learning assertion skills (less aggressive, less passive)

_____ 5. Developing self-esteem

_____ 6. Stress management

_____ 7. Coping with grief and loss

_____ 8. Dealing with alcohol and drugs

_____ 9. Learning to make better decisions

_____ 10. Relaxation skills

_____ 11. Dealing with bullies and cliques

_____ 12. Transition from elementary to middle/junior high school and middle/junior high school to high school

_____ 13. Getting along at home (parents and siblings)

_____ 14. Dating relationships

_____ 15. Getting along with teachers

_____ 16. Dealing with abuse in the home

_____ 17. Sexual activity, STD's, pregnancy

_____ 18. Dealing with learning problems (AD/HD, other)

_____ 19. Other _____

_____ 20. Other _____

Comments:

Name _____ Date _____

Return to _____

Student Group Counseling Needs Assessment

Dear Student:

Your school counselors will be providing group counseling experiences for you during the year. Group counseling is a way for six to eight students to work with a counselor on such topics as learning to manage stress, friendship skills, learning to manage anger, learning to make better decisions, dealing with a divorce in the family, understanding feelings, and other issues. Please tell us what group topics you would be interested in or that you think we need at our school. Please put a check mark next to any subject you think would be helpful. Please circle any subject if you would like to have a counselor speak with you about the possibility of being included in a group on that topic. SIGN YOUR NAME ONLY IF YOU ARE INTERESTED IN BEING CONTACTED ABOUT BEING IN A GROUP.

_____ 1. Anger management skills

_____ 2. Dealing with a divorce in the family

_____ 3. Meeting, making, and keeping friends

_____ 4. Learning assertion skills (less aggressive, less passive)

_____ 5. Developing self-esteem

_____ 6. Stress management

_____ 7. Coping with grief and loss

_____ 8. Dealing with alcohol and drugs

_____ 9. Learning to make better decisions

_____ 10. Relaxation skills

_____ 11. Dealing with bullies and cliques

_____ 12. Transition from elementary to middle/junior high school and middle/junior high school to high school

_____ 13. Getting along at home (parents and siblings)

_____ 14. Dating relationships

_____ 15. Getting along with teachers

_____ 16. Dealing with abuse in the home

_____ 17. Sexual activity, STD's, pregnancy

_____ 18. Dealing with learning problems (AD/HD, other)

_____ 19. Other _____

_____ 20. Other _____

Comments:

Sign your name only if you want to be contacted about a group.

Name _____ Date _____

Return to _____

Letter to School Faculty

Dear Faculty Member:

The counseling staff will soon be starting a series of group counseling experiences for the youth in our school. Group counseling has been found to be very helpful in assisting certain youths in learning important personal and social skills, and in developing more healthy attitudes. Group leader(s) will work with six to eight students for eight or nine sessions of approximately 50 minutes each.

It is important to distinguish between group guidance and group counseling. *Group guidance* involves sharing information with a large group, such as an entire class. This information can help students make better life decisions about such matters as the use of drugs/alcohol, career paths, and so forth. Group guidance is designed to prevent issues from becoming problems and is something every student needs and deserves on a regular basis. *Group counseling,* on the other hand, is remedial in nature. It is meant to help those who are already having problems with developmental issues and to prevent such problems from becoming out of hand. In group counseling, small groups are selected by the counselor to receive this service.

Group counseling is not appropriate for every youth who has problems. Some need more intense, individualized help and would best be served by individual counseling or family therapy. For example, a child who is involved in a crisis of some sort would not be an appropriate candidate for group counseling. A youngster who is so shy that he or she cannot interact in a group would also not be suited. And a youngster who is very aggressive or who needs constant attention would not be a good candidate. So, although a student might need help very badly, group counseling might not be the best type of service. If you know of such students, the counseling staff would be happy to assist in finding appropriate help.

The group counseling experiences coming up are on the following topics:

_____

_____

_____

They will meet from _____ to _____ . If you have students you think could benefit from this experience, please let us know as soon as possible. We will be happy to meet with you and plan how we can cooperate to make this a special learning experience for the youngsters of our school.

Sincerely,

School Counseling Staff

Letter to Parent/Guardian

Dear Parent or Guardian:

During the school year, your school counseling staff will be offering students in need of services the opportunity to participate in group counseling. About six to eight youths are selected to be in the group.

Group counseling is an excellent way for some students to learn new skills, develop self-confidence, become more aware of how others see them, practice new behaviors, and better understand how to deal with the many problems life presents.

Your child has expressed interest in participating in a group that will be starting soon. Enclosed is a form that asks you to give your consent for your child to participate. He or she has not been selected yet and will not be considered until you give your permission. Only a few students will be able to have this opportunity at a time. If your child is not selected but is an appropriate candidate for future services, he or she will have other opportunities to participate. Participation in the group is completely voluntary and will not affect your child's grades in any way.

Please read the Parent/Guardian Consent Form thoroughly and return it by _____ (date). If you have questions, concerns, or comments, please call us at the number and times listed below. Thank you very much for considering this opportunity for your child.

Sincerely,

School Counseling Staff

Telephone number _____

Best times to call _____

Parent/Guardian Consent Form

Your permission is requested for your child, _____ (name), to participate in group counseling activities at _____ (school). The group counseling will run for approximately _____ (number of weeks), from _____ (date) to _____ (date). A total of _____ (number of sessions) of _____ (number of minutes) each is scheduled. The group is entitled _____ (topic/title) and will include discussion of ideas, behaviors, feelings, attitudes, and opinions. Some of the subjects to be covered in the group are as follows:

_____

_____

_____

Participants will have the opportunity to learn new skills and behaviors that may help their personal development and adjustment. The group will be led by _____ (name/s), of the school counseling staff.

Because counseling is based on a trusting relationship between counselor and client, the group leader(s) will keep the information shared by group members confidential except in certain situations in which there is an ethical responsibility to limit confidentiality. In the following circumstances, you will be notified.

1. If the child reveals information about harm to himself/herself or to any other person

2. If the child reveals information about child abuse

3. If the child reveals information about criminal activity or the court (a judge) subpoenas counseling records

4. Other _____

By signing this form I give my informed consent for my child to participate in group counseling. I understand that:

1. The group will provide an opportunity for members to learn and practice interpersonal skills, discuss feelings, share ideas, practice new behaviors, and make new friends.

2. Anything group members share in group will be kept confidential by the group leader(s) except in the above-mentioned cases.

Please return this form to _____ (name) by _____ (date).

Parent/Guardian _____ Date _____

Parent/Guardian _____ Date _____

Student _____ Date _____

Harm
(to self or others)

Abuse

Courts

TAP-IN STUDENT SELECTION CHECKLIST

Date _____ Interviewer _____

Name of student _____

Age _____ Grade _____ Group _____

TELL

_____ 1. The name, purpose, and goals of the group.

_____ 2. Where, when, and how often the group will meet.

_____ 3. The name(s) of the group leader(s).

_____ 4. The number of students to be selected (not everyone who wants to be in the group will be selected).

_____ 5. Both student and parents must give permission.

_____ 6. Members will be expected to share some personal things about themselves, such as ideas, feelings, attitudes, and behaviors, but no one will force you to share anything you do not wish to.

_____ 7. Benefits of being in the group (be specific to group topic).

_____ 8. Risks of being in the group (negative feelings or behaviors from self and others as a result of learning new things or making changes).

_____ 9. In group, we agree to keep whatever is said confidential (no one tells what is said to anyone outside the group). Since none of us has complete control over all of the members, we can't guarantee that another group member will not break your confidence. Also, there are times when the group leader(s) would have to share what you say with other adults, such as your parents.

   • If you say anything about doing harm to yourself or someone else, or if you say you know about others who are being or might be harmed

   • If you tell about child abuse

   • If you tell about criminal activity or the court (a judge) subpoenas records about the group

_____ 10. All group members are expected to be on time for each meeting. A close bond forms in the group because members are sharing and learning together. It therefore affects everyone when one person is absent.

_____ 11. You may stop being a member of the group at any time, but you need to discuss this first with the leader, and then come to one last group and say good-bye to the other group members who were working with you.

_____ 12. No physical abuse, verbal abuse, or drug use is allowed in group.

_____ 13. Each group member is expected to do some self-improvement practice between sessions. This is like "personal homework."

_____ 14. Each group member is expected to work on behavior-change goals.

ASK

_____ 1. What would you like to ask me about the group from what I've told you so far?

_____ 2. Are you going to any other counselor, social worker, family counseling, or psychologist outside of school? Any other group counseling?

_____ 3. If selected for the group, will you be able to and agree to attend every session (any school or outside-of-school activities or classes that would be scheduled at the same time)?

_____ 4. Are you willing to share personal things about yourself, such as your ideas, thoughts, feelings, and behaviors?

_____ 5. Are you willing to do self-improvement exercises between meetings?

_____ 6. What goals would you like to work toward? In other words, how do you want to be different at the end of the group?

_____ 7. Would you allow the leader to invite a student counselor to co-lead during group? (Ask only if applicable.)

_____ 8. On a scale of 1 to 10, 1 meaning not at all and 10 meaning very much, how much do you want to be a member of the group?

Interviewer _(signature)_ _____ Date _____

PICK

Note: Complete this part after the interview with the student is finished.

_____ 1. Does this student seem to understand the purpose and goals of the group?

_____ 2. Does this student appear to want to participate in the group and be a productive group member?

_____ 3. Does this student have some positive behaviors, attitudes, coping skills, or other qualities from which other members could learn?

_____ 4. Does this student seem compatible with others tentatively selected?

_____ 5. Does this student appear to be making the decision to join the group independently or under the influence of others?

_____ 6. Does this student appear to be giving informed assent?

_____ 7. What is this student's motivation factor (on a scale of 1 to 10)?

Selected _____ Not selected _____

Potential for future group? Yes_____ No _____

Comments:

PRETESTS/POSTTESTS

Girlfriends: Understanding and Managing Friendships

Name _____ Date _____

Instructions: Each of the statements below concerns your ideas, beliefs, attitudes, or feelings about personal and friendship issues. After each statement is a response you could choose. Circle the response that is how you think or feel now.

1 = never
2 = hardly ever
3 = sometimes
4 = most of the time
5 = always

Example: I like to eat pizza and drink Dr. Pepper.   1 ② 3 4 5

You hardly ever like to eat pizza and drink Dr. Pepper.

1. I am able to express my feelings to my family and friends.   1 2 3 4 5
2. I am aware of stresses caused by friends and peers with negative attitudes.   1 2 3 4 5
3. I can tell when someone is not good for me to hang out with.   1 2 3 4 5
4. I know how to end a friendship that is not good for me.   1 2 3 4 5
5. I can tell when a situation means trouble, and I can avoid it.   1 2 3 4 5
6. I am aware of how my body reacts to too much stress.   1 2 3 4 5
7. I can tell exactly what is and what is not gossip.   1 2 3 4 5
8. I know what my values are, and I make decisions based on them most of the time.   1 2 3 4 5
9. I know what to do if someone is sexually harassing me.   1 2 3 4 5
10. I have a positive attitude about being a girl.   1 2 3 4 5

Jugglers: Middle School Transition Issues

Name ——————————————————————— Date ———————————————

Instructions: Each of the statements below concerns your ideas, beliefs, attitudes, or feelings about the many changes and emotions you are experiencing. After each statement is a response you could choose. Circle the response that is how you think or feel now.

1 = never
2 = hardly ever
3 = sometimes
4 = most of the time
5 = always

Example: I like watching sports events on TV.   1 2 ③ 4 5

You like watching sports events sometimes.

1. I know how to be a good listener.   1 2 3 4 5
2. I am aware that I am going through physical, emotional, and   1 2 3 4 5
   educational changes.
3. Sometimes I feel that all these changes are very confusing.   1 2 3 4 5
4. I know that big mood changes are part of growing up.   1 2 3 4 5
5. Sometimes I feel very irritated and frustrated by so many changes.   1 2 3 4 5
6. I feel like I have a lot of skill in relationships.   1 2 3 4 5
7. I am flexible and able to change and adjust to situations easily.   1 2 3 4 5
8. I am aware of the long-term consequences of certain of my behaviors.   1 2 3 4 5
9. I realize that my emotions change from very low to very high,   1 2 3 4 5
   sometimes quickly.
10. I have a positive attitude about my future.   1 2 3 4 5

Dating and Relating: Male/Female Relationship Issues

Name _____ Date _____

Instructions: Each of the statements below concerns your ideas, beliefs, attitudes, or feelings about dating relationships. After each statement is a response you could choose. Circle the response that is how you think or feel now.

1 = never
2 = hardly ever
3 = sometimes
4 = most of the time
5 = always

Example: I like playing games on the computer.   1   2   3   ④   5

You like playing computer games most of the time.

1. I know how being passive, aggressive, and assertive are different.   1   2   3   4   5
2. I know what I like and don't like in someone I would date more than once.   1   2   3   4   5
3. Sometimes I feel dating is very confusing.   1   2   3   4   5
4. I understand loyalty and keeping personal secrets.   1   2   3   4   5
5. I have a right to stop dating someone without a big hassle.   1   2   3   4   5
6. I would stand up to a date who wanted me to do something wrong.   1   2   3   4   5
7. I know how to express positive and negative feelings to a date.   1   2   3   4   5
8. I believe it is OK to have differences of opinion with a person I would date.   1   2   3   4   5
9. I could express anger to a date in a respectful way.   1   2   3   4   5
10. I am aware of what behaviors would be considered "sexual harassment."   1   2   3   4   5

"Teaching Tolerance": Understanding and Valuing Individual and Cultural Differences

Name _____ Date _____

Instructions: Each of the statements below concerns your ideas, beliefs, attitudes, or feelings about different cultures, races, religions, and personal abilities. After each statement is a response you could choose. Circle the response that is how you think or feel now.

1 = never
2 = hardly ever
3 = sometimes
4 = most of the time
5 = always

Example: I think summer vacation is the best time of the year.   1 ② 3 4 5

You think summer is hardly ever the best time of year.

1. I think people of all cultures deserve respect for who they are and what they believe.   1 2 3 4 5

2. I choose my friends for who they are, not what color or religion they are.   1 2 3 4 5

3. Everyone has abilities and disabilities.   1 2 3 4 5

4. I think people can get along if they get to know and respect one another.   1 2 3 4 5

5. I can learn a lot from people from different countries.   1 2 3 4 5

6. Feeling "different" is very uncomfortable.   1 2 3 4 5

7. I think I can learn to get along with people better if I try to understand them   1 2 3 4 5

8. I have trouble expressing anger to friends.   1 2 3 4 5

9. I could express anger better if I learned some new skills.   1 2 3 4 5

10. I feel I would like to contribute to a peaceful world by learning some negotiation skills.   1 2 3 4 5

Give a Little, Take a Little: Relationships at Home

Name _____ Date _____

Instructions: Each of the statements below concerns your ideas, beliefs, attitudes, or feelings about getting along at home. After each statement is a response you could choose. Circle the response that is how you think or feel now.

1 = never
2 = hardly ever
3 = sometimes
4 = most of the time
5 = always

Example: I like to rent video movies and watch them with my friends.   1 2 3 4 ⑤

You always like to rent movies and watch them with your friends.

1.	I am happy with the way I get along with my parent(s).	1 2 3 4 5
2.	I get along with my brother(s) and sister(s) most of the time.	1 2 3 4 5
3.	I want more freedom to do things on my own.	1 2 3 4 5
4.	I think parents don't understand kids.	1 2 3 4 5
5.	I know how to negotiate with my parents for what I want.	1 2 3 4 5
6.	I feel I have to argue with my brother(s)/sister(s) to get what I want.	1 2 3 4 5
7.	Sometimes I feel no one at home respects me.	1 2 3 4 5
8.	Sometimes I am too hard on my mom and dad.	1 2 3 4 5
9.	I realize I have to give and take to get along at home.	1 2 3 4 5
10.	I need to learn how to express anger without being hurtful to my family.	1 2 3 4 5

The Brain Laundromat: Cognitive Coping Skills

Name _____ Date _____

Instructions: Each of the statements below concerns your ideas, beliefs, attitudes, or feelings about having control over your negative feelings and behaviors. After each statement is a response you could choose. Circle the response that is how you think or feel now.

1 = never
2 = hardly ever
3 = sometimes
4 = most of the time
5 = always

Example: I like to hang out at the mall with my friends.   1   2   ③   4   5

You sometimes like to hang out at the mall with your friends.

1.	I feel I have to be mean to get my point across.	1 2 3 4 5
2.	I feel I am not responsible for my behavior.	1 2 3 4 5
3.	I can't seem to deal with so much schoolwork.	1 2 3 4 5
4.	I get depressed and don't feel like going out with my friends.	1 2 3 4 5
5.	I know how to express positive feelings.	1 2 3 4 5
6.	I feel I have to pitch a tantrum to get what I want.	1 2 3 4 5
7.	Sometimes I feel like I am out of control.	1 2 3 4 5
8.	I would like to have some help with schoolwork.	1 2 3 4 5
9.	I can't seem to keep new friends more than a few weeks.	1 2 3 4 5
10.	I know how to make decisions and stick with them.	1 2 3 4 5

Agree to Disagree:
Learning to Manage Anger

Name _____ Date _____

Instructions: Each of the statements below concerns your ideas, beliefs, attitudes, or feelings about dealing with anger and other negative emotions. After each statement is a response you could choose. Circle the response that is how you think or feel now.

1 = never
2 = hardly ever
3 = sometimes
4 = most of the time
5 = always

Example: I like to eat onion rings and drink Coke.   1 ② 3 4 5

You hardly ever like to eat onion rings and drink Coke.

  1. It isn't good for you to hold all your anger inside.   1 2 3 4 5
  2. Anger is caused by things other people say and do.   1 2 3 4 5
  3. When I get really angry I think it is OK to hurt someone else.   1 2 3 4 5
  4. I can tell when a situation is going to turn out in a fight, and I leave.   1 2 3 4 5
  5. Some ways to express anger are better than others.   1 2 3 4 5
  6. Keeping control of my temper is important to me.   1 2 3 4 5
  7. I feel comfortable expressing anger to family and friends.   1 2 3 4 5
  8. I need to improve my anger management skills.   1 2 3 4 5
  9. It is scary to get really angry.   1 2 3 4 5
10. I would feel better about myself if I could control my anger better.   1 2 3 4 5

Guys' Club:
Issues from a Male Perspective

Name _____ Date _____

Instructions: Each of the statements below concerns your ideas, beliefs, attitudes, or feelings about getting along at school, with friends, and with family. After each statement is a response you could choose. Circle the response that is how you think or feel now.

1 = never
2 = hardly ever
3 = sometimes
4 = most of the time
5 = always

Example: I like to watch TV after school. 1 2 3 ④ 5

You like to watch TV after school most of the time.

1. I know how to express positive and negative feelings.	1 2 3 4 5
2. I can tell how a person is feeling by his/her body language.	1 2 3 4 5
3. I am loyal to my friends.	1 2 3 4 5
4. It is important to be a trustworthy friend.	1 2 3 4 5
5. Honesty is an important part of being a friend.	1 2 3 4 5
6. Being in control is very important to me.	1 2 3 4 5
7. I like to be in control of friendships.	1 2 3 4 5
8. I need to improve my friendship skills.	1 2 3 4 5
9. It is important to me to have at least one or two close friends.	1 2 3 4 5
10. Calling people hurtful names is just part of growing up.	1 2 3 4 5

ASSOCIATION FOR SPECIALISTS IN GROUP WORK BEST PRACTICE GUIDELINES

Approved by the Executive Board March 29, 1998
Prepared by Lynn Rapin and Linda Keel, ASGW Ethics Committee Co-Chairs

The Association for Specialists in Group Work (ASGW) is a division of the American Counseling Association whose members are interested in and specialize in group work. We value the creation of community; service to our members, clients, and the profession; and value leadership as a process to facilitate the growth and development of individuals and groups.

The Association for Specialists in Group Work recognizes the commitment of its members to the Code of Ethics and Standards of Practice (as revised in 1995) of its parent organization, the American Counseling Association, and nothing in this document shall be construed to supplant that code. These Best Practice Guidelines are intend to clarify the application of the ACA Code of Ethics and Standards of Practice to the field of group work by defining Group Workers' responsibility and scope of practice involving those activities, strategies, and interventions that are consistent and current with effective and appropriate professional ethical and community standards. ASGW views ethical process as being integral to group work and views Group Workers as ethical agents. Group Workers, by their very nature in being responsible and responsive to their group members, necessarily embrace a certain potential for ethical vulnerability. It is incumbent upon Group Workers to give considerable attention to the intent and context of their actions because the attempts of Group Workers to influence human behavior through group work always have ethical implications. These Best Practice Guidelines address Group Workers' responsibilities in planning, performing, and processing groups.

SECTION A: BEST PRACTICE IN PLANNING

A.1. Professional Context and Regulatory Requirements

Group Workers actively know, understand, and apply the ACA Code of Ethics and Standards of Best Practice, the ASGW Professional Standards for the Training of Group Workers, these ASGW Best Practice Guidelines, the ASGW diversity competencies, the ACA Multicultural Guidelines, relevant state laws, accreditation requirements, relevant National Board for Certified Counselors Codes and Standards, and insurance requirements impacting the practice of group work.

A.2. Scope of Practice and Conceptual Framework

Group Workers define the scope of practice related to the core and specialization competencies defined in the ASGW Training Standards. Group Workers are aware of personal strengths and weaknesses in leading groups. Group Workers develop and are able to articulate a general conceptual framework to guide practice and a rationale for use of techniques that are to be used. Group Workers limit their practice to those areas for which they meet the training criteria established by the ASGW Training Standards.

A.3. Assessment

a. *Assessment of self.* Group Workers actively assess their knowledge and skills related to the specific group(s) offered. Group Workers assess their values, beliefs, and theoretical

---

orientation and how these impact upon the group, particularly when working with a diverse and multicultural population.

b. *Ecological assessment.* Group Workers assess community needs, agency or organization resources, sponsoring organization mission, staff competency, attitudes regarding group work, professional training levels of potential group leaders regarding group work, client attitudes regarding group work, and multicultural and diversity considerations. Group workers use this information as the basis for making decisions related to their group practice, or to the implementation of groups for which they have supervisory, evaluation, or oversight responsibilities.

A.4. Program Development and Evaluation

a. *Group Workers identify the type(s) of group(s) to be offered and how they relate to community needs.*

b. *Group Workers concisely state in writing the purpose and goals of the group.* Group workers also identify the role of the group members in influencing or determining the group goals.

c. *Group Workers set fees consistent with the organization's fee schedule, taking into consideration the financial status and locality of prospective group members.*

d. *Group Workers choose techniques and a leadership style appropriate to the type(s) of group(s) being offered.*

e. *Group Workers have an evaluation plan consistent with regulatory, organization, and insurance requirements, where appropriate.*

f. *Group Workers take into consideration current professional guidelines when using technology, including but not limited to Internet communication.*

A.5. Resources

Group Workers coordinate resources related to the kind of group(s) and group activities to be provided, such as: adequate funding; the appropriateness and availability of a trained co-leader; space and privacy requirements for the type(s) of group(s) being offered; marketing and recruiting; and appropriate collaboration with other community agencies and organizations.

A.6. Professional Disclosure Statement

Group Workers have a professional disclosure statement which includes information on confidentiality and exceptions to confidentiality, theoretical orientation, information on the nature, purpose(s), and goals of the group, the group services that can be provided, the role and responsibility of group members and leaders, Group Workers' qualifications to conduct the specific group(s), specific licenses, certifications and professional affiliations, and address of licensing/credentialing body.

A.7. Group and Member Preparation

a. *Group Workers screen prospective group members if appropriate to the type of group being offered.* When selection of group members is appropriate, Group Workers identify group members whose needs and goals are compatible with the goals of the group.

b. *Group Workers facilitate informed consent.* Group Workers provide in oral and written form to prospective members (when appropriate to group type): the professional disclosure statement; group purpose and goals; group participation expectations including voluntary and involuntary membership; role expectations of members and leader(s); policies related to entering and exiting the group; policies governing substance use; policies and procedures governing mandated groups (where relevant); documentation requirements; disclosure of information to others; implications of out-of-group contact or involvement among members; procedures for consultation between group leader(s) and group member(s); fees and time parameters; and potential impacts of group participation.

c. *Group Workers obtain the appropriate consent forms for work with minors and other dependent group members.*

d. *Group Workers define confidentiality and its limits (for example, legal and ethical exceptions and expectations; waivers implicit with treatment plans, documentation and insurance usage).* Group Workers have the responsibility to inform all group participants of the need for confidentiality, potential consequences of breaching confidentiality, and that legal privilege does not apply to group discussions (unless provided by state statute).

A.8. Professional Development

Group Workers recognize that professional growth is a continuous, ongoing, developmental process throughout their career.

a. *Group Workers remain current and increase knowledge and skill competencies through activities such as continuing education, professional supervision, and participation in personal and professional development activities.*

b. *Group Workers seek consultation and/or supervision regarding ethical concerns that interfere with effective functioning as a group leader.* Supervisors have the responsibility to keep abreast of consultation, group theory, process, and adhere to related ethical guidelines.

c. *Group Workers seek appropriate professional assistance for their own personal problems or conflicts that are likely to impair their professional judgment or work performance.*

d. *Group Workers seek consultation and supervision to ensure appropriate practice whenever working with a group for which all knowledge and skill competencies have not been achieved.*

e. *Group Workers keep abreast of group research and development.*

A.9. Trends and Technological Changes

Group Workers are aware of and responsive to technological changes as they affect society and the profession. These include but are not limited to changes in mental health delivery systems; legislative and insurance industry reforms; shifting population demographics and client needs; and technological advances in Internet and other communication and delivery systems. Group Workers adhere to ethical guidelines related to the use of developing technologies.

SECTION B: BEST PRACTICE IN PERFORMING

B.1. Self Knowledge

Group Workers are aware of and monitor their strengths and weaknesses and the effects these have on group members.

B.2. Group Competencies

Group Workers have a basic knowledge of groups and the principles of group dynamics, and are able to perform the core group competencies, as described in the ASGW Professional Standards for the Training of Group Workers. Additionally, Group Workers have adequate understanding and skill in any group specialty area chosen for practice (psychotherapy, counseling, task, psychoeducation, as described in the ASGW Training Standards).

B.3. Group Plan Adaptation

a. *Group Workers apply and modify knowledge, skills, and techniques appropriate to group type and stage, and to the unique needs of various cultural and ethnic groups.*

b. *Group Workers monitor the group's progress toward the group goals and plan.*

c. *Group Workers clearly define and maintain ethical, professional, and social relationship boundaries with group members as appropriate to their role in the organization and the type of group being offered.*

B.4. Therapeutic Conditions and Dynamics

Group Workers understand and are able to implement appropriate models of group development, process observation and therapeutic conditions.

B.5. Meaning

Group Workers assist members in generating meaning from the group experience.

B.6. Collaboration

Group Workers assist members in developing individual goals and respect group members as co-equal partners in the group experience.

B.7. Evaluation

Group Workers include evaluation (both formal and informal) between sessions and at the conclusion of the group.

B.8. Diversity

Group Workers practice with broad sensitivity to client differences including but not limited to ethnic, gender, religious, sexual, psychological maturity, economic class, family history, physical characteristics or limitations, and geographic location. Group Workers continuously seek information regarding the cultural issues of the diverse population with whom they are working both by interaction with participants and from using outside resources.

B.9. Ethical Surveillance

Group Workers employ an appropriate ethical decision making model in responding to ethical challenges and issues and in determining courses of action and behavior for self and group members. In addition, Group Workers employ applicable standards as promulgated by ACA, ASGW, or other appropriate professional organizations.

SECTION C: BEST PRACTICE IN GROUP PROCESSING

C.1. Processing Schedule

Group Workers process the workings of the group with themselves, group members, supervisors or other colleagues, as appropriate. This may include assessing progress on group and member goals, leader behaviors and techniques, group dynamics and interventions; developing understanding and acceptance of meaning. Processing may occur both within sessions and before and after each session, at time of termination and later follow up, as appropriate.

C.2. Reflective Practice

Group Workers attend to opportunities to synthesize theory and practice and to incorporate learning outcomes into ongoing groups. Group Workers attend to session dynamics of members and their interactions and also attend to the relationship between session dynamics and leader values, cognition and affect.

C.3. Evaluation and Follow-Up

a. *Group Workers evaluate process and outcomes.* Results are used for ongoing program planning improvement and revisions of current group and/or to contribute to professional research literature. Group Workers follow all applicable policies and standards in using group material for research and reports.

b. *Group Workers conduct follow-up contact with group members, as appropriate, to assess outcomes or when requested by a group member(s).*

C.4. Consultation and Training with Other Organizations

Group Workers provide consultation and training to organizations in and out of their setting, when appropriate. Group Workers seek out consultation as needed with competent professional persons knowledgeable about group work.

ABOUT THE AUTHOR

Distinguished Teaching and Service Professor at Indiana University Southeast in New Albany, Dr. Rosemarie Smead is an accomplished teacher and training consultant, with over 30 years experience working with children and adolescents in school, mental health, inpatient, and family therapy settings. She has presented workshops and training seminars both nationally and internationally to professional groups, state departments of education, school systems, juvenile treatment facilities, and business and industry. Dr. Smead is past president and fellow of the Association for Specialists in Group Work and has received state, ASGW, and systemwide university awards for her distinguished teaching and service to the profession in group work. She holds a doctorate in counseling psychology from Auburn University and is a licensed marriage and family therapist and mental health counselor, as well as a clinical member of the American Association for Marriage and Family Therapists. In addition to her teaching responsibilities, she consults with and conducts workshops for school systems, mental health agencies, government agencies, professional organizations, and hospital treatment facilities. Her professional interests are in counselor education and group counseling research with children and adolescents, and she maintains a private practice in marriage and family therapy. She is the author of the widely acclaimed books *Skills for Living: Group Counseling Activities for Young Adolescents* (Volume 1) and *Skills for Living: Group Counseling Activities for Elementary Students* (both written under the name Rosemarie Smead Morganett). Her book *Skills and Techniques for Group Work with Children and Adolescents* and her two-part video series *Skills and Techniques for Group Counseling with Youth* are, along with the previous titles, available from Research Press.

DATE DUE

APR 1 9 2007		